RUHETAG: THE DAY-TO-DAY LIFE OF THE GERMAN SOLDIER IN WWII

VOLUME I: HEALTH AND HYGIENE

LTC (RETIRED) JIMMY L. POOL

Other Schiffer Books by the Author:
Pool, Jim and Tom Bock. *Rations of the German Wehrmacht in WWII.* (Schiffer Military/Aviation History, 2010).

Other Schiffer Books on Related Subjects:
Gassend, Jean-Loup, *Operation Dragoon: Autopsy of a Battle: The Allied Liberation of the French Riviera August-September 1944,* (Schiffer Military/Aviation History, 2014)

Mason, Chris. *Personal Effects of the German Soldier in World War II.* (Schiffer Military/Aviation History, 2006).

Palinckx, Werner with Dr. J.F. Borsarello. *Camouflage Uniforms of the German Wehrmacht.* (Schiffer Military History, 2002).

Weaver, W. Darrin. *Kunststoffe: A Collectors's Guide to German World War II Plastics and their Markings.* (Schiffer Military/Aviation History, 2008).

Library of Congress Control Number: 2015945073

Designed by Justin Watkinson
Cover design by Molly Shields
Type set in BaseTwelveSansSC/Minion Pro

ISBN: 978-0-7643-4919-5
Printed in China

Published by Schiffer Publishing, Ltd.
4880 Lower Valley Road
Atglen, PA 19310
Phone: (610) 593-1777; Fax: (610) 593-2002
E-mail: Info@schifferbooks.com

FOR MY WIFE AND FOUR FURRY KIDS WHO MADE THIS POSSIBLE.

TABLE OF CONTENTS

ACKNOWLEDGMENTS

I would like to thank the many individuals, organizations, and dealers who have given so generously of their valuable time and expert knowledge to bring these two volumes to life. Without their generosity this project would not have been possible.

Steve Androsko Collection
Kevin Barrett Collection
Andrea Bartoli Collection.
Thomas Bock Collection
Jerry Bozentko
Clay W. Chambers of Bunker Militaria
George Cone Collection
Michael Davis of VirtualGrenadier
Klaus Peter Emig of Militaria-Versand Emig
Espenlaub Militaria
Carsten Fries Collection
Jean-Loup Gassend
Terry Gest Collection
Jim Haley Collection
Frank Heukemes Collection
Bob Hritz Collection
Ruben Kant Collection
Jim Kreunen of Militaria Plaza
Chris Liontass Collection
Chris Mason Collection
Brian Matthews of Tomahawk Films WW-II German Archive-UK
Drew Maynard
Patrick Ott Collection
Bill Petz Collection
Rich Prandoni Collection
Henrik Rask of RASKANTIK
Ron Richter Collection
Eugeniu Rotari Collection
Frédéric Ruelle Collection
Thomas Salazar of Ostfront Militaria
Bill Shea of The Ruptured Duck
Kamleithner Siegfried Collection
Jeff Slaker
Gerard Stezelberger of Relic Hunter Militaria
Ed Stroh Collection
Helmut Weitze, Hamburg
Peter Whamond of the Collector's Guild
Michel Verberkt Collection
Sammlung Zeugmeister
Bundesarchiv-Federal Archives, Potsdamer Str. 1, D-56075 Koblenz
United States National Archives and Records Administration (NARA)

INTRODUCTION

Soldiers are dreamers; when the guns begin
they think of fire lit homes, clean beds, and wives.
– SIEGFRIED SASSOON

Soldiering is 99% boredom and 1% sheer terror.
– UNKNOWN CIVIL WAR SOLDIER

If you are a fan of war movies, you might get the mistaken impression that war is one continuous state of combat. The reality of war is more likely to be short periods of very intense combat preceded and followed by long interludes of relative quiet. It is those periods of quiet that are the focus of this book. It was during these times that the German soldier saw some return to normalcy in his or her life. Of course, "normal" is a relative term, depending on the type of unit you were assigned to and where you were stationed. Generally, the closer to the front line you were the greater the hardships and sacrifices a soldier endured. The conditions of a soldier stationed in Paris can hardly be considered a hardship when compared to a soldier living in a log bunker outside of Leningrad.

When viewed in isolation toothpaste, toilet paper, sewing kits, mail, etc., do not seem all that important. However, as part of the larger picture of caring for the needs of the soldier, whether it be spiritual, personal, or intellectual, they all served to reinforce the soldier's willingness to fight. The German military was sensitive to these requirements and aggressively supported programs and policies that met these needs. There is no way of accurately assessing the effectiveness of the German approach except as a part of the overall German military machine. Maybe it is fitting that I offer this assessment from one of Germany's enemies conducted within weeks of Germany's total collapse. In *TM-E-38-451 Handbook on German Military Forces, 15 March, 1945*, the United States War Department had this to say about the German military machine:

> After five and a half years of ever growing battle against ever-stronger enemies, the German Army in 1945 looks, at first glance, much the worse for wear. It is beset on all sides and is short of everything. It has suffered appalling casualties and must resort to old men, boys, invalids, and unreliable foreigners for its cannon fodder. Its weapons and tactics seem not to have kept pace with those of the armies opposing it; its supply system in the field frequently breaks down. Its position is obviously hopeless, and it can only be a question of time until the last German soldier is disarmed, and the once proud German Army of the great Frederick and of Scharnhorst, of Ludendorff and of Hitler, exists no more as a factor to be reckoned with.
>
> Yet this shabby, war-weary machine has struggled on in a desperate effort to postpone its inevitable demise. At the end of 1944 it was still able to mount an offensive calculated to delay for months the definitive piercing of the western bulwarks of Germany. Despite the supposed chronic disunity at the top, disaffection among the officer corps, and disloyalty in the rank and file, despite the acute lack of weapons, ammunition, fuel, transport, and human reserves, the German Army seems to function with its old precision and to overcome what appear to be insuperable difficulties with remarkable speed. Only by patient and incessant hammering from all sides can its collapse be brought about.
>
> The cause of this toughness, even in defeat, is not generally appreciated. It goes much deeper than the quality of weapons, the excellence of training and leadership, the soundness of tactical and strategic doctrine, or the efficiency of control at all echelons. It is to be found in the military tradition which is so deeply ingrained in the whole character of the German nation and which alone makes possible the interplay of these various factors of strength to their full effectiveness.
>
> The German Army of 1939 was a model of efficiency, the best product of the concentrated military genius of the most scientifically military of nations. A study of the German Army of 1945, however, older and wiser, hardened and battle tested, cornered and desperate as it is, show best how this military science and military genius operate in the practical exigencies of long-drawn-out total war.

Since the target audience of these books are collectors and reenactors, it should come as no surprise that they are filled with wartime and contemporary pictures of artifacts used by the German soldier in WWII. While the items shown were supplied to the

German soldier by various means, the bulk of them were available as *Marketenderwaren*, (Author's note: The US Army Intelligence reports referred to these as Post Exchange [PX] items.) All units were allowed to set up a *Kantine* to carry luxury articles and voucher payment goods. Field Manual H. Dv. 86/1 was the governing regulation covering PX items. PX items supplied to the Kantines were either requisitioned and distributed via the ration supply system or procured locally. Here is the section from H. Dv. 86/1 that covered PX items:

> The unit commander is responsible for operating the PX program. Suitable merchandise for the PX are: Beer, wine, soft drinks, liquor, cigars, cigarettes, snuff, cigarette wrap (sleeve and cigarette paper in booklets), pipes, cigar/cigarette cases, cigar/cigarette holders/filters, cigar/cigarette purses, tobacco cans/bags, lighter with fluid, matches, electric lamp with battery and bulb, writing paper with envelopes, post cards, post instructions, report listings, note books, ink, pen nibs, fountain pens, pencils, copy pencils, color pencils, pencil holders, pencil sharpeners, sketch materials, erasers, packs of paper, letter boxes, playing cards, simple parlor games, sewing kits, needles-all sorts, thimbles, scissors, buttons, neck purse-for dog tags and money, money purse, wallets, knives, forks, spoons, pocket knives, can openers, combs, hairbrushes, tooth brushes, tooth paste, mouth wash, straight razors, razor blades, razor soap brushes, safety razor kits, razor mirrors, rub stone, hair tonic, skin cream, foot powder, handkerchiefs, toilet paper, shoe polish, string, insoles, styptic stick, mouth harmonicas, photo film. These daily living and luxury items, as well as food items (except for wine and tobacco), should be stocked for purchase.
>
> To purchase a PX item the soldier takes out a single debit advancement of 2 RM from the unit, based on the soldiers salary. Soldiers are not allowed to borrow the funds from their canteen enterprise. The advance payment must be paid back as soon as possible, but not to exceed four weeks. After that the military will automatically take the payment out of the soldier's reserve fund.

The bulk of the items available through the Kantine systems appear to have been standard, off-the-shelf commercial items. Fortunately for the collector, very little effort has gone into reproducing commercial items. Germany was an industrial nation of the first order and thousands of items were produced in Germany prior to and during the war that could have found their way into the hands of the soldier. Many items were supplied to the soldier via the normal supply system, but could just as easily been mailed to them from home or purchased in the local economy. Some of the methods of authenticating items as wartime are covered in the two-volume series on German rations.

The majority of the information used to tell the story of German personal items came from wartime sources. Technical aspects of selected industries were assessed in numerous British and American intelligence reports written during and after the end of the war. German regulations, as well as US Army Intelligence Studies, Field Manuals, and Technical Manuals show how the German military operated in the field. While all branches of the German military are covered to some degree, the overall focus is on the German Army.

I have tried to present the story from the point of view of those that lived it; the German and Allied soldiers. I cannot overstate that fact. In many cases, I used direct quotes from credited sources. In certain discussions I wove the narrative using facts from several sources. In those cases, I credited the major source and state that additional information was taken from other minor sources. In no way do I take credit for any of the facts or thoughts being conveyed. In certain cases, I attempt to clarify a position, state a fact, or offer my "two cents." These examples are usually offered as (Authors note).

All the photographs in this volume come from wartime publications, individual collections, private companies, or government archives and are used with the belief that there are no copyright infringement issues. In certain cases a single caption will be used to explain a number of items contributed by numerous individuals or organizations. Due to the difficulty of trying to credit each source in those cases, I have elected either to omit the credit or to credit the person or organization that provided the most photographs in that sequence.

I hope this series of books, along with the two volumes on rations, will round out the coverage devoted to the life and times of the German soldier in WWII.

CHAPTER 1

YOU'RE IN THE ARMY NOW!

To most Germans of the period, serving in the military was an obligation and an honor. A strong sense of patriotism based in part on its strong military tradition ran deep in the German character. Before Hitler came to power, the German Army was composed entirely of professional soldiers. By the time Germany went to war on 1 September 1939, soldiers classified as non-professional or conscripts filled the ranks. The classification of professional or non-professional soldier was important because it affected a soldier's pay, allowances, and pensions. In general terms, every soldier was provided housing, rations, and clothing, either directly or by adjustments in their pay. The military pay system also provided allowances for family members. Women Auxiliaries (Helferinnen) were treated as civil servants for most of the war, but like their male counterparts were provided housing, rations, and clothing.

The earliest memories of military service for most soldiers is tied to their initial training post or camp. It was here that he or she was first exposed to the discipline and regimen required to be a soldier. Giving up a civilian lifestyle in favor of a soldier's life, where every activity was dictated and privacy was nonexistent, was certainly not an easy adjustment. Prior participation in certain paramilitary organizations like the Hitler Youth or *Reichsarbeitsdienst* (German Labor Service, or RAD) certainly made that transition less traumatic.

The initial phase of military life consisted of basic training, which was conducted at one of the numerous *kasernes* in Germany and later in the occupied territories. Conditions in the German Kasernes were relatively comfortable. Under Hitler, a concerted effort was made to modernize the older Kasernes to bring them up to the living standards of the period. The soldier was generally billeted in a room with several comrades, each of which was assigned a bed and a wall locker to store both military and personal items. Depending on the size of the room, other furniture like a table or chairs could be issued to make life more comfortable. Some military members—mostly cadre or married members—lived in civilian-style homes.

Basic training was conducted by "training units" of the soldier's assigned unit. At the beginning of the war basic training was sixteen weeks long, but was reduced to eight weeks by the end of the war. Basic training was generally divided into three parts: individual, squad, and platoon level. After basic training was completed, soldiers were sent to their unit of assignment. Sometimes soldiers were sent to advanced or specialized training before joining their unit.

The soldier's life after he joined his unit was largely dictated by the leadership, unit's location, weather conditions, unit mission, and of course, the enemy situation. A soldier stationed in a modern city or town most likely had access to all the creature comforts, like electricity, showers, and toilets. Soldiers in forward positions did the best they could to make their environment more livable. The longer a unit occupied a position, the more likely that some level of comfort could be attained.

Aspects relating to the logistics of supporting the soldier were highlighted in *German Clothing, Equipment and Rations, Office of the Quartermaster General Military Planning Division Research and Development Branch, 5 September 1945*:

> Providing supplies needed in billets and quarters which are handled by the Quartermaster Corps must not be confused with billeting. The latter is a question of deciding in what places troops will actually be quartered. That is considered a command function and so is not handled by the supply branches. The duties of the Quartermaster Corps are restricted to providing all equipment and supplies they will need in the billets. Providing supplies for billets and quarters falls into the following chief groups:
>
> 1.) Supplying equipment.
> 2.) Supplying housekeeping linen, especially for hospitals.
> 3.) Supplying expendables such as soap, candles.
> 4.) Supplying heating and cooking fuel.
>
> This division was necessary, as the supplies were made available in different ways. It was very unusual for troops to be equipped with equipment like beds, tables, etc., except where supplied to hospitals and to the most essential units whose work compelled them to use shelters; only a little equipment was supplied during the war to those troops who remained inactive for rather long periods on a stabilized front. In a fluid situation, it was impossible to move this equipment because of the limited capacity of railroads or columns.

Supplying wash basins, knives, forks, spoons, brooms, and similar equipment was generally necessary, even though the quantity was not too great and diminished after the beginning of air raids and the consequently greater need for these things for the civilian population at home. This equipment was sometimes carried forward in whole trains, usually to the army group. There were special loading plans for such trains, which could rarely be used. The hospital requirements of such items were naturally filled at any cost.

Textile items, such as bed clothes, towels, etc., were supplied only in small quantities because of the shortage of raw materials.

Both soap and lighting materials were carefully rationed per head per month. Each man received one piece of toilet soap (80 grams or 2.8 oz) per month, one piece of laundry soap (80 grams) per month, and once every three months one piece of shaving soap (30 grams or 1.1 oz.). Additional rations were given to such individuals as motor repairmen, WACs (Author's note: female auxiliary) and doctors. The lighting material ration was determined by the type of duty of the troops. Where there was electric light, only emergency lighting was given. On the other hand, combat and committed fortifications troops received up to four candles and twelve Hindenburg lights (flat, bread candles in paste board cups) per man per month. Such cleaning materials as IMI and ATA were also transported in supply trains. Lighting materials trains also carried carbide and similar lighting materials. Electric light bulbs and lamps were not supplied in this way, but were considered construction materials and were supplied by the Army Construction Corps. Although the raw materials for soap were critical, it was possible during the whole war to supply them regularly and in the authorized quantities without more than local interruptions. The largest quantities of supplies for billets and quarters consisted of heating and cooking fuels, and these often took up a very large percentage of the amount of rail transportation allocated to the Quartermaster Corp. (Author's note: A detailed look at the soap industry is provided in chapter 8.)

As mentioned, the German soldier relied on the standard supply system, which included the unit Kantine to provide most of the day-to-day personal hygiene products. The Feldpost, scrounging, bartering, or the local economy were additional sources of supply. Modern plumbing and toilets were nonexistent in some theaters of operation, like Russia or North Africa. The soldiers' shovels allowed them to do their business on the move. If a soldier was expected to remain stationary for an extended period more permanent arrangements were made. Toilet paper was not always available and the soldier would improvise, using leaves, magazines, or the ever-popular propaganda leaflet.

If the German soldier was fortunate, he could find himself billeted in a fixed structure. Bunkers or other temporary positions were made more comfortable with the addition of a few pieces of furniture. *BIOS Final Report No.952. Item No.22, Design Investigation in Selected German Consumer Goods Industries* investigated a number of specialty industries, including furniture production. Some of the highlights in the report include:

60% of Germany's furniture trade including bulk production is in Westfalen, one of the centers being Herford. The average firm employs 50-60 workers, 200 or more being unusual—firms such as Bock and Feil in Stuttgart, Bartels in Langenberg, or May in Zeulenroda with 900 or more are exceptional.

Under the Nazis the industry came under two headings: firms in which the different stages of production are allocated to different personnel came under the Reichsgruppe-Industrie and smaller firms in which one man saw the job all the way through came under the Reichsgruppe-Handwerk. Dove tailing is always done by machinery; the use of glued on press moldings is unusual, but the cheaper firms also having carving machines for the production of such ornamentation.

Training for the furniture industries was given at the Fachschulen für Textilien, Tischlerei, Holztechnikum and Holzbearbeitung, and Polstermoebel. Cabinet making schools were to be found at Detmold and Blankenburg, and boys would enter direct from school; those who wished to improve the quality of their work would probably go to a Kunstgewerbeschule in South Germany or even to a wood-carver in Italy. The chief schools for wood technology were at Rosenheim, Bayern, and Holzminden and here, for example, men destined to become managers of saw mills would be trained. There were five schools for upholstered furniture: at Blankenburg (distinct from the cabinet making school referred to), Frankfurt a.d. Oder, Frankfurt a. Main, Hildesheim and Hamburg, of which the last two were the best, that at Hamburg being a private school under Neckermann.

Tents were also available, but were only seen as a temporary means of billeting troops. The subject of tents was discussed in *German Clothing, Equipment and Rations*:

Wherever possible, the Germans attempted to get on without using their heavy tentage. Under most conditions it was considered enough to let the men find themselves billets or to pitch their shelter tents (Author's note: Zeltbahn). Only when the climate was severe and when other shelter was not available, such as in the less thickly inhabited parts of Russia in the winter or in Africa, was it thought to be essential to supply heavy tentage. A number of different reasons were given for this. Under most conditions, houses and permanent buildings were thought to give better protection against the weather and better concealment from the enemy. Problems of sanitation were not thought to be great since the buildings could be cleaned. Generalstabsarzt (Major General of the Medical Corps) Haubenreisser, Chief Surgeon of the Commander-in-Chief of the West, said that nearly all Surgeons in Russia preferred to use buildings because they could be properly heated and that they were cleaned easily enough so that almost no infections came as a result. Another reason was to reduce the amount of equipment that needed to be transported. A third reason was to conserve on fabrics, which were critically short in Germany.

In places where billets were not available, the men often pitched their shelter tents. The commonest method was to make a pyramidal tent of four of the triangular shelter tent sections, each of which could also be used as a poncho. Sometimes eight men pitched theirs together to make a larger tent. If more headroom was needed for a command post or signal tent, straight sides could be made with eight sections or sloping sides with twelve, on top of which a four section pyramidal roof was erected. The German soldier found the shelter tent section extremely useful both for pitching tents and for use as a poncho. Nearly all men complained, however, about the lack of size.

At the beginning of the war, there were many different types of tents issued by the Army (Heer), such as the large and small staff tents, mountain squad tent, medical tents, etc. As the war progressed, the different types of personnel tents were eliminated in favor of the M-70 and the M-100. Only the Medical Corps kept its own tents. The M-70 and the M-100 got their names from the height in centimeters at the eaves. Both were nearly identical in design, being standard A-type tents. The M-70 which had only 2 center poles was designed to hold 10 men, while the four pole M-100 tent held 20 men.

The Luftwaffe had an additional type of tent, a square straight walled tent with a fly type of roof. This was commonly used near air strips.

A large special purpose tent was the stable tent. This was made up of three sections.

Early in the war there were special purpose, light weight mountain tents intended for two men. These proved to be impractical since the men could usually build themselves snow shelters where the weather was too severe for shelter tents. Loads of the mountain troops were such that they could rarely be carried. The two man Afrika Korps tent was similarly not essential although it was useful in the desert where dispersal was necessary and where the shelter tent gave insufficient protection in sandstorms.

The Germans never reimpregnated their tents in the field. They were neither mildew-proofed or fire-proofed.

German Clothing, Equipment and Rations provided the following observations on sleeping in cold climates:

Sleeping in the Winter: On a stabilized front in the winter sleeping presented no great problem to the German soldier. Wherever *any* house or shelter was available the German soldier took it over after cleaning it up and used it as quarters. In wooded areas, he built log huts, etc. With stoves and adequate shelter and the four blankets he was allowed on the Eastern Front in winter, he usually slept comfortably enough. In some instances he added to the insulation of the house and to its camouflage by piling snow around and over it. In other stabilized areas he set up portable plywood houses, known as "Finnish Tents" (Finnenzelte). Only in rare instances did he live in tents.

It was in fluid situations that the German soldier had a more difficult time sleeping. Many of the ordinary infantry units were not given adequate training or were in situations where it was impossible to do anything but throw up a snow wall as a windbreak and sleep as well as they could behind it, wrapped up in blankets. Each man could carry one or at most two blankets and so two or three men pooled their blankets and slept together. More highly trained troops such as mountain troops ordinarily operated in more difficult terrain and climates. These men were taught how to build brush lean-tos in wooded country where the snow was not deep or snow shelters in deeper snow. Under some circumstances they built igloos, but more commonly it was a snow burrow or snow cave. The snow burrow was usually a hole large enough to hold two or three men lying closely together. It was roofed over by placing sticks, skis, etc., over the hole to support a shelter half which in turn was covered with snow. A snow cave was more elaborate, being dug into a snow bank. The mountain troops were the only troops with sleeping bags which were down filled. These were organizational and often blankets were used. In bivouacs, each soldier removed boots, changed his socks for dry ones and slipped his feet into his rucksack. Then about three men pooled their blankets and went to sleep. Even the lightweight mountain tents were rarely used because of their weight and the fact that they were colder than snow shelters.

Entrance to Kaserne housing elements of Infantry Regiment Grossdeutschland.

Standard barracks furniture.
Photos: US National Archives and Records Administration (NARA)

A barracks wall locker.

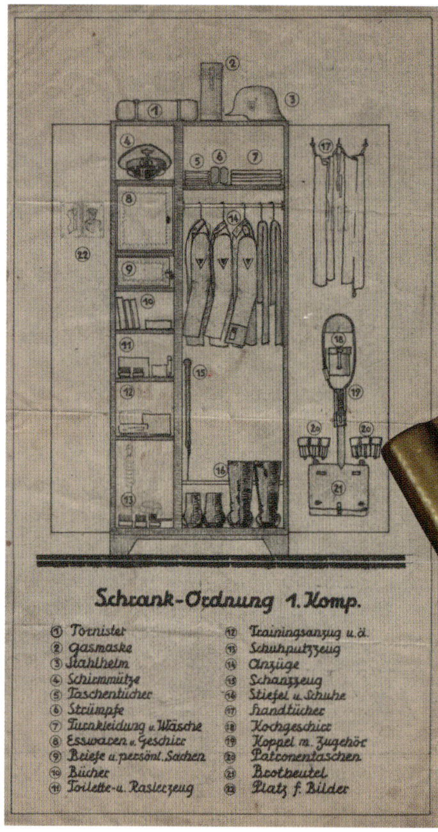

Standardized unit layout for a wall locker.

A 1944 dated lock used to secure wall lockers. *Bunkermilitaria.com*

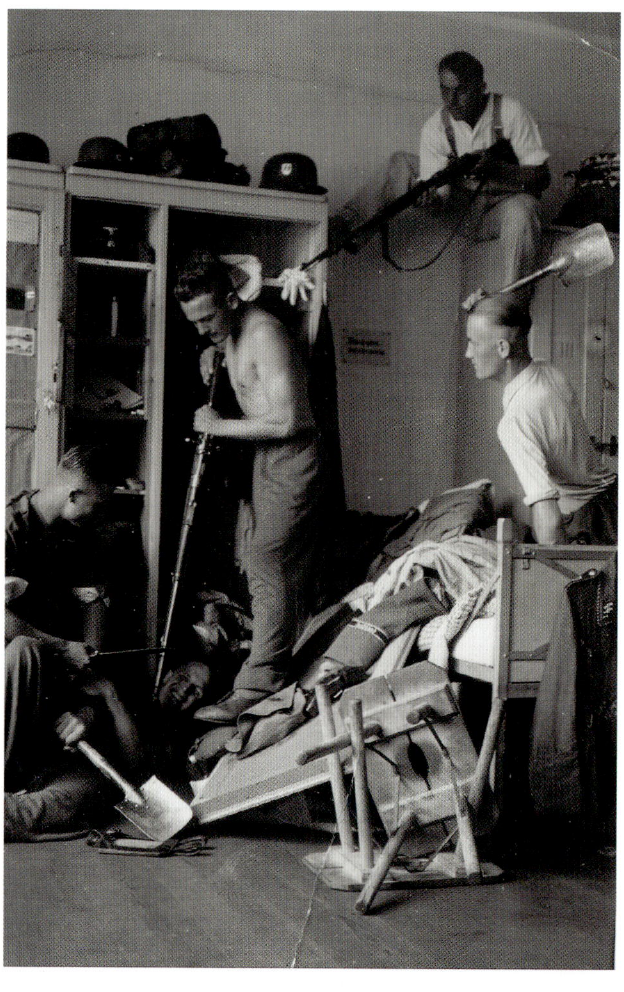

Inside the wall locker.

A barracks stool.
Bunkermilitaria.com

A chair stamped as army property.

Rifle rack insert
that fit into recessed
areas built into the walls of troop
barracks. *Bunkermilitaria.com*

Typical rifle rack found in a German Kaserne.

Blue light bulbs became common after the allies started their nighttime bombing campaign.[1] *Bunkermilitaria.com*

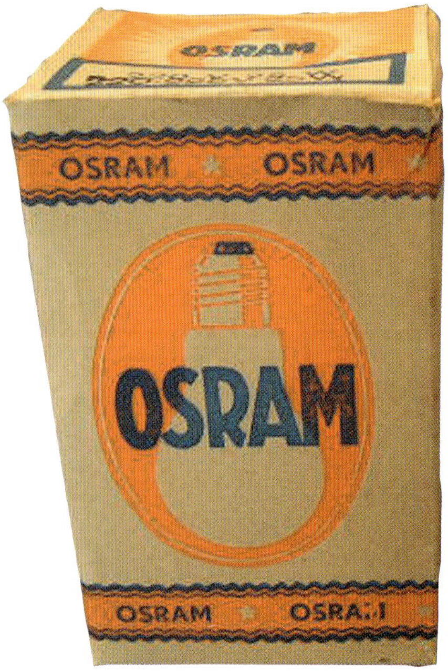

A soldier stands by a table full of personal items, including a light bulb. *OSTFRONT Militaria*

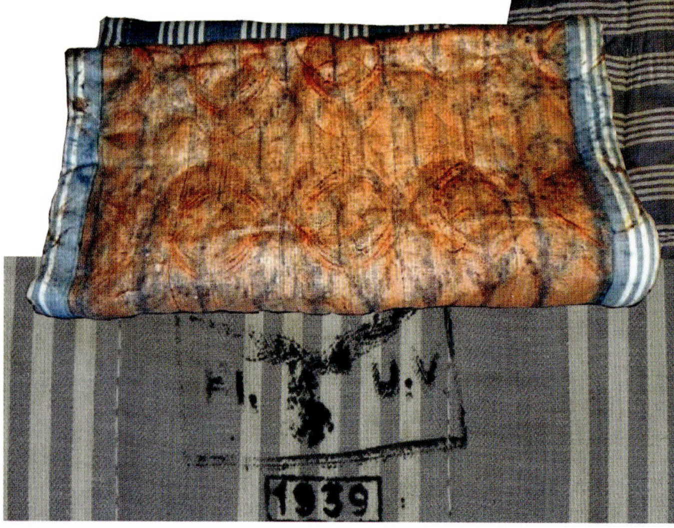

Several styles of mattresses. *www.raskantik.com*

Sheets were manufactured from a variety of materials.

Mattress covers could be filled with other materials to provide support.

Pillow cases. *Helmut Weitze, Hamburg*

Two issue blankets. *Michael Davis-VirtualGrenadier and The Collectors Guild*

For troops with access to electricity, electric blankets were an option. *OSTFRONT Militaria*

A variety of tents including two-man versions to large staff tents were manufactured in plain as well as camouflaged colors.

Commercially manufactured tents were also used by the military.

B W. Söhngen & Co. O. H. G., Wiesbaden.

Haus-Zelte:

Diese Zelte sind aus prima wasserdichtem, imprägniertem, feldgrauem Zeltstoff hergestellt.

This tent in field gray cloth was available through a Red Cross catalog.

Each soldier was issued a Zeltbahn that could be joined together to make a tent.

Everything needed to make a tent, except the rope. *The Collectors Guild*

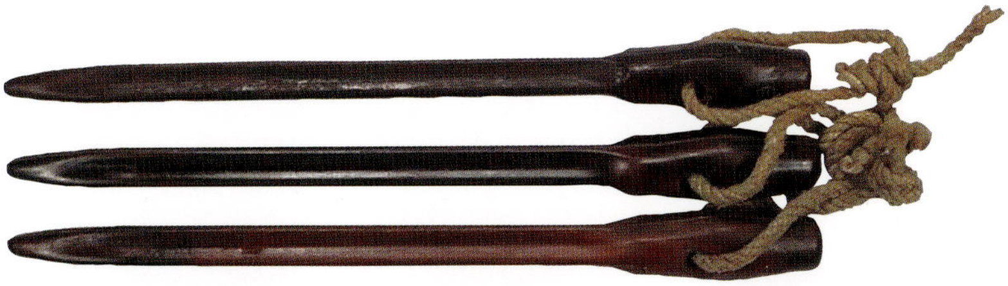

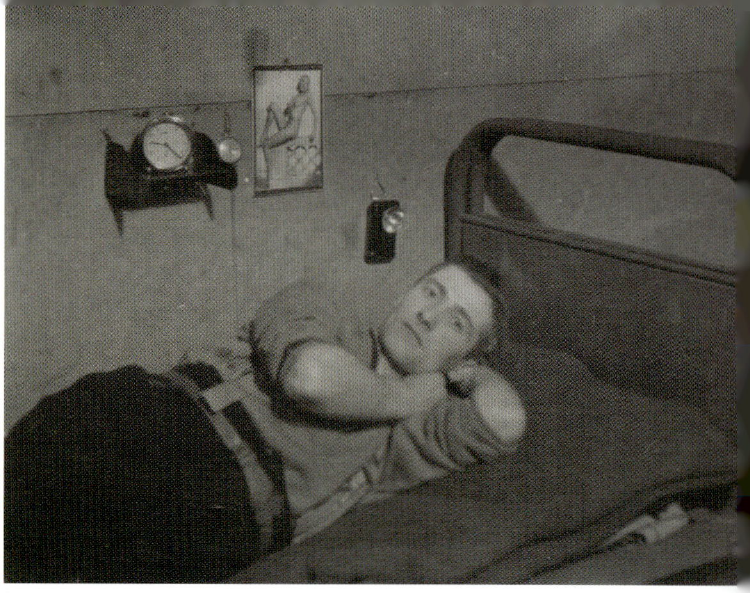

Soldiers brought as many creature comforts with them as available transportation allowed.

Young SS soldiers at rest. *Photo: National Archives and Record Administration (NARA)*

Staff call! *Bundesarchiv-Bild-101I-187-0203-15A, Foto: Gehrmann, Friedrich Juli 1941*

A field cot.
www.raskantik.com

Hammocks like this Navy version were also popular with ground forces.

Mobile troops could carry larger items like this cot.

Hammocks were only practical if you had something to tie them to.

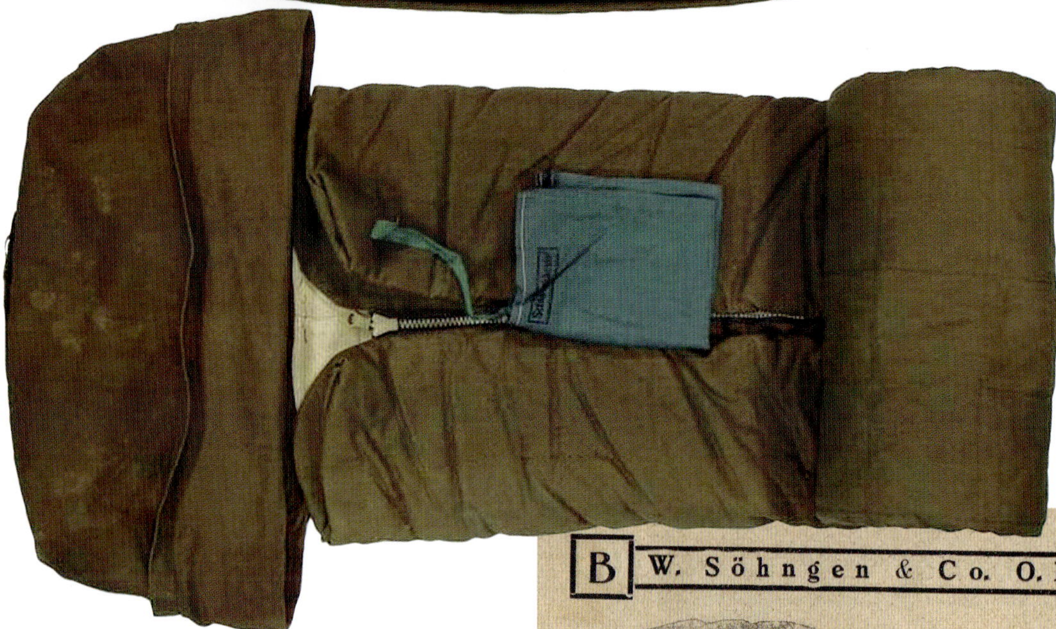

Sleeping bags were generally issued to special troops like mountain troops, or those serving in extreme cold. Commercial versions were also available. *The Collectors Guild*

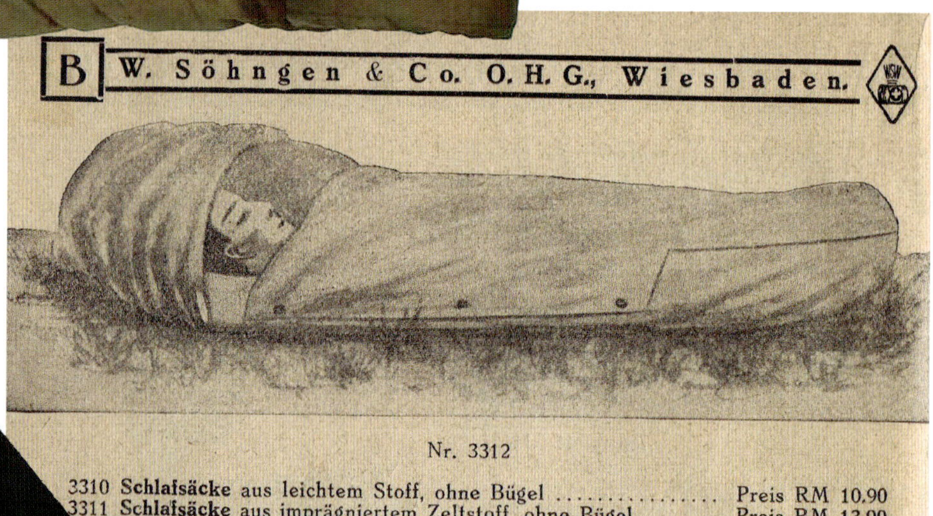

Air mattresses were lightweight and comfortable. *www.raskantik.com*

These soldiers have scrounged some furniture to make their lives more comfortable.

A folding stool.

Inside a bunker. *Bundesarchiv-Bild-101I-034-0095-21A, Foto: Eckart 1939 Herbst*

Soldiers quickly learn how to adapt to their environment.

Eagle brand candles. *www.kpemig.de*

Standard candles like these were used in the field.[2]

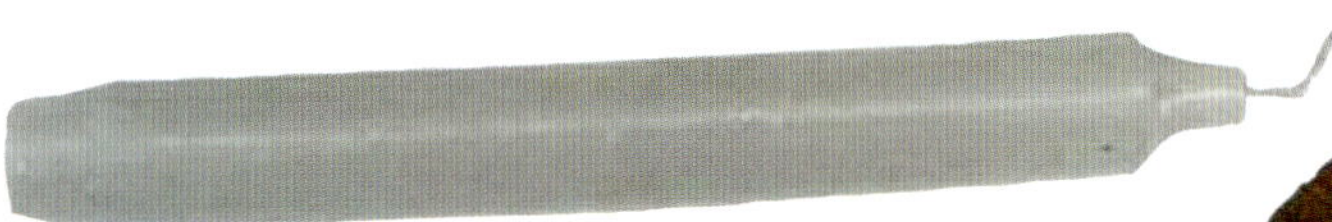

Combat troops received up to four standard candles and twelve of these Hindenburg lights per man per month.

Writing a letter by candlelight.

These soldiers are sorting candles for distribution.

This style of lantern used candles to generate light. *Jim Kreunen of Militaria Plaza*

Flamex brand scrubbing powder.[3] *Bunkermilitaria.com*

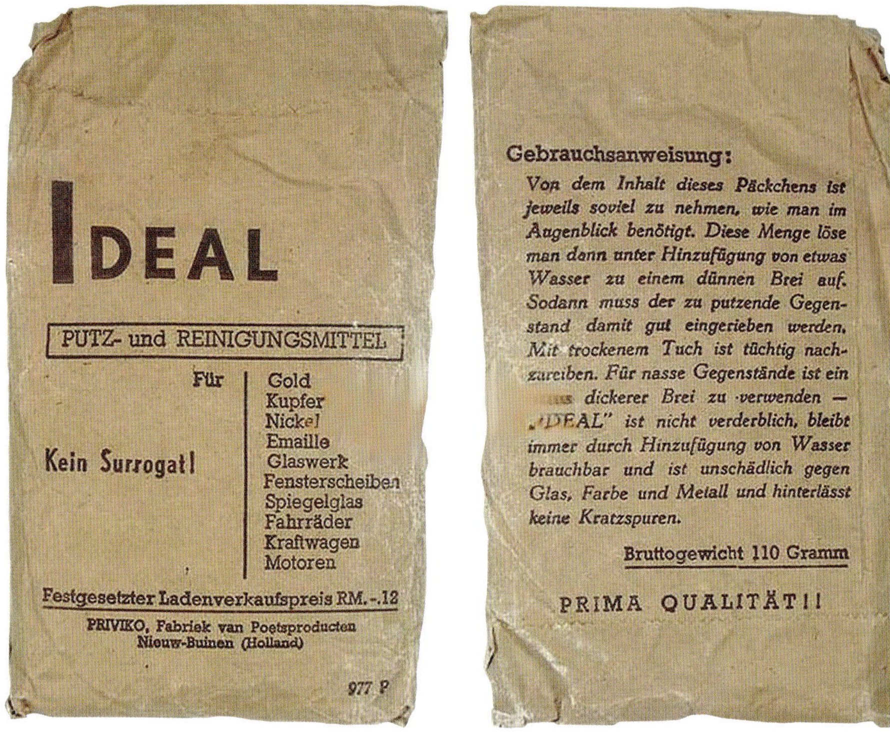

Ideal brand cleaning soap. *Bunkermilitaria.com*

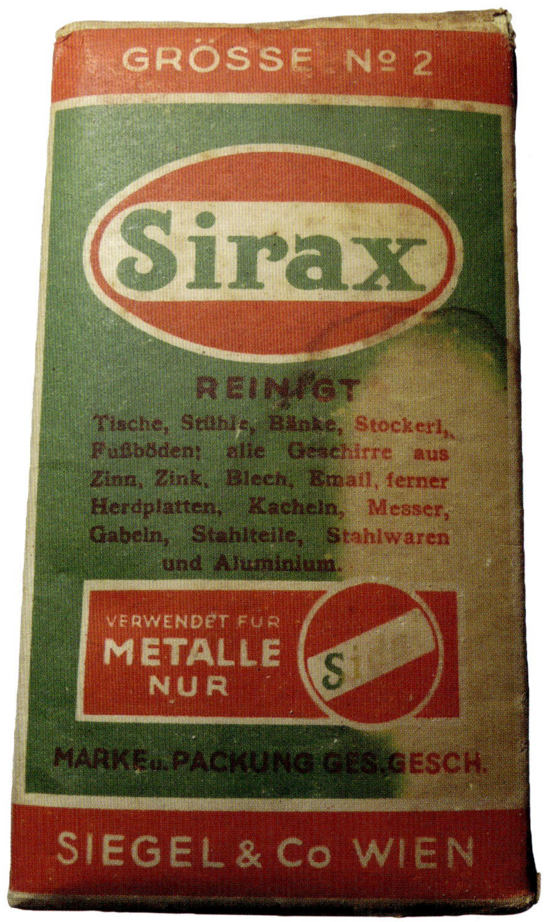

Sirax brand metal cleaner. *Frédéric Ruelle Collection*

Purit brand cleaning soap.

A gathering of young and old soldiers. *Bunkermilitaria.com*

ATA was a very popular cleaning product. *Frédéric Ruelle Collection*

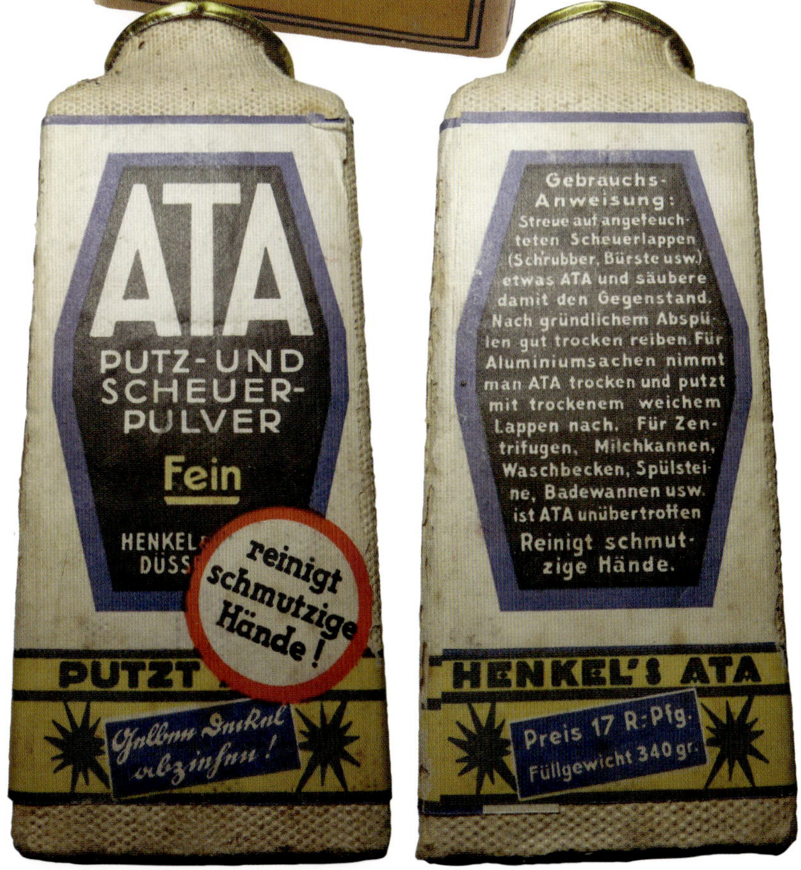

Dust pan and brush.

A hand mop.

VIM was frequently mentioned in Allied intelligence reports. *Frédéric Ruelle Collection*

A tin of Sigella brand floor wax.

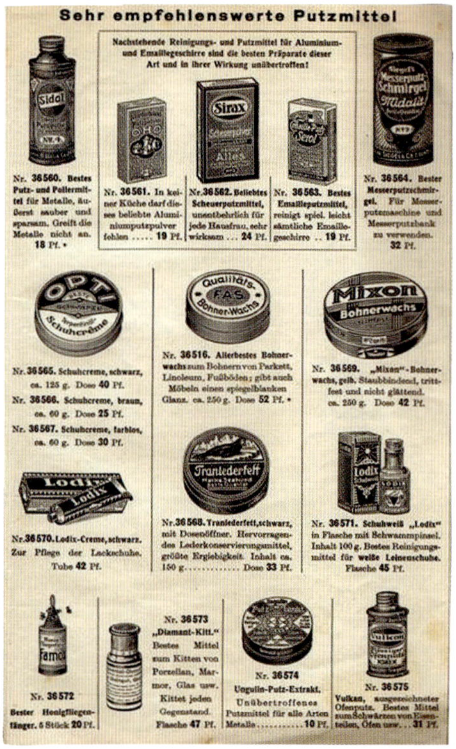

Wartime advertisement for cleaning products.

Scrub brushes. *Helmut Weitze, Hamburg*

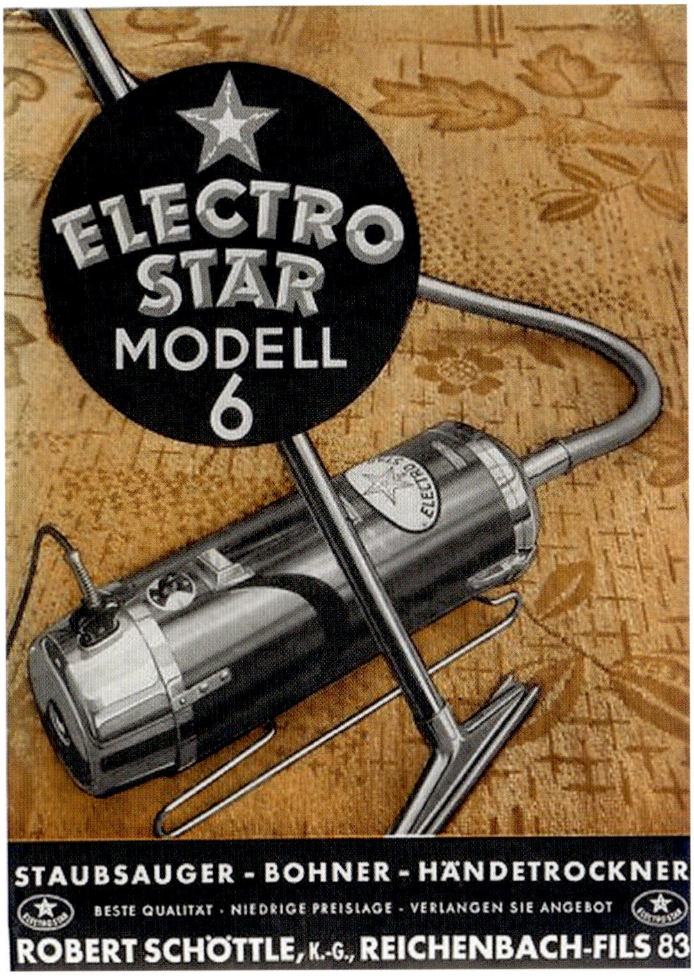

If you lived in a house or apartment, this vacuum cleaner could come in handy.

Spring cleaning!

A variety of toilet paper brands available on the commercial market.

A disposable hygiene kit that included toilet paper.[4]

Toilet paper packaged so it could be shipped via Feldpost.

Toilet paper for the person on the go.

Zelltex toilet paper. *Bunkermilitaria.com*

Nature calls.

This sign for 2nd Battalion, 110th Infantry Regiment is from Campbell Barracks, Heidelberg, Germany, former headquarters of the United States Army in Europe. Prior to May 8, 1945, the Kaserne was occupied by the German 110th Infantry Regiment (112th Infantry Division).

A wartime photograph of Grossdeutschland-Kaserne which became Campbell Barracks, Heidelberg, Germany.

CHAPTER 1 ENDNOTES

1. As a company, OSRAM traces its roots back to 1919. OSRAM was the result of a merger between three companies: AEG, Siemens & Halske AG, and Auer-Gesellschaft. All three companies were pioneers in the development of the electric light. The company is in business today as OSRAM SYLVANIA. Here is a wartime advertisement.

2. The A. Riebeck'sche Montanwerke AG was a German mining company in the form of a public company that existed from 1883 to the 1990s. Here is their listing in the 1929 Mosse Register of Firms.

Riebeck'sche Montanwerke A.-G., A. Vorstand: Direktor Dipl. Ingenieur Dr. Otto Scharf, Vorsitzender des Vorstandes; Direktor Bergassessor Erich Schulze, Direktor Fritz Feiler, Direktor Dipl. - Bergingenieur Paul Franke, Direktor Emil Eberlein. Geschäftshaus I, Riebeckplatz 1, Sammeln. für Stadtgespr.: 27821, für Ferngespr.: 28031 bis 33; Geschäftshaus II

3. The Kraemer & Flammer firm was founded in 1871. The company became a well known detergent and soap producer in Germany. It closed in 1970. Here is their listing in the 1929 Mosse Register of Firms.

Seifenfabr. ×Krämer&Flammer

4. As best as I can determine, Compagnie Ray was founded around 1900. No other history was found. Here is their listing in the 1929 Mosse Register of Firms.

Compagnie Ray GmbH, ℌ 44145, Seifenfabr., Nossener Str. 2–6. *RMC*.

CHAPTER 2

SKIN CARE

Personal hygiene is described as practices performed by an individual to care for one's bodily health and well being through cleanliness. What is considered proper personal hygiene can be cultural, religious, gender, or geographically specific and may change over time. Grooming is an extension of personal hygiene as it pertains to the maintenance of a good personal and public appearance, which is not necessarily hygienic in nature.

Elementary cleanliness is generally considered common knowledge and in a perfect world is easy to achieve. In a combat environment, the simple task of bathing or shaving is not always so easy to accomplish. The German military had bath units as part of their chemical decontamination equipment, but these were rarely employed for the general bathing of German troops. It was largely up to the individual German soldier or his unit to find solutions to this problem. Considering the large number of cologne bottles found in German positions on the Eastern front, it is probably fair to say that no universal solution was found.

Taschenbuch für den Winterkrieg (Handbook for Winter Warfare), dated 1943, provided detailed survival information for German units operating in a winter environment. I took note of those aspects relating to the care and use of individual or unit equipment and reproduced them below. While focusing on winter operations, many procedures were applicable throughout the year.

> The clothing and equipment intended for winter warfare must afford not only comfort but freedom of movement for combat, and especially for attack in severe cold, deep snow, and strong wind. If supplies issued to the unit are not sufficient, they must be augmented by improvisations and substitutes of all kinds. The ingenuity of the individual soldier and of the leader in contriving makeshifts keeps the unit efficient and reduces casualties.
>
> The following are basic requirements for clothing, equipment, and weapons in winter:
>
> a. Clothing should not be too warm, but it must be windproof. It should permit quick movements (jumping, creeping, shooting). Extra underwear for changing after sweating, and additional warm clothing (such as a slipover sweater), should be carried for wear during rest periods and bivouacs.
>
> b. Camouflage suits should be supplied at least to patrols and sentries. If such suits are not available they must be improvised.
>
> c. Footgear is especially important. Felt boots are best, but they must be kept dry. Keep the uppers of leather boots from freezing hard by wearing overboots or cloth covers over them. In addition, paper and foot cloths should be wrapped on the feet in addition to socks. Footgear must be roomy enough to permit moving the toes.
>
> d. Bivouac equipment makes one independent of permanent shelters. Cloth tents of the Finnish type are the best, but in emergencies, shelter halves (which may also be used as ground sheets) will do. The equipment should also include plywood shelters, portable stoves, and individual cooking utensils so that the men can cook their own food.
>
> e. Skis should be provided for ski troops, scouts, messengers, and signal and medical personnel of all ranks. These classes of personnel should also be provided with felt boots and over boots if possible, otherwise with laced shoes. Snowshoes may be used as expedients.
>
> f. Sleds must be substituted for most wheeled vehicles. The sleds must be light, and of standard width, and horses should be harnessed one behind the other (tandem). Field kitchens and heavy weapons must be loaded on sleds or runners.
>
> g. Snow-clearing equipment is needed to facilitate movement, especially off the road. Snow plows should be provided or improvised.
>
> h. Weapons must be mobile, and therefore their weight and caliber must be limited. They must be in condition to fire in any weather. For close combat many automatic weapons are needed, but it is better to have a large abundance of ammunition rather than a large number of weapons with only a limited amount of ammunition.
>
> i. Individual motor vehicles, tanks, and assault guns are often valuable aids in winter combat and must be ready for operations in any kind of weather. Snow must be cleared to facilitate their movement.
>
> j. Medical equipment must be provided in greater quantities than in other seasons. Provisions must be made for adequate transportation of the wounded, even in front lines, and for protecting them against the cold.

Health measures for troops quartered in billets during the winter were also discussed in the *Taschenbuch für den Winterkrieg*:

> It is best to wash oneself with cold water in the morning and with warm water at night. Wash cloths of rough fabrics are desirable. A warm shower should be taken at least once a week. Finish it with a short cold shower; otherwise there is danger of catching cold. After washing, grease the face and hands with Vaseline, boric-acid ointment, or water-free cold cream (Vaseline, Borsalbe, wasserfreie Hautcreme) before going outside. It is advisable to shave at night to avoid chapping of the skin. Hair should be cut short as a safeguard against lice. Regular brushing of the hair is very important.
>
> In permanent billets, soldiers should work in shifts so that all will have rest periods. Duties outside barracks should be carried out around midday, when the sun is shining; duty inside barracks, when it is cold and dark. Loitering in the open air, especially after physical exertion and perspiration, should be avoided. Rest periods during fatigue in the cold, open air do more harm than good, as it is unwise to lie or sit down. During practice firing, soldiers should be relieved frequently, and huts and fires must be at hand for their comfort.
>
> Vermin can communicate dangerous contagious diseases to human beings. The best method of fighting them is by keeping quarters, clothing, and the body clean. Lice can transmit spotted fever, and "five-day fever" (Fünftagefieber), a sickness which occurs frequently during the winter, when people live in close contact. Fleas from rats can communicate the plague. The sooner you fight vermin, the easier it will be to destroy them. Fix regular hours for delousing. Body lice usually are found in pleats and seams of clothing, bedding, and equipment. During inspection special attention should be paid to these hidden places.
>
> Lice may be eradicated by washing clothing with a cresol-soap solution or with kerosene, and then pressing the garment with a hot iron. Regular use should be made of Russla louse powder. If clothes are too heavily infested with lice, they should be treated in delousing stations by means of dry heat or steam, or, in the case of underclothing, by boiling.
>
> If bedbugs appear in great numbers, the quarters should be fumigated with gas. For this purpose, the men must move temporarily to other quarters, but only after having cleaned their bodies thoroughly and deloused their clothes. When returning to their original quarters, the men must observe the precautionary measures laid down by the fumigators.
>
> Places where pipes have been removed should be especially protected against the rats. Use traps continuously against mice and rats. Poisoned grain, meat, bacon, fish, and intestines should be used as bait. The bait and the location of the traps should be frequently changed. If rats or other rodents run around dizzily or let themselves be caught, or if a remarkable number of the bodies of these rodents are found, there is danger of an outbreak of plague. The unit medical officers should be notified immediately so that countermeasures can be taken in time. Each plague of human beings is preceded by a plague of rats.
>
> Keeping animals for combating rats and mice is not advisable; dogs and cats can easily communicate rat-bite disease, tapeworm, and rabies to human beings with whom they live in close contact. Rabies is not infrequent in Eastern Europe, because of the wolves indigenous there. Wolves and stray dogs and cats should be destroyed. If an animal which has bitten a person is suspected of having rabies, it should not be shot through the head because examination of the brain is necessary.
>
> If possible construct an emergency delousing station. Such stations consist of a steam bath, or sauna (common in Finland), which may be built in existing rooms that meet the necessary specifications. In field positions, these stations may be constructed in the form of log huts, but suitable drainage must be provided.
>
> Heat retaining walls and ceilings are essential. In the log-cabin type, for example, insulation is provided by filling all cracks with straw and earth, and insulating the roof with an upper layer of clay, with sand filler. Stone-lined ditches are installed under the floor for drainage.
>
> A furnace of field stones, preferably granite, is made without cement on a solid rock foundation. A chimney is not necessary; the smoke is drawn up through the ventilating pipe in the ceiling.
>
> For fuel, use birch, alder, or pine wood. The furnace is heated for several hours until the room temperature reaches 140 to 158 degrees F. Then remove the fire from the furnace and pour a small quantity of hot water over the hot stones. The steam will drive the remaining smoke up through the ventilator in the roof. When the smoke has been cleared out, the ventilator vent is closed to prevent loss of steam. The sauna bath is then ready for use. During the bathing process, hot water is poured on the rocks from time to time in order to create more steam.

German Clothing, Equipment and Rations emphasized the importance of training and leader involvement to prevent serious health issues from occurring. While that particular reference focused on operations in winter climates, the Germans emphasized training in every operating environment.

> The enormous importance which the Germans placed on extensive training in the proper use of winter clothing and equipment and in living in cold weather was clearly shown in the interrogations. Some of the most interesting observations given by higher ranking officers were made by the following: Generaloberstabsintendant (Lieutenant General of the Quartermaster Corps) Kleberger, the Quartermaster General of the German Field Army (Feldheer); Generalstabsintendant (Major General of the Quartermaster Corps) Fritsch, Chief Quartermaster of the Commander-in-Chief West; Generalstabsarzt (Major General of the Medical Corps) Haubenreisser, Chief Surgeon of the Commander-in-Chief West; Generalarzt (Brigadier General of the Medical Corps) Wischhusen, Chief Surgeon of the 1st German Army; Generalstabsintendant (Major General of the Quartermaster Corps) Berndt, Chief Quartermaster of the 6th German Air Force; Colonel Michelowsky, Chief

Surgeon of the 6th German Air Forces; Lt. Col. Detterde, Quartermaster of the XIII Waffen SS Corps. In addition to the observations of these high ranking officers, a number of company officers were interviewed. These officers were able to give an account of the actual training and how it was carried out. Coming from infantry, armored infantry, armored, mountain, paratroop and artillery units, they were able to tell how it had been done in different parts of the Eastern front, from Northern Finland to the steppes of the Ukraine, in the Balkans, Italy, and Western Europe.

As has been said the importance placed by the Germans on training soldiers in the use of their cold weather clothing and equipment and in living under winter conditions cannot be overemphasized. All officers, from top to bottom, stated unanimously that the best equipment was useless unless it was used properly. For instance General Wischhusen stated half of the problem of preventing trench foot was providing the soldiers with properly fitted, waterproof (preferably rubber) footgear. Supply difficulties often curtailed this. The other half of the problem was no less important. That was training the men to change their socks to dry ones, massage the feet, to dry their socks, to carry their extra socks with them, in short, *training the men to use their clothing and equipment properly in cold weather*.

Material for instructing the troops was made up either by the Quartermaster or Medical Departments or by both jointly. These were then issued out to the troops at least down to company level and in some cases to each soldier. These consisted of pamphlets, manuals, instructional sheets, training films, etc. Particular emphasis was put on issuing new information on improvisations and instructions on new clothing and equipment. Typical of the written information are the "Handbook for Winter Warfare" (*Taschenbuch für den Winterkrieg*) published in English as *M.I.S., Special Series #18*, "German Winter Warfare." "Tentative Instructions for the Training and Tactics of Ski Troops" (*Verläufige Richtlinien für Ausbildung von Skitruppen*) published in English as *M.I.S. Special Series #20*, "*German Ski Training and Tactics; 'From the Front for the Front'*, (*Von der Front für die Front*), a periodical of improvisations; and leaflets like "Injuries from the Cold," given out to each soldier to be pasted into his paybook (Author's note: See chapter 7). The higher echelons kept sending out instructional material to the units throughout the winter months.

From the material which was sent out to them, as well as from first-hand experience, the company commander or the medical officer or both was required to give instructional courses during the winter months. A check of company officers in the Army (Heer), Luftwaffe, and Waffen SS revealed that except in the most unusual cases instruction was given once a week. Not one single officer reported that it was given less often. Mountain troop officers from Finland said that their troops received instruction twice a week. This was definite instruction and must not be confused with the foot inspections which were supposed to take place every 48 hours. The subjects stressed for the most part were the same subjects which have been emphasized by the U.S. Quartermaster training course in cold weather living. The similarity was striking. Important points of the many taught included the following: changing the socks; drying them; avoiding standing still; seeing a medical officer if feet got numb; not dressing too warmly; stripping off clothing before getting too hot; washing socks at every opportunity; using foot powder; etc.

Contrary to the belief of many Americans, the Germans did not suffer badly from the cold after the disastrous winter of 1941-1942. This was emphasized by all from General Kleberger down to company officers. Even accounts in the N.Y. Times coming from U.S.S.R. have pointed this out. All the German officers felt that the training was one of the primary causes for this change. Indeed it was very striking that every officer from the highest echelon to company level emphasized the importance of the training and the necessity of repeating it continually under almost all circumstances to prevent the disastrous casualties which would otherwise be suffered in winter warfare.

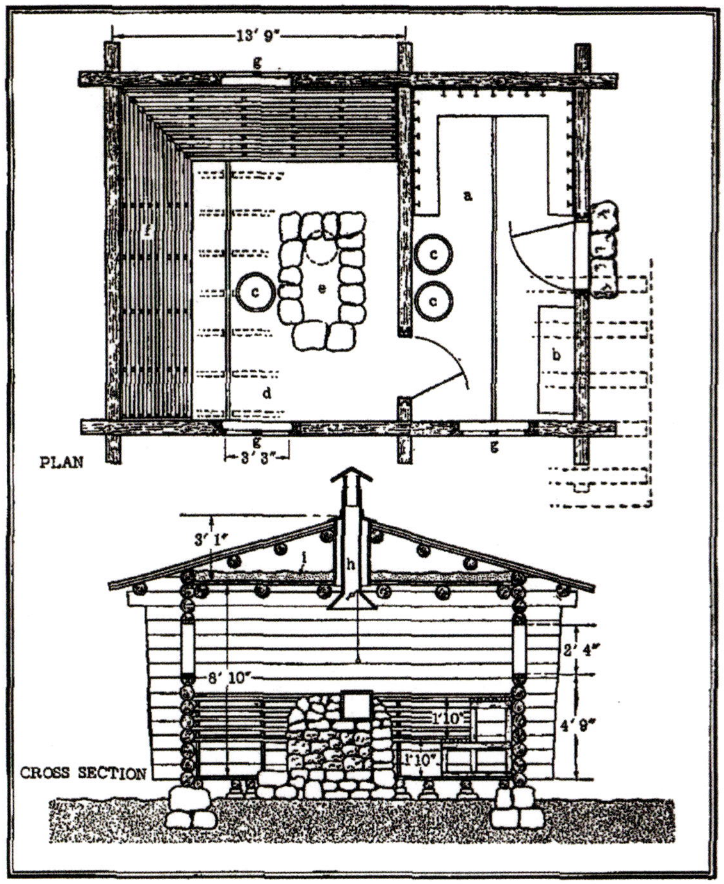

Figure 73.—Sauna (Finnish steam bath) in log cabin.

a. Anteroom with bench
b. Woodpile
c. Water tanks
d. Bathrooms
e. Furnace with hot-water tank
f. Benches in tiers
g. Windows
h. Chimney with vent
i. Roof insulation (humus and earth)

Diagram of a Finnish sauna.

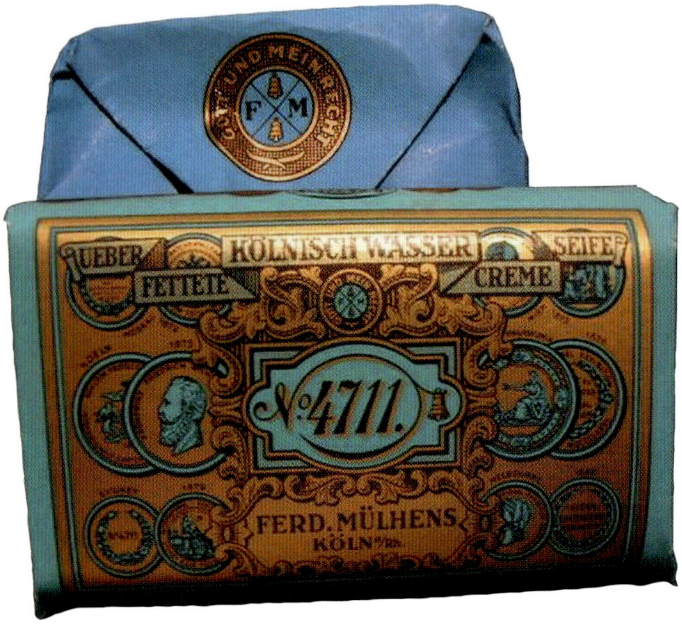

A bar of 4711 brand soap.[1] *OSTFRONT Militaria*

A bar of Abralin brand soap.[2] *Bunkermilitaria.com*

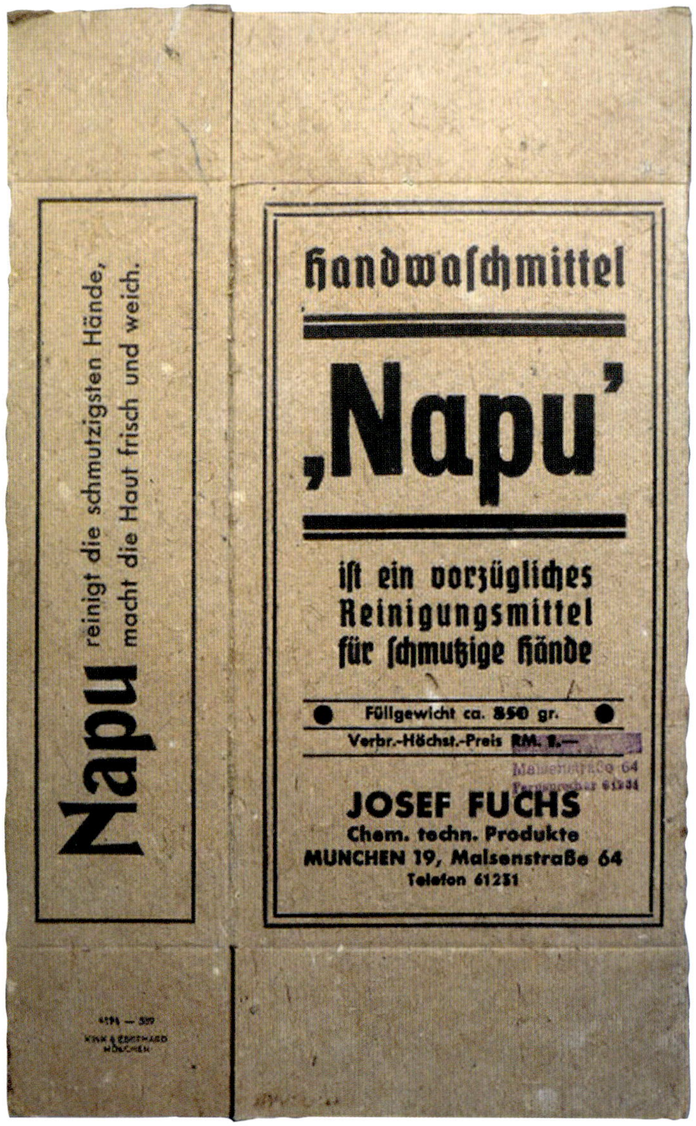

Napu brand hand soap. *Bunkermilitaria.com*

Puck is actually a general purpose cleaning product, but could also be used for washing hands. *Bunkermilitaria.com*

Zaza brand hand soap.[3] *Bunkermilitaria.com*

Hygienic soap sheets for soldiers in the field. *www.kpemig.de*

A bar of Edel Kernseife.[4]

Palm oil soap manufactured by the Pfeilring-Werke.[5]

A bar of OBE soap.[6] *Bunkermilitaria.com*

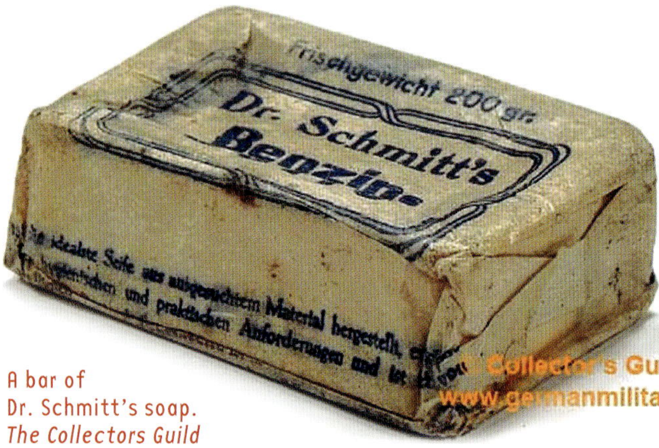

A bar of
Dr. Schmitt's soap.
The Collectors Guild

Two bars of kernseife.

Box of soap from the firm of M. Kappus.

PIK-AS brand soap. *Jim Kreunen of Militaria Plaza*

Dalli soap.[7]

AoK brand skin cleanser.[8] *Frédéric Ruelle Collection*

Schwan brand soap. *Frédéric Ruelle Collection*

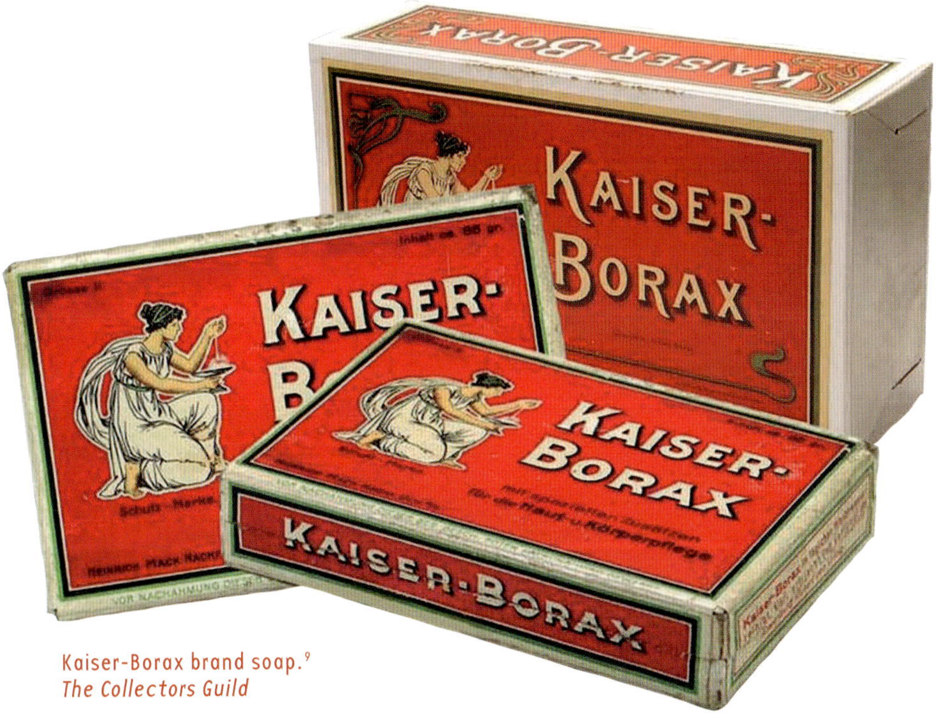

Kaiser-Borax brand soap.[9] *The Collectors Guild*

Time for cleaning and freshening up.

Issue wash basin. *www.kpemig.de*

Soap dishes came in a variety of colors, sizes, and materials. *Frédéric Ruelle Collection*

A pair of Air Force swim trunks. *Helmut Weitze, Hamburg*

These SS soldiers donned swimming trunks as they washed up. *National Archives and Records Administration (NARA)*

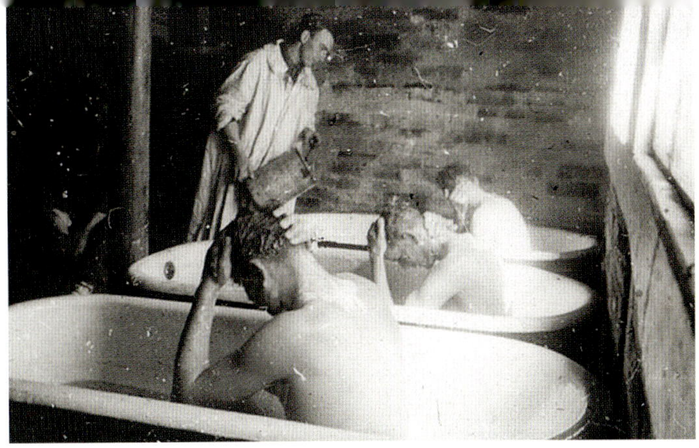

It felt good to wash away the dirt and grime. *Photos: US National Archives and Records Administration (NARA)*

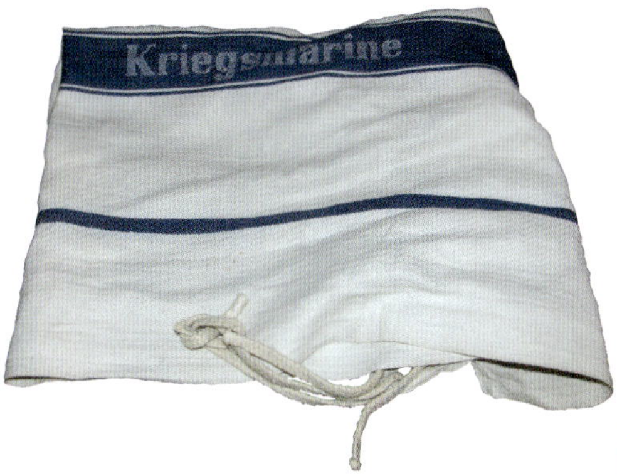

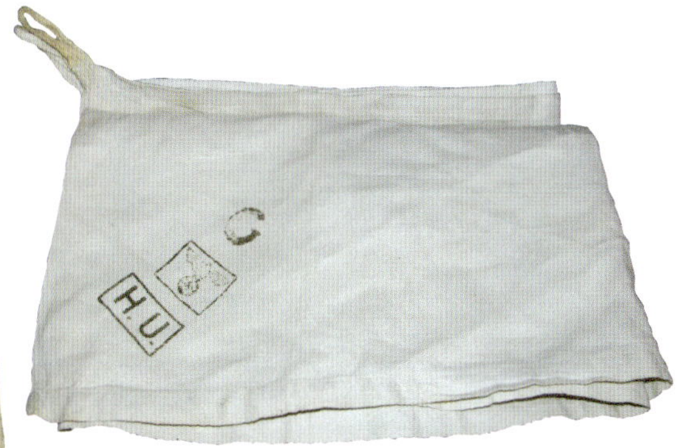

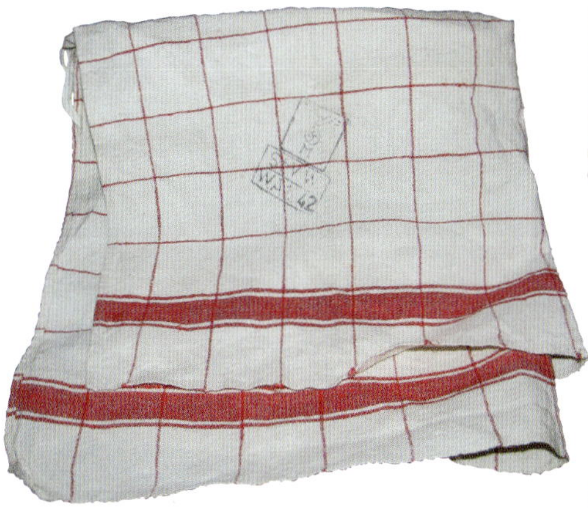

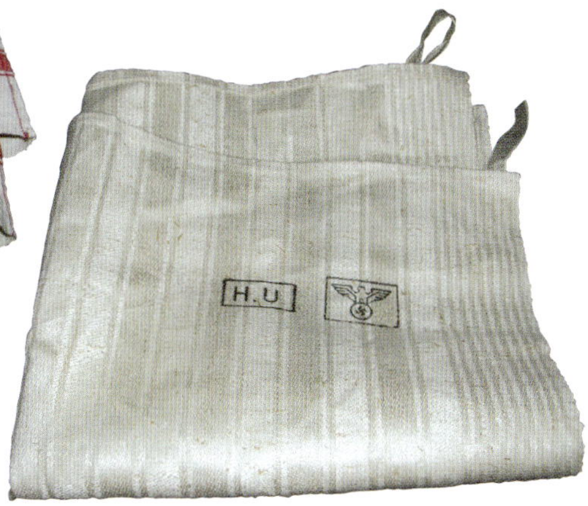

Various bath and hand towels. *Bunkermilitaria.com*

Bathing products as advertised in the *Officers Clothing* catalog.

Talcum powder.

Nivea brand body powder. [10]

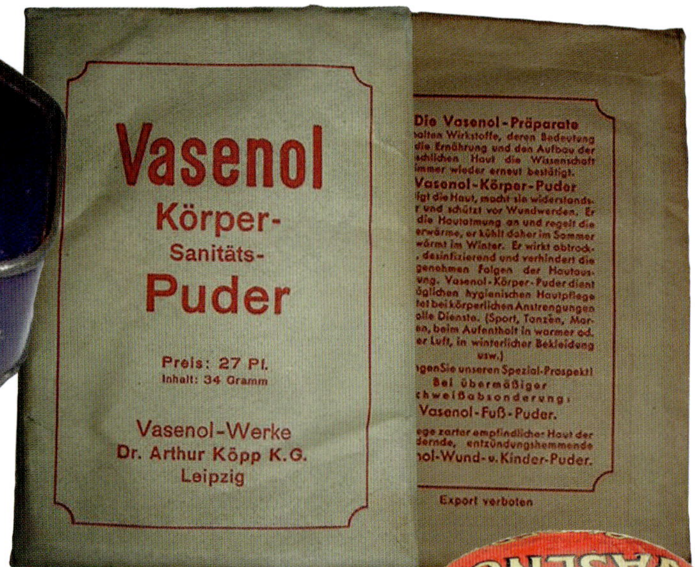

A variety of Vasenol products.[11]

Divenus brand body powder.

Silvana brand powder.

Scented powder by Heinz Pabst, Leipzig. *Michel Verberkt Collection*

Nivea cream was very popular with the troops. *Frédéric Ruelle Collection and The Collectors Guild*

Nivea skin oil and cologne.

Peri body cream and Lenicet skin protection cream.[12] *Zeugmeister Collection*

A tin of Socco brand Vaseline. *Frédéric Ruelle Collection*

Eukutol cream.[13] *OSTFRONT Militaria*

Blendax brand skin cream.[14]

Mayolin brand skin cream.

A tin of skin cream manufactured by A. Waldheim. *Michel Verberkt Collection*

Diaderma oil.[15] *Zeugmeister Collection*

Sparta 4711 cream.

A few more examples of skin cream products. *Frédéric Ruelle Collection*

Pigmentan brand skin cream. [16]

Leokrem.[17] *Jim Kreunen of Militaria Plaza*

Sixtolin oil for sun burns, insect bites, and frostbite manufactured by Richter and Co., Schliersee.[18] *Michel Verberkt Collection*

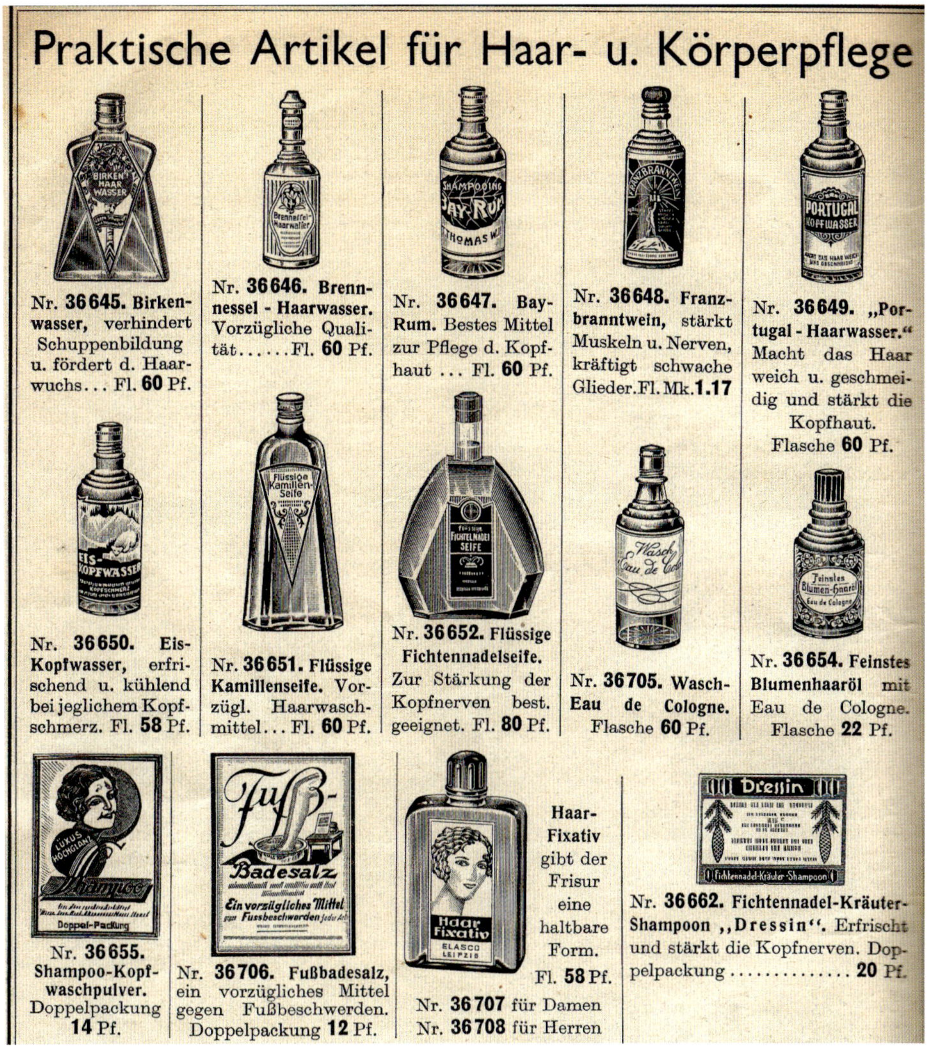

Wartime advertisement for a variety of hair and body products.

Getting ready for a night on the town. *Helmut Weitze, Hamburg*

The sign says this is the entrance to an indoor swimming pool. *Bundesarchiv-Bild-101I-100-0754-17 Foto: Krumme 1942*

CHAPTER 2 ENDNOTES

1. During the eighteenth century, Italian expatriate Johann Maria Farina created a new fragrance and named it *Eau de Cologne* (water from Cologne) after his new residence, Cologne, Germany. In the late 1880s, "4711" was selected as the company name (after an office address). During the war, German U-Boat crew members were routinely issued 4711 perfume to improve the odor aboard their vessel. In many cases, the crew members would take home bottles as presents for mothers, wives, or girlfriends. Here is a wartime advertisement.

2. Luhns GmbH is a German manufacturer of washing and cleaning products. The company was founded on January 8, 1869, in Wuppertal-Barmen, Germany, and is still in business. The factory was heavily bombed during the war and on March 13, 1945, an aerial attack destroyed the factory. Here is a wartime advertisement.

3. In 1848, the M. Kappus soap and perfume factory was founded in Offenbach, Germany. When WWII began, the company only produced sand soap (pumice) and floating soap. By 1945, over 80% of the factory was destroyed. The company is still in business. Here is their listing in the 1929 Mosse Register of Firms.

Kappus, M. (Ad., Ludw. u. Mart. Kappus), Seifenfabr., 𝔉 Sa. 83241, Ps 7295 Fr., Bk S. Merzbach, TA Kappus.

4. The Schlüchterner Seifenfabrik Meier Wolf was originally a Jewish-owned firm. The owners were forced to sell in 1938 and the name was changed to Schlüchterner Seifenfabrik E. Heinlein. The company remained in operation until 1987. Here is their listing in the 1929 Mosse Register of Firms, when it still belonged to the Wolf family.

Seifenfabr. (Dampf-). ×Wolf GmbH, M., 𝔉 25, Ps 258 Fr. – **Wolf, Victor,** 𝔉 4 u. 24, [G], Ps 260 Fr., TA Seifenindustrie, RUC

5. The Pfeilring-Werke, Berlin, Germany, was founded in 1872. I believe they were finally acquired by L'Oreal in 1973. Here is a wartime advertisement.

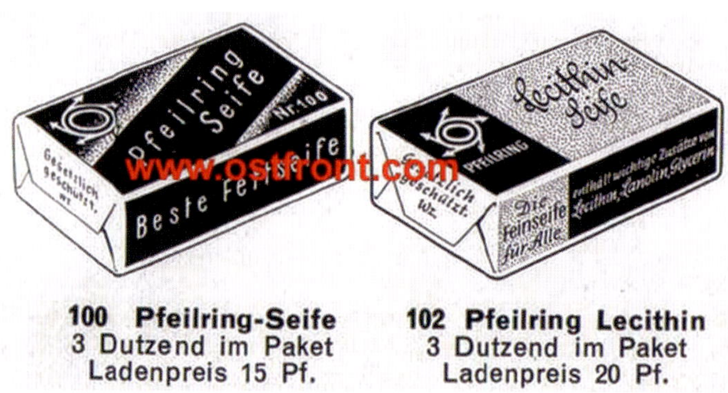

6. OBE soap was manufactured by Gebrüder Kiefer, Seifenfabrik, Kehl, Germany. No history of the firm was found. Here is their address in the 1929 Mosse Register of Firms.

Kiefer, Gebrüder (Karl K.), Seifenfabrik, 𝔉 33, Ps 4959 Ka.

7. The Mäurer and Wirtz Seifen-Fabrik was founded in 1848 in Stolberg, Germany. The brand name DALLI SOAP was first used in 1885. In 1938, the firm acquired factories in Berlin and Vienna. The company is still in operation. Here are some prewar letterheads.

8. Pharmacist Wilhelm Anhalt of Bad Kolberg (currently in Poland) founded the AOK firm in 1885. The firm specialized in pharmaceutical and cosmetics, and also went by the name C. Lück. The AOK brand was officially registered in 1903. The three letters stand for the roots of the company: A for Wilhelm Anhalt, O for Ostseebad (Baltic Ocean), and K for Kolberg. By autumn 1943, production had ceased due to a lack of raw materials. In March 1945, the factory burned down. AOK cosmetics are still being produced.

9. Kaiser Borax is a traditional brand established in 1849 as the Heinrich Mack Firm, Illertissen, near Ulm, Germany. In 1939, the company got into the bee business, producing a rheumatic agent (Forapin), as well as a honey-based sedative and cough suppressant. It is currently a part of Pfizer Manufacturing GmbH Germany. Here is a prewar advertisement.

10. Nivea crème traces back to 1911, and is still being manufactured today. The last wartime Nivea crème can was introduced in 1943. The Nivea website provides a good history with photographs of the various types of packaging used by the company. Here is a wartime advertisement.

11. The Vasenol-Werke, Dr. Arthur Köpp was founded at the end of the nineteenth century. In 1903, Vasenol became a registered trademark for wound and skin care products. In 1946, the company became part of a state-owned East German enterprise named VEB Vasenolwerke, Leipzig. The company was sold several times after the war and it is still in business under the Unilever brand name. Here is a wartime advertisement.

12. Peri cream was manufactured by Dr. Korthaus, Frankfurt A.M., Germany. The company traces its history to the Dr. Albersheim perfumery founded in Frankfurt in 1892. This Jewish firm was sold to Schering AG for a price substantially below its actual value in 1938. The company was taken over by Dr. Korthaus, a former senior manager at the "IG Farben" concern. Fritz Scherk—the principal heir of the deceased firm founder—returned to Germany in 1950 and bought the company back from Schering. Here is a wartime advertisement.

13. No history was found on the Chemische Fabrik Promonta. I believe they are still in business as Promonta Lundbeck Arzneimittel GmbH and Co. Here is a wartime advertisement.

14. The term Blendax for dental products was first registered on 4 January 1910. Blendax GmbH was founded in 1932 in Mainz, Germany, with production starting in 1936. Their product range included toothpaste, shampoo, soap, skin cream, and mouthwash. The company's headquarters in Mainz was almost completely destroyed during the war. The factory in Gera became part of the state-owned East German system, first as VEB Blendax and later as VEB Gerana. It went under the name Gerana Cosmetic GmbH until it closed in 2007. The Mainz plant was rebuilt in 1949. In 1987, the company was acquired by Procter & Gamble. Here is a wartime advertisement.

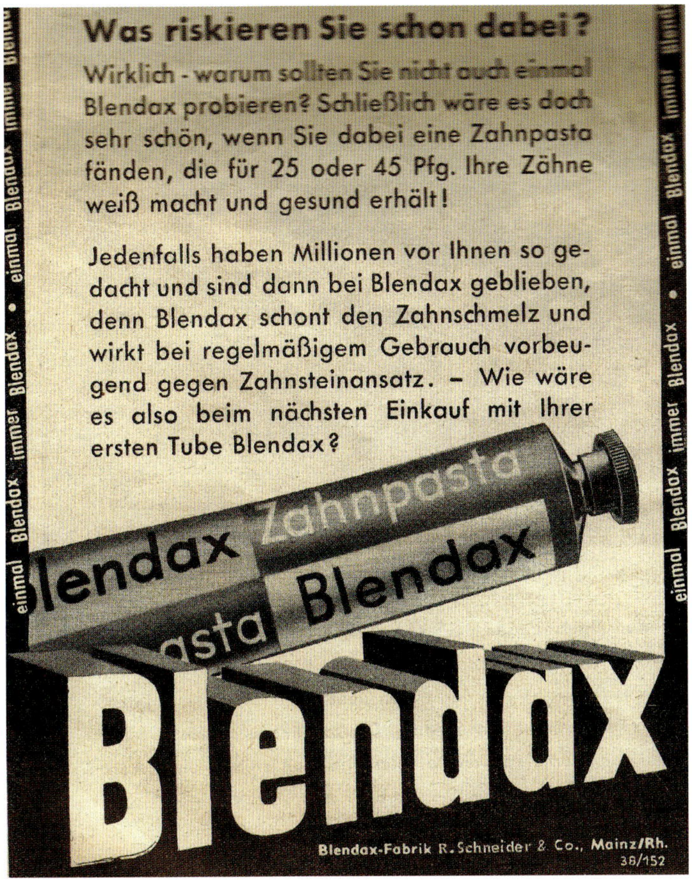

15. The origin of Diaderma-house dates back to 1905, when MEG Gottlieb began selling hygiene and diet products in Heidelberg, Germany. Diaderma—from the Greek word for "through the skin"—was an oil-based skin care product. A Javelin thrower was chosen as the firm's logo. The firm survived the war and is known today as Arya-Laya, which specializes in cosmetics and other health care products. Here is a wartime advertisement.

16. No detailed history was found on Obermeyer and Company, Hanau A/M, Germany. It appears that Pigmentan cream was sold from 1935 into the 1960s. The company is currently named Halajot Germany GmbH. Here is their address in the 1929 Mosse Register of Firms.

Obermeyer & Cie., A-G, Pharmazeut. Präparate, ℱ 2145, [G], Ps 2473 Fr., RUC.

17. Leokrem was produced by Leo-Werke, which was founded in Dresden, Germany, in 1907. They produced the famous Chlorodont toothpaste in 1917. Chlorodont is derived from the words *chloros* (Greek for green, as a symbol of freshness and the peppermint flavor) and *odon* (Greek for tooth). Chlorodont was produced until the early 1980s. By 1924, Leo-Werke was Europe's largest toothpaste manufacturer, with twenty-seven subsidiaries in Germany, Europe, and overseas. The Leo Werke factory was badly damaged in February 1945, but was back in operation by November 1945. In 1952, the company became a state-owned enterprise and was renamed VEB Elbe-Chemie. In 1992, the Munich-based ARGENTA International Investment Company mbH became sole proprietor over what was originally Leo-Werke. Here is a wartime advertisement.

18. Sixtus Werke, Richter and Co. Schliersee, Germany, was founded in 1931. The company is still in business.

CHAPTER 3
ORAL HYGIENE

Oral hygiene is the practice of keeping the mouth and teeth clean to prevent dental problems, especially dental decay, cavities, gingivitis, bad breath, etc. Poor oral hygiene practices can lead to more serious issues which left untreated could affect unit readiness.

I utilized numerous substantiated online articles as the basis for the background discussion and history of oral hygiene. One of the most important tools in dental hygiene is the lowly toothbrush. The earliest use of a toothbrush dates back to 1600 BC. During the 1900s, celluloid handles gradually replaced bone handles in toothbrushes. Natural animal bristles were also replaced by synthetic fibers—usually nylon—by DuPont in 1938. Nylon—or Perlon as it was known in Germany—probably had little impact on the German toothbrush industry, since other wartime requirements most likely took priority.

Tooth powders for use with toothbrushes came into general use in nineteenth century Britain, using chalk, pulverized brick, or salt as ingredients. By 1900, a paste made of hydrogen peroxide and baking soda was recommended for use with toothbrushes. Pre-mixed toothpastes were first marketed in the nineteenth century, but did not surpass the popularity of tooth powder until WWI. In 1892, Dr. Washington Sheffield of London manufactured toothpaste inside a collapsible tube called Dr. Sheffield's Creme Dentifrice. Fluoride was first added to toothpastes in the 1890s. The German toothpaste industry seems to have kept pace with worldwide trends, but was influenced by a lack of resources as the war intensified. Mouthwashes were also available and were used to enhance oral hygiene, but were not as effective as brushing.

It was common practice for the German soldier to place his toiletry items in a ditty bag that was placed in his bread bag or pack.

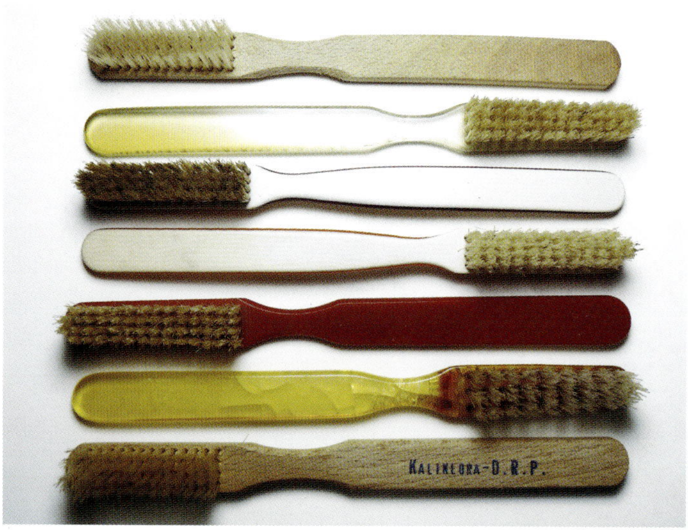

A selection of period toothbrushes. Frédéric Ruelle Collection

A travel container for a Chlorodont brand toothbrush.

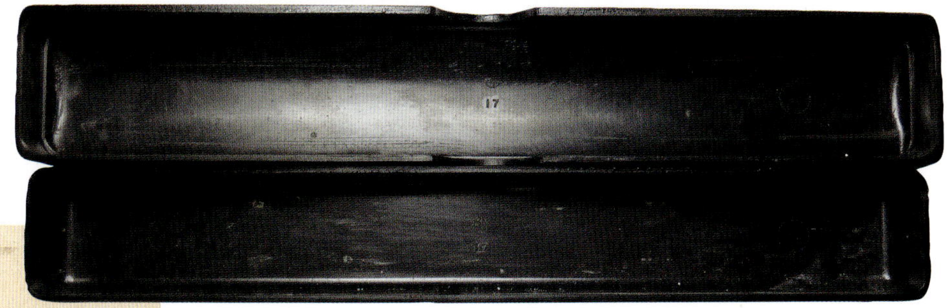

A plain toothbrush container. *Frédéric Ruelle Collection*

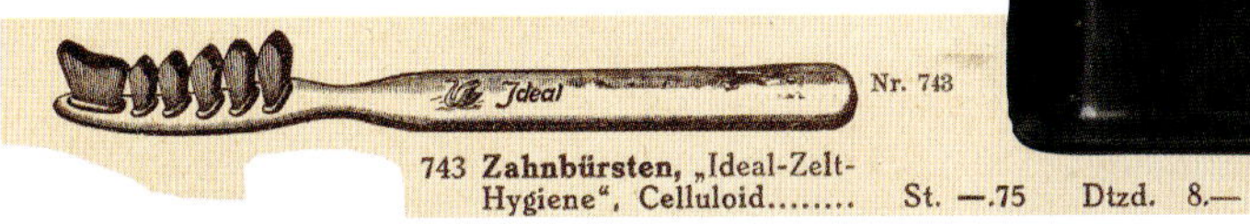

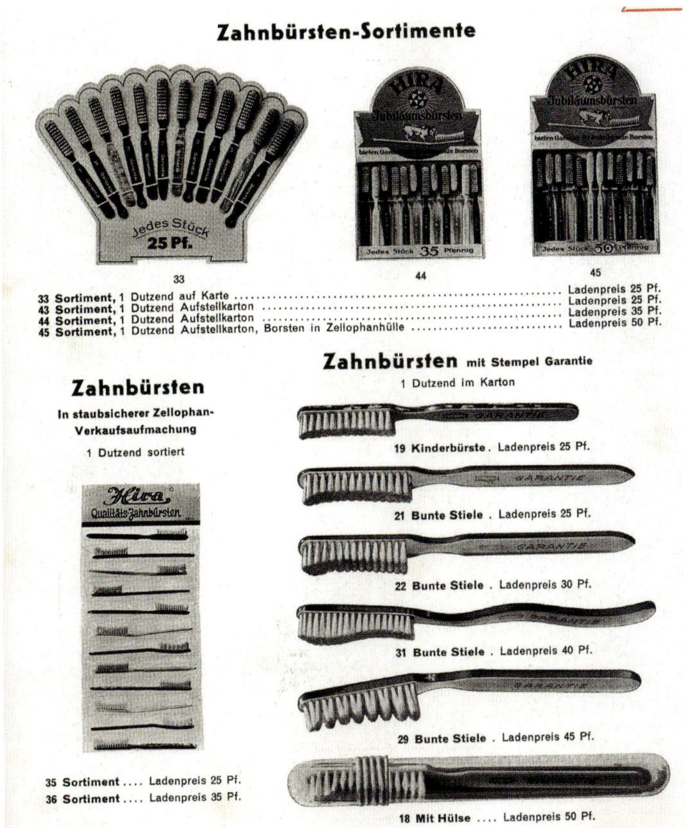

Zahnbürsten-Sortimente

33 Sortiment, 1 Dutzend auf Karte .... Ladenpreis 25 Pf.
43 Sortiment, 1 Dutzend Aufstellkarton .... Ladenpreis 25 Pf.
44 Sortiment, 1 Dutzend Aufstellkarton .... Ladenpreis 35 Pf.
45 Sortiment, 1 Dutzend Aufstellkarton, Borsten in Zellophanhülle .... Ladenpreis 50 Pf.

Zahnbürsten

In staubsicherer Zellophan-Verkaufsaufmachung

1 Dutzend sortiert

35 Sortiment .... Ladenpreis 25 Pf.
36 Sortiment .... Ladenpreis 35 Pf.

Zahnbürsten mit Stempel Garantie

1 Dutzend im Karton

19 Kinderbürste . Ladenpreis 25 Pf.
21 Bunte Stiele . Ladenpreis 25 Pf.
22 Bunte Stiele . Ladenpreis 30 Pf.
31 Bunte Stiele . Ladenpreis 40 Pf.
29 Bunte Stiele . Ladenpreis 45 Pf.
18 Mit Hülse .... Ladenpreis 50 Pf.

Some wartime toothbrush advertisements.

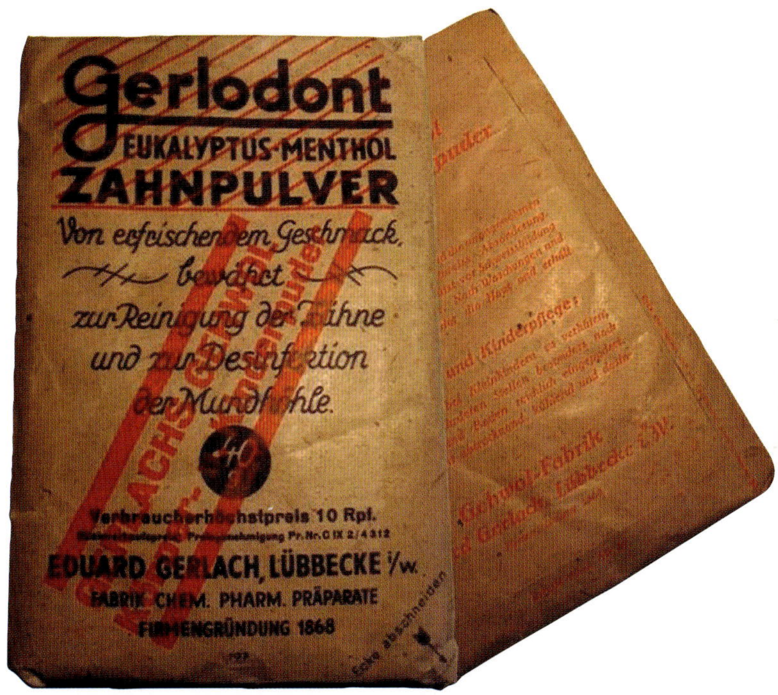

Gerlodent brand tooth powder.[1]

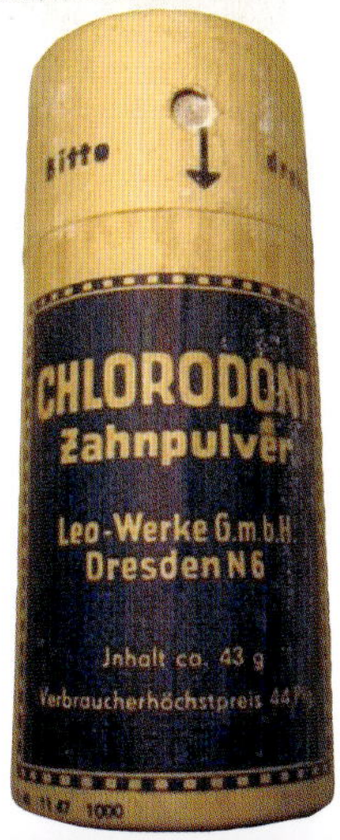

Chlorodont toothpaste and powder.

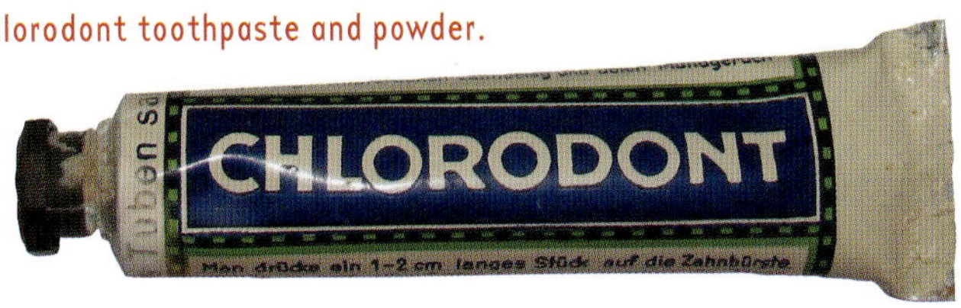

Dallidont brand tooth powder.

Rosodont tooth powder.[2] *Frédéric Ruelle Collection and Bunkermilitaria.com*

TOLA brand tooth powder. *Michel Verberkt Collection*

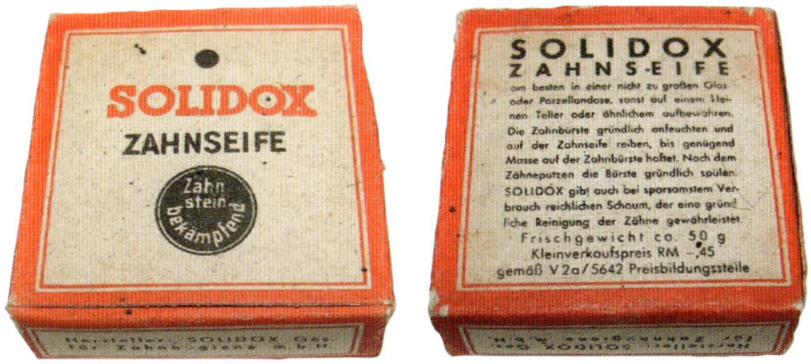

Solidox brand tooth powder.[4]

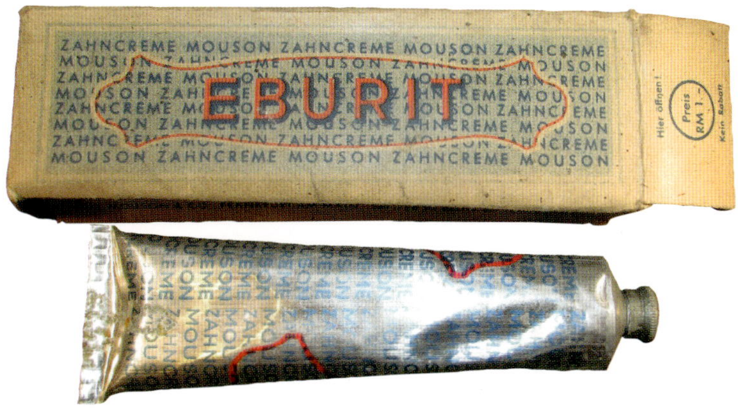

Eburit brand toothpaste.[5]

Paschadont brand tooth powder. *Michel Verberkt Collection*

Kaliklora brand tooth powder.[3]

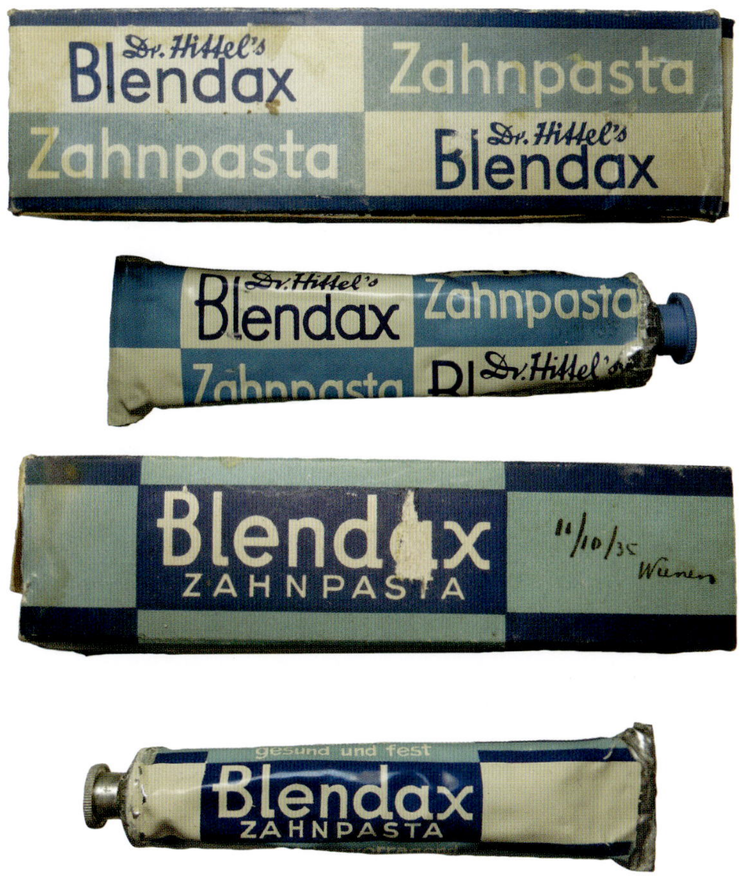

Blendax brand toothpaste. *Frédéric Ruelle Collection*

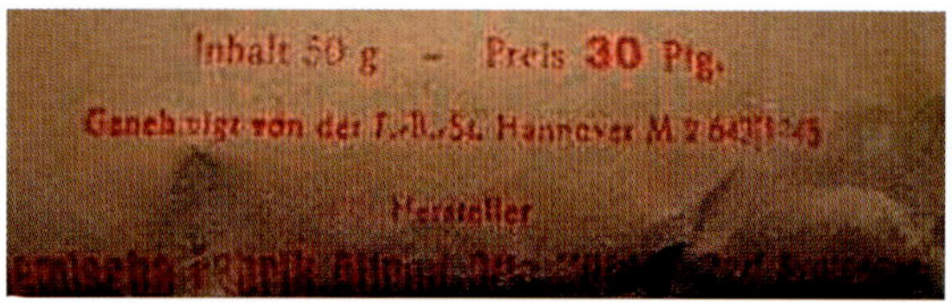

Cosis tooth powder manufactured in Hannover. *Bunkermilitaria.com*

Odol brand toothpaste.[8]

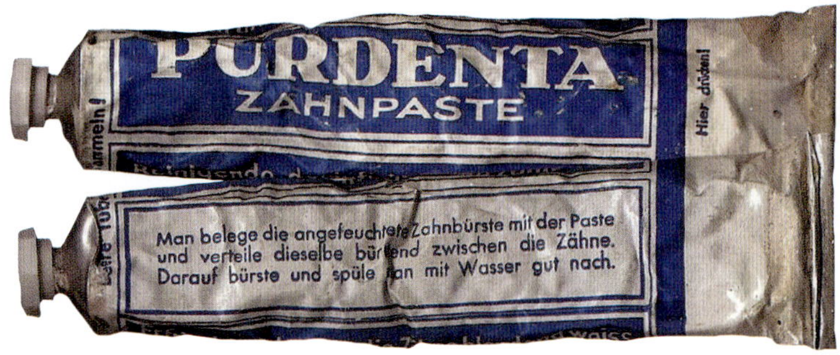

Purdenta brand toothpaste.

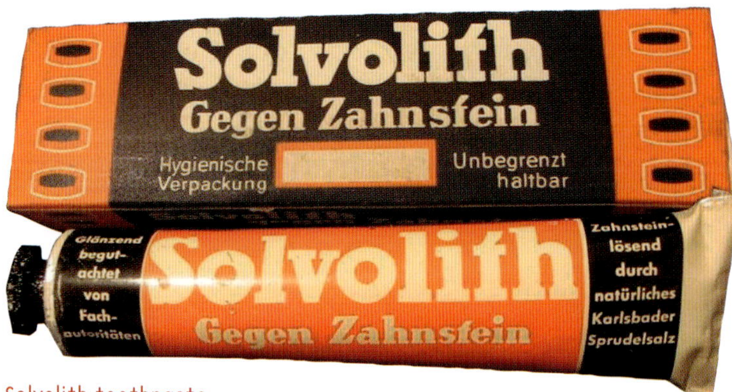

Solvolith toothpaste manufactured by Fattinger Werke, Frankfurt.[9]

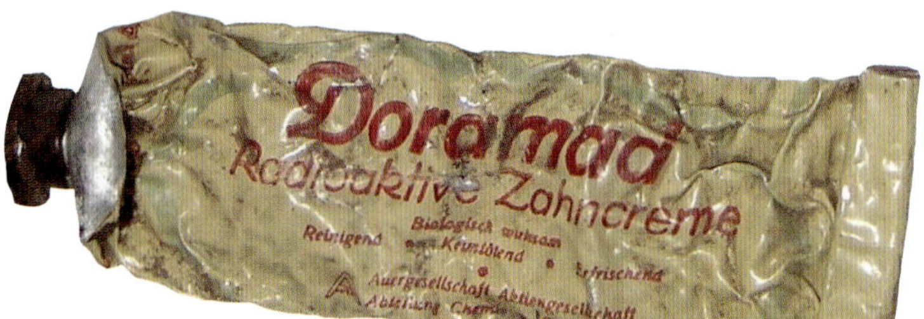

Doramad brand radioactive toothpaste![6] *Kevin Barrett Collection*

COLIBRI brand toothpaste.[7] *Michel Verberkt Collection*

Vademecum tooth powder.[10]

Nivea brand tooth powder.

Mouson tooth powder was over-wrapped in paper prior to shipping. *Frédéric Ruelle Collection*

Tooth powder manufactured by F. Wolff and Sohn, Karlsruhe.[11]

Oral hygiene set from Apotheker Seeger, Landshut. *Michel Verberkt Collection*

Peri toothpaste, along with a wartime advertisement. *Frédéric Ruelle Collection*

Everon toothpaste. *Frédéric Ruelle Collection*

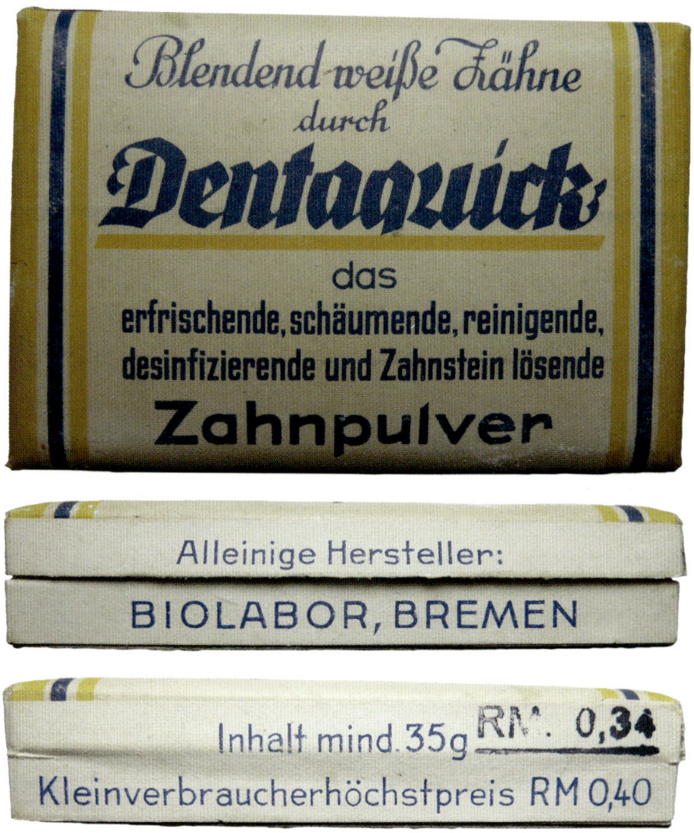

Dentaquick tooth powder manufactured by Biolabor, Bremen. *Frédéric Ruelle Collection*

Odol brand mouthwash.

Oral hygiene in the field.

Formamint germ killing tablets.[12] *OSTFRONT Militaria*

Horse-drawn wagons were commonly used to move supplies in infantry units. *Bundesarchiv Bild 101I-725-0190-24 Foto: Reimers. 1943/44 Winter/ Licence CC-BY-SA 3.0*

CHAPTER 3 ENDNOTES

1. The firm Eduard Gerlach, Lübbecke i/w, Germany was founded in 1868. It was a pioneer in the foot care industry and is still in business as Gewol. There is an excellent book on the company website that provides a detailed history of the firm. Here is a wartime advertisement.

2. The A.H.A. Bergmann firm was founded in 1852, in Waldheim, Germany. The brand name Rosodont was patented in 1904. It became a state-owned factory in East Germany. It is still in operation as Florena Cosmetic GmbH. Here is a wartime advertisement.

3. Queisser and Company was founded in Hamburg, Germany, in 1897. It moved to Flensburg in 1987. The current Queisser Pharma arose from the merger of two companies: Queisser and Doppelherz Pharma. It is an international firm. Here is a wartime advertisement.

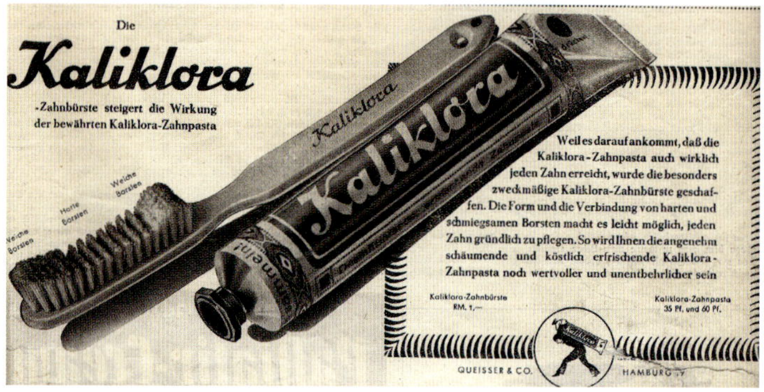

4. Lilleborg AS is a major hygiene company in Norway. It was established in 1833, and was one of the first companies in Norway to start manufacturing brand name products, i.e., Lano, Solidox, Blenda, and Lux. During the 1920s and 1930s, Lilleborg developed a close relationship with Denofa (a Norwegian cooking oil company) and the British company Lever Brothers (Unilever). As part of this agreement, Lilleborg acquired ownership and production of several well-known Lever Brothers brands, Sunlight being perhaps the best known. It is still in business. Here is a wartime advertisement.

5. J. G. Mouson & Cie. was founded in 1798 in Frankfurt am Main, Germany. By the 1870s, it had gained international renown. It produced a wide range of products, including tooth powder/paste, mouthwash, hair tonic, shaving soaps, perfumes, and other cosmetics. The lack of resources made production difficult during the war. In early 1944, 70% of the factory was destroyed during an air raid. It survived the war and finally shut down in 1972. Here is their address in the 1929 Mosse Register of Firms.

Mouson & Co., J. G. (Aug. Frdr. Mouson u. E. Bieber), Я Ca. 40351, Toiletteseifen- u. Parfümeriefabr., Gwinnerstr. 9. [G], Ps 2572, TA Mousonco, RUC

6. Doramad radioactive toothpaste was produced during WWII by Auergesellschaft of Berlin, Germany. The toothpaste did contain very low levels of thorium. Auergesellschaft was founded in 1892 in Berlin. Until the end of WWII they conducted research in gas mantles, luminescence, rare earths, radioactivity, and uranium and thorium compounds. In 1934, the corporation was acquired by the German corporation Degussa. In 1939, their Oranienburg plant began the development of industrial-scale, high-purity uranium oxide production. In 1958, Auergesellschaft merged with the Mine Safety Appliances Corporation, a multinational US corporation. Auergesellschaft became a limited corporation in 1960. Here is a wartime advertisement.

7. The Georg Dralle firm was founded in 1852 in Altona, Hamburg, Germany. It was in operation until 1991. Here is a wartime advertisement.

8. In 1892, Dresden, Germany, businessman Karl August Lingner introduced Odol mouthwash to the market. Odol is from the Greek word Od (ous, teeth) and the Latin word *ol* (eum, oil). The factory was destroyed during the war. The Odol firm is still in business. Here is a wartime advertisement.

9. No history was found on Solvolith Fattinger Werke, Frankfurt, Germany. Here is a wartime advertisement.

10. Barnängens Vademecum GmbH is a Swedish firm founded in 1868. It manufactured pharmaceutical and cosmetic preparations like Vademecum toothpaste. It is still in business. Here are some prewar advertisements.

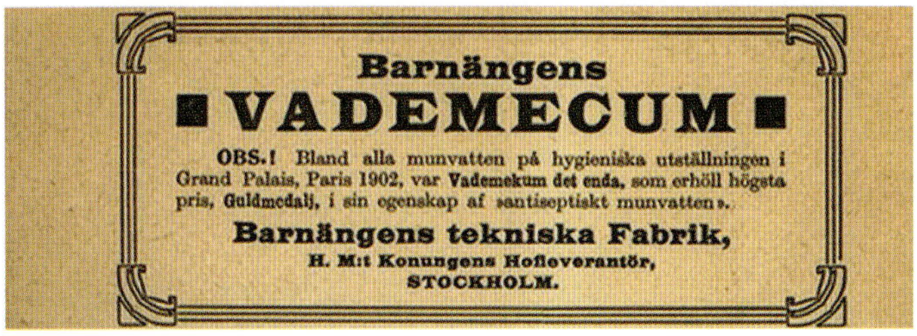

11. F. Wolff and Sohn began operations in 1857, in Karlsruhe, Germany. The Kaloderma brand name gained international renown. From 1911 to 1935, the company had a branch office in Basel, which was responsible for the marketing products manufactured in Germany. In 1935, it was renamed Kaloderma AG. The Karlsruhe operation was closed and auctioned off after 1945. The firm Wolff & Son was established in Zurich in 1951. In 1973, Hans Schwarzkopf GmbH Wolff & Son took over the firm. Berlin Cosmetics GmbH & Co. KG received ownership of the Kaloderma brand in 2001. Here is a prewar advertisement.

12. Formamint germ killing tablets were produced by Bauer & Cie, Gronau, Germany. During the war the firm address was Firma Johan A. Wulfing, Bauer & Cie, Graf-Adolf-Str. 18, Dusseldorf 4000. I could not locate a history of the firm. Here is a prewar advertisement.

CHAPTER 4
FOOT CARE

Non-battle casualties associated with the improper care of soldiers' feet were considerable during WWII. While foot care was an important requirement throughout the year, it became even more critical during times of extreme dampness or cold. Immersion foot symptoms caused by prolonged exposure to water or dampness were unfortunately all too common in the European Theater. According to a 1985 article in the *Journal of Military Dermatology* by Lewis J. Adnot titled "Immersion Foot Syndromes," American forces sustained 11,000 cases of trench foot in November 1944, with more than 6,000 in the Third US Army alone. In *German Clothing, Equipment and Rations* the authors point out that trench foot was practically unknown in the German Army, however:

> This misconception was due to differences in terminology. The Germans group injuries to the feet under a single heading, known as freezing (Erfrierung). Only in rare cases do they make a distinction between frost bite and trench foot.

The highest casualty rates occurred during wet, cold weather. German officers all agreed that trench foot—as known in the United States—rather than frostbitten feet was the more serious problem. Trench foot was a serious problem in the Eifel region during the Battle of the Bulge.

Properly manufactured and fitting footwear, as well as proper care of the feet can help prevent many foot problems. The Germans made a concerted effort to ensure all soldiers were aware of the dangers and implemented preventative measures to keep their feet in good shape. After all, an immobile soldier is an ineffective soldier. In *German Clothing, Equipment and Rations*, the authors examined certain aspects relating to the care of the German soldier, especially when operating in conditions of extreme cold or dampness (Author's note: The following narrative is a combination of direct quotes or paraphrases from *German Clothing, Equipment and Rations*, along with information from a few other select sources.):

The importance of issuing large enough footgear was realized by the German Army early in the war. In 1941, orders were given to fit all footgear, summer or winter, over two pairs of woolen socks or over one pair of socks and one pair of foot wraps. The fitting was supposed to be carefully supervised by supply sergeants who had been told repeatedly of the need for issuing large enough footgear. Some difficulties on this score did however arise and some shoes were issued that were too small. Particular difficulties were had with the ski-mountain boot, where the men did not realize the importance of the added size and took boots that were too small for use on skis in extreme cold. Paratroops always bandaged their ankles before jumping, but the tapes were removed as soon as possible after a jump in the winter to prevent constriction of the blood flow.

Some of the men preferred foot wraps to a second pair of socks. The foot wrap was a rectangular piece of woolen or flannel cloth which was wrapped around the foot. In moderately loosely fitting boots, the men who were skilled at wrapping them could place more material over those parts of the foot where there was the most room and make the boot fit better. They felt they could wrap more thickness around their feet where it was needed and thus get more insulation. Foot wraps were more comfortable than mended socks. They were easier to wash and after washing, there was no sizing problem as there was if the socks shrank. However, it took the men a rather long time to acquire skill at using them.

Footless stockings which come up above the knees were popular in extreme cold since the men believed they kept their knees and legs warm and helped keep their feet warm. They were especially liked by men in vehicles.

The most important thing to do to prevent trench foot, according to General Wischhusen, was to provide properly fitted, preferably rubber, waterproof footgear (to keep the feet dry) and to see that the men change their socks when they did get moist. From the highest echelon to the company officers, all insisted on the necessity of having each man carry at least one pair of extra socks at all times. In fact, long range patrols in Finland carried one extra change of socks for each day that the patrol was expected to last. For instance, on a four day patrol, the soldiers carried four changes of socks because they realized the importance of dry footgear and the difficulty of drying anything while they were on the move. The greatest drying difficulties were obviously encountered during very fluid situations. Every possible means of drying was used. Extensive use of formalin foot powder was recommended to reduce moisture from sweating. Although the plan was obviously not directed from the top, since higher echelons knew nothing about it, in a few motorized infantry (Panzergrenadier) divisions a sock exchange system was set up. Dry, clean socks were sent forward with the rations and wet ones were picked up to be washed, dried, and sent forward again. The Panzergrenadier officers emphasized, however, the necessity of still having an extra pair in case the rations were delayed. This system was by no means universal and most officers had never heard of it, but those who had used it, were high in their praise of it.

Special drying tents or shelters were unheard of. On a stabilized front, the troops were for the most part quartered in billets or dugouts, where they could build fires, wash their socks and dry them. Various types of stoves, mostly for wood, briquettes, or charcoal were used. The size of the stove differed considerably according to the expected size of the billet and the carrying capacity of the unit. Some of the stoves were only about 8 inches high and 3 inches in diameter, while others were rather large. In this respect the Luftwaffe was generally better off than the Army.

Insoles were not issue items, those that were supplied being post exchange articles. However, in cold weather nearly all men used either PX insoles made of woven paper, fur, felt, etc., or improvised them some out of paper. The importance of having extras was realized by the troops themselves, who carried a second pair with them at all times. (Author's note: Gaiters and puttees were worn by soldiers equipped with low shoes or mountain boots. They helped secure the pant legs, as well as offering some protection to the legs. Rolled up socks were also a popular method of securing pant legs.)

All personnel were carefully instructed and continually reminded in their weekly instruction courses about what they needed to do to avoid unnecessary trench foot and frostbite. Aside from having medical officers conduct the training, it was the responsibility of the company officers to ensure that the necessary precautions were taken. The men were also accountable and could be disciplined if they were grossly negligent in carrying out precautions which they were responsible for knowing. Foot inspections were supposed to be conducted every 48 hours, but under combat conditions it was often much less frequent. The company commander had to see that the men carried out such steps as changing their socks, adding paper for warmth, drying their footgear, massaging their feet, etc.

Figure 70.—Method of wrapping foot cloths.

Many soldiers preferred foot wraps over socks, even though they required a bit of skill to fit correctly.

A pair of socks manufactured from wool with Perlon reinforcement. The use of Perlon became more frequent later in the war. Since Perlon is a true synthetic thread, most collectors will dismiss Perlon reinforced socks as fake.

A pair of socks for use in tropical climates.

Several pair of socks believed to be of wartime manufacture. The size rings were done in a variety of colors.

Commercially manufactured socks were also worn by soldiers. *Ed Stroh Collection*

Commercial socks were also manufactured with size rings, which could make it difficult to distinguish military issue socks from commercial pairs.

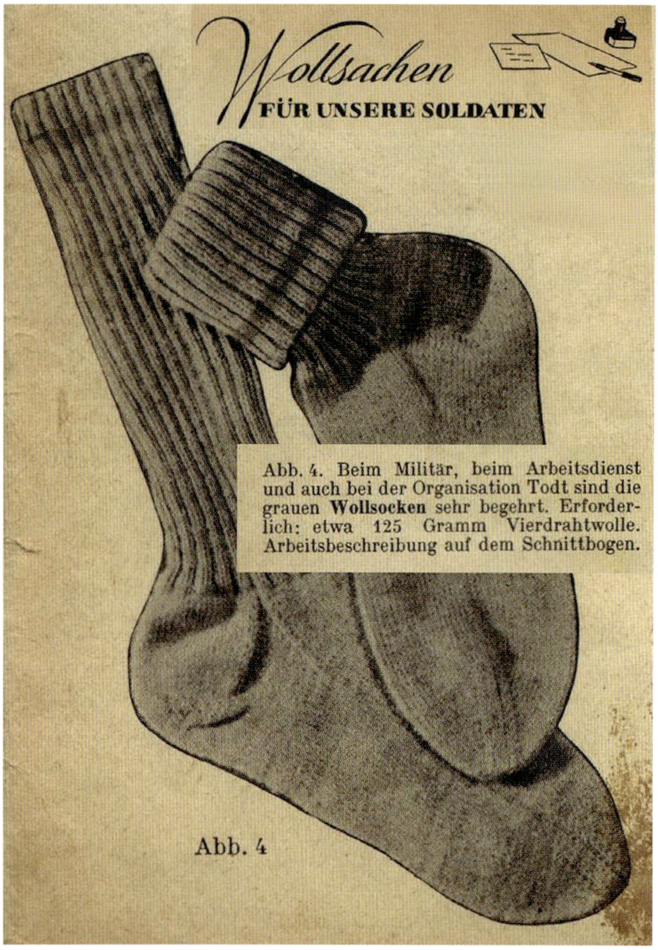

The size rings are clearly seen here.

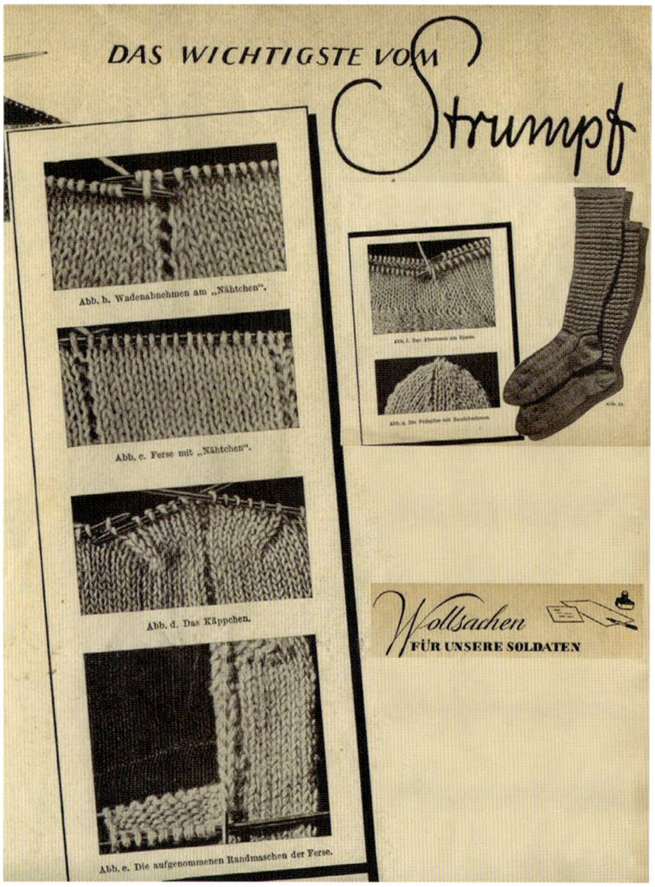

Family members were encouraged to knit items of clothing for soldiers serving at the front.

It was important to issue properly fitted foot gear.

Insoles were available in unit Kantines. *Bunkermilitaria.com*

A pair of tropical puttees. *Helmut Weitze, Hamburg*

A pair of gaiters. *Jim Kreunen of Militaria Plaza*

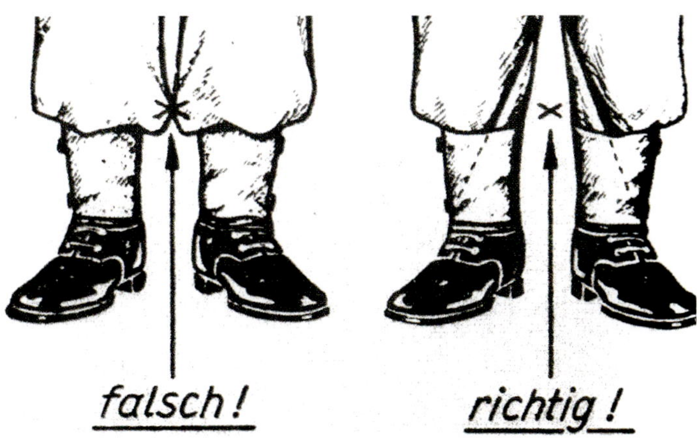

The right and wrong way to put on a pair of gaiters.

A pair of Styrian gaiters worn with mountain boots. *Helmut Weitze, Hamburg*

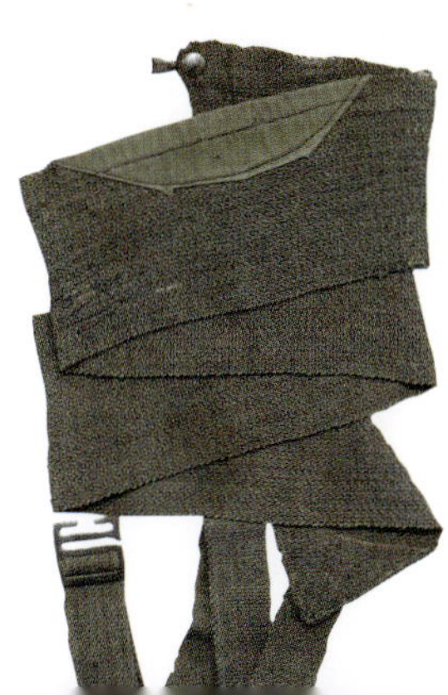

A pair of puttees worn by mountain troops and other infantry members.

The *Taschenbuch für den Winterkrieg* (*Handbook for Winter Warfare*) provided soldiers with the following guidance on cold weather protection, much of it dealing with the care of the feet:

> Put felt lining inside the steel helmet-preferably the crown of an old hat. If nothing else is available, use a handkerchief or crumpled newspaper. The strap should be worn loose so that circulation of the blood will not be impaired. The feet are especially susceptible to frost bite. Socks should be changed frequently. A proved measure for preventing frostbite of the feet is to use inner soles of straw, cloth, or paper; the straw should be cut to the right size and arranged carefully; if newspaper is used, it should be wrapped carefully around the foot to avoid wrinkles. Foot cloths (also paper 'foot cloths') are warmer than socks.
>
> An especially effective measure for protecting the feet is to wear paper between two pairs of socks, and another layer of paper or foot cloths over the top pair of socks. All wrinkles must be smoothed out. If ski boots are worn, a piece of cloth should be sewed over the heels of the socks in order to prevent wear at that point.
>
> Boot leather can be kept from freezing by covering the shoes or boots with the foot of a sock or a casing made of fur or similar material. An illustration is provided that shows how to make a toe protector.
>
> Clean underwear will keep the soldier warmer than underwear which has been worn for a long time. Therefore, all laundry facilities should be used. Special protective measures for the genitals should be taken if the weather is very cold or the wind very strong. The soldier should wear short trunks, if they are available, in addition to his underwear, or should place paper between his drawers and his trousers.
>
> Mounted men should wrap cloth remnants, woven straw, or string around their stirrups. A protective cap for the toe of the boot, made of woven straw and fixed to the stirrup, is recommended. In case of a shortage of felt boots, sentries and drivers may wear shoes of straw over their regular footgear. Use the natives to manufacture straw shoes. Motorcyclists should put layers of newspaper between the shirt and sweater to protect the chest from wind. Wrap several layers of newspaper around the knees as protection against the cold, inserting them between the drawers and the outer knee-length stockings.
>
> The sleeve straps of the field blouse should be buttoned or tied, and gloves should be drawn over the sleeves. Put paper, hay, or straw loosely in boot tops. Trousers should not be put into the boots flat, but should hang over the top of the boots, or outside the boots and tied at the bottom. Another method is to tie the sections of the skirt of the overcoat around the legs and wrap an improvised legging around them to keep them secure over the boot tops. The use of issue cloth for improvising wrap leggings is forbidden. Units which are not equipped with infantry boots should wear laced shoes with short woolen spiral puttees. If laced shoes must be worn without leggings, then the trousers should be pulled over the ankles, and the socks drawn over them. If the soldier wears two pairs of socks, he should roll down one pair, like ski socks.
>
> As protection against the cold, units are provided with the following emergency paper articles in sufficient quantities: caps, vests and drawers (both of which are worn between the underwear and outer clothing, foot cloths, sleeping bags, and bed sheets).

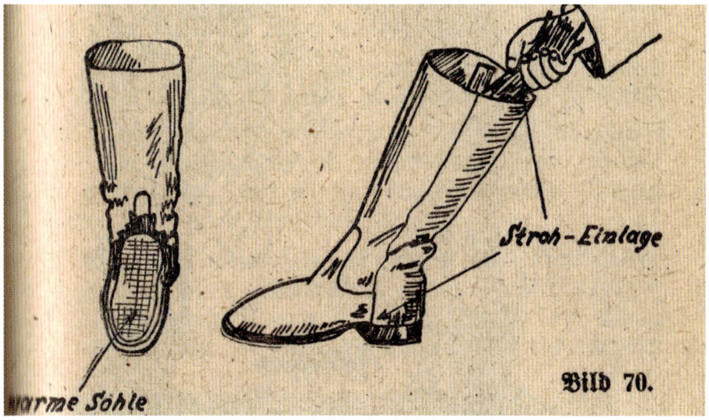

Soldiers were instructed on various methods to keep their feet warm.

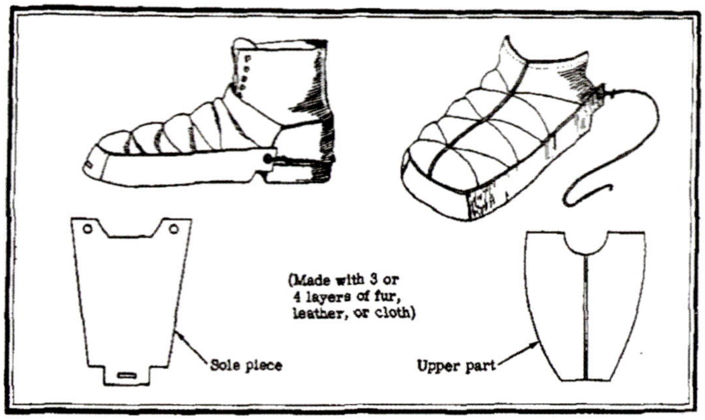

Figure 71.—Improvised protector for shoes and boots.

Bild 71b. Papierweste aus Zeitungsbogen.

Bild 69 c. Kapuze aus Zeitungspapier.

Bild 69 d. Gesichtsmas aus Kreppapier.

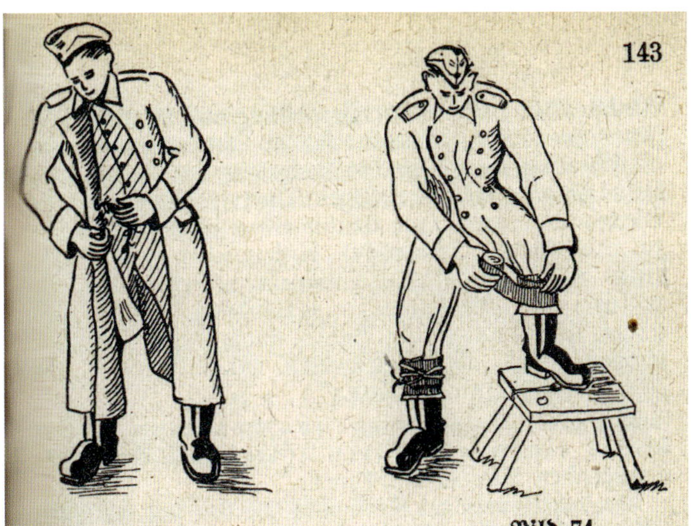

Bild 73.

Bild 74.

A number of lessons learned were disseminated to the troops to help them keep warm.

Carton for a compact boot puller. *Ed Stroh Collection*

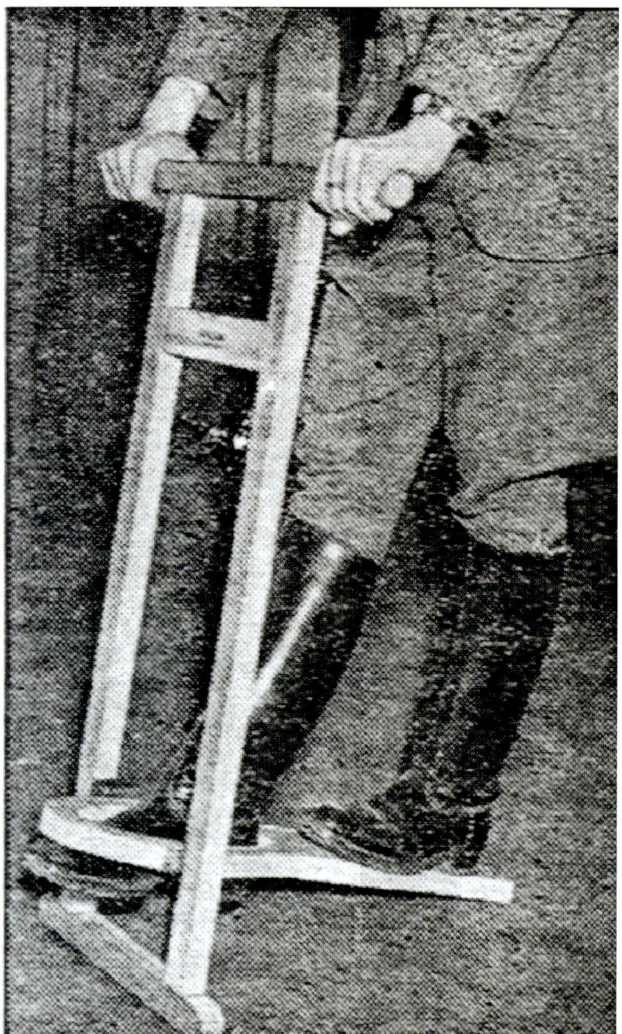

Diesen neuartigen Stiefelknecht

A new style of boot puller.

Small folding wooden boot puller. *The Collectors Guild*

Shoe horn. *Bunkermilitaria.com*

German Clothing, Equipment and Rations provided the following discussion on German footgear, especially pertaining to keeping feet warm and dry:

> Almost all German soldiers agreed that the best type of footgear for extreme cold was the felt boot. The only exceptions to this were German mountain troops serving in Northern Finland who preferred ski-mountain boots for active operations. The mountain troops removed their boots during any long halt and if they were not continuing, they changed their socks. For less active combat and for manning defensive positions, they preferred the Lap type of mukluks, which they felt were warmer than the German felt boot.
>
> The German felt boot was an adaptation of the Russian Valenki. The Germans found the plain all felt Russian boot unsatisfactory for two reasons. The Germans wanted the greater arch support and better traction afforded by a regular sole and they needed greater water repellency in the foot of the boots. The boots stayed dry enough in extreme cold, provided the men were outdoors all the time, but in defensive positions or around emplacements etc., the men got a chance to go into dugouts and shelters. There their boots got warm and when they came out, they picked up snow which melted on them. This led the Germans to sole the boot and face the foot portion with leather. The commonest sock combination used with felt boots was two pairs of ordinary wool socks and insoles improvised from paper.
>
> Other types of footgear were used locally. Officers from the Waffen SS Mountain Division Nord were very enthusiastic about the Finnish felt ski boot for use in the deep powder snow which lay in the flat thick forests where they were operating. The chief advantage of this type of boot was the hooked toe, which made it possible to use a simple toe strap type of ski binding and to kick the skis on and off without effort. They agreed that in rough terrain, those boots and bindings could not have been used. For warmer weather similar boots of leather were used.

Canvas winter boots with a felt interlining on the foot were not widely used. Whenever they appeared they were worn only because of a lack of felt boots. Generaloberstabsintendant (Lieutenant General of the Quartermaster Corps) Kleberger, Quartermaster General of the German Field Army (Heeresintendant), stated that they were manufactured only because wool and hair shortages prevented the manufacture of felt boots exclusively. Fur boots were used in a few cases in such elite units as the Grossdeutschland Panzer Division and the Waffen SS, but these proved impractical, especially because of the difficulty in drying them and were satisfactory only for sentries.

It was, however, in wet/cold weather that the ordinary German soldier suffered the most, as their trench foot record shows. The ordinary soldier did not have any waterproof footgear that kept his feet dry for any period of time. His leather boots resisted it longer, but they too finally became wet. So the leather footgear was unsuited to colder weather and the felt to warmer. Therefore either one or the other had to be kept with company supplies, where they were a definite burden. It was difficult to be sure that they would be available at the right time. Some units on the Western Front tried to solve this problem by keeping a few pairs of felt boots with company supplies as organizational equipment.

The best answer to the difficult problem of keeping the feet dry, according to members of elite units who had experience with it was rubber footgear. It was only elite units, such as the Waffen SS, the mountain troops and the Grossdeutschland Panzer Division that received the limited amount of rubber foot gear that was available. There were two chief types of rubber footgear: an ordinary rubber boot and a kind of rubber over boot. The former was ill fitting, poor for marching and pulled off in mud. The later, shaped somewhat like the U.S. Army mukluk, was worn over ordinary footgear. It was too light to stand wear and tear. The German Quartermaster Research and Development organization knew how to solve the problem, but was unable to because of the critical shortage of materials. U.S. Army cold weather footgear was designed to accommodate and was issued with felt insoles. The German soldier was equally aware of the need for insoles and although he was not issued them, either bought them for himself at the Post Exchange or improvised them.

German felt and leather boots.

These winter boots appear to be manufactured from leather, wood, and some type of quilted cloth.

The felt and leather boot was very popular with the troops. *Photo: US National Archives and Record Administration (NARA)*

A pair of white felt and leather boots. *Zuegmeister Collection*

Information from the following intelligence reports was woven together to present the following narrative on the use of rubber in the production of German foot gear: *German Clothing, Equipment and Rations*, *The German Rubber Footwear Industry*, *The German Sole and Heel Industry*, and *Investigation of Certain German Paper and Board Mills with Particular Reference to the Production of Leatherboard, Carton and Shoe Board and Coated Papers*.

The German military did not use rubber footgear except under extreme conditions, such as the Russian front in the winter of 1942–43. During 1941, the Germans produced approximately 2,200,000 pairs of rubber boots for the military. In 1943, production decreased to 1,400,000 pairs and by 1944, it saw further decline. The Germans used Buna—a synthetic rubber made by polymerizing butadiene—in the production of footgear. Both the United States and Germany experienced manufacturing problems producing footgear using Buna. However, Germany was further constrained by the need to use spun rayon fabrics and the lack of rubber cement and Latex. After 1942, cotton fabric was discontinued, except as the "form" in gas protection boots. The use of spun rayon fabrics required an increase in the amount of Buna because of the slickness of the fabric.

The sole and heel industries in the United States and Germany encountered similar problems in the development of synthetic rubber soles. Generally speaking, top quality US soles were superior to top quality German synthetic rubber soles. In most cases, German soles were harder than American soles. The reality of war made it impossible to improve the quality of materials used to make soles. The quality of German synthetic rubber soles was regulated by the Public Materials Testing Office in Berlin/Dahlem. Before the war ended, Germany had made substantial progress in the development of a brown no-mark sole material, chiefly through the use of a new pigment called TEG. This was an aluminum oxide gel (Tonerdegel) that appears to have value as a reinforcing pigment for non-marking soles.

Synthetic rubber heels made in Germany were generally thinner than the Junior 3/8 inch heels produced in the United States. Because of the shortage of synthetic rubber, only a combination two-compound heel could be produced. The back or wearing portion was made from a reasonably good compound. The fore-part or breast portion was made of a much lower grade compound. The combined quality was so poor that efforts were made to improve quality in 1942. The increase in quality meant that fewer units were required, resulting in a reduction of the amount of synthetic rubber consumed.

The use of substitute materials for leather soles increased in the latter stages of the war. These materials were made from varying proportions of chrome and vegetable tanned leather in conjunction with binding materials, such as polyvinyl acetate and a suitable plasticizer.

Shoe counters (Author's note: The area that sits behind the heel of the foot, used to stiffen the back part of the shoe and to give it structure.) made from the same basic combinations were generally used in preference to leather counters. It is claimed that the substitute counter was more substantial and longer-lived than the best leather counter.

No new adhesives were developed for use in the manufacture of shoes. In prewar Germany, latex and crude rubber cement were universally used. As crude rubber became scarce, polyvinyl acetate emulsions and Oppanol (polyisobutylene) were substituted. It appears the Germans did not use thermoplastic cements for the shoe industry. The "Ago" process, which used nitro-cellulose cements to attach synthetic rubber soles in shoe factories and repair shops, was considered unique by the Allied investigators.

Plastic sole materials were used extensively during the last few years of the war. In 1942, "P-Soling"—a high molecular weight, un-chlorinated polyvinyl chloride—was developed by Dr. Hans Roser. Large quantities were used on new shoes and for repairs during 1943 and the first ten months of 1944. Successful performance of "P-Soling" required the use of leather midsoles on men's shoes but was not necessary on women's shoes.

The German military was generally not receptive to the use of rubber sole bottoms for military combat foot gear. However, towards the end of the war, sole leather shortages became so critical that the Wehrmacht was obliged to consider using synthetic rubber soles. Extensive walking tests to simulate walking over various types of terrain supplemented by tests by some individual shoe manufacturers resulted in the approval of a synthetic rubber sole. The war ended before any of these soles were fielded. (Author's note: The authors were probably referring to shoes issued to combat troops like "Jack boots" and the combat low shoe. Experimental combat shoes/boots and footgear not intended for wear in combat were manufactured and issued to the troops. The use of rubber soles for mountain boots is discussed below.)

It was common practice in Germany to conduct field trials before any new item was approved for Wehrmacht distribution. The Army Quartermaster Corps sent specially trained observers to the field under combat conditions to see what the field needed in the way of new items, to talk with the troops and bring back ideas and hear complaints on existing items. These observers showed how newer items should be used and explained why an inferior item was being issued. A suggestion program was established that allowed soldiers to send suggestions for improvements or to submit new ideas directly to the Army Research and Development Staff without interference.

Mountain troop officers of the Waffen SS and army were questioned on the German ski-mountain boot. The army mountain troops were equipped with this type of boot in any temperature in Alpine terrain. They did state that the square-toed Austrian type—which was both a ski and mountain boot, and which came to be standard for the German Army—was better than the rounder-toed German boot that was standard in the German Army before the *Anschluss*, since the latter was only a mountain boot. They all emphasized that the ski-mountain boot must not be too high at the ankle and experiments to raise its height failed for skiing and climbing.

The first rubber lug soles for shoes were invented by an Italian, Vitale Bramani. Mr. Bramani was driven to develop a new climbing sole after six of his friends were killed in a mountaineering accident in 1935 that was partially blamed on inadequate footwear. Two years later, he patented his invention and launched the first rubber lug soles on the market with a tread design called the "Carrarmato," or tank tread. Leopoldo Pirelli of Pirelli Tires provided the financial backing for the venture. The sole was designed to provide excellent traction on a wide range of surfaces, had a high degree of abrasion resistance, and was manufactured using the latest vulcanized rubber of the time. These soles were first used on mountain boots, replacing leather soles fitted with hobnails or steel cleats that were commonly used at the time.

Most of the German officers who had experience with rubber cleated (Bramani) soles were enthusiastic about them. The army model made of synthetic rubber had not worked out well because the ersatz rubber cleats broke off, so they were not procured after the first year or two of the war. The army mountain troop officers expressed a preference for Tricouni nails. (Author's note: A Tricouni is a metal nail used on mountain climbing shoes because of its improved gripping properties. Tricounis are also referred to as hobnails, boot nails, cleats, and shoe studs.) The Waffen SS high mountain troops apparently got a better type of rubber and were highly satisfied with them. One officer of a high mountain unit in Italy received a pair in the spring of 1945. These officers thought they were perfect except on steep grass. They also did not grip on smooth ice, requiring crampons. These rubber-cleated soles were lighter, quieter, wore better, etc. (Author's note: At the end of the war, the 5th Mountain Division was selected to test a mountain boot with replaceable rubber soles and heels, which is probably the same boot mentioned in the previous sentence. The sole/heel was screwed into the bottom of the boot and was easy to replace.)

The Germans were forced to abandon their old leather jackboot primarily because of leather shortages and to extend the issue in its place of the laced service shoe that had previously been used as a second pair, or as the standard footgear for service troops, artillery, etc. This change was looked upon as a mistake by most officers. General Wischhasen, surgeon of the 1st German Army, pointed out that jackboots were better than service shoes because there were no laces to cut down the circulation of the blood; there were not any lacing holes to let in the water and because of the greater height. Generalstabsintendant (Major General of the Quartermaster Corps) Fritsch, Chief Quartermaster of the Commander in Chief of the West, stated the change from the old type service shoe to the heavier M-1944 was made primarily because of the need for a more waterproof construction. The new boot also had a stitched-in bellows tongue in an attempt to cut down leakage through the lacing eyelets. This boot also had a stiffer sole and a box toe to make it better suited for use on skis.

This mountain trooper is wearing a pair of rubber boots. *Bundesarchiv_Bild_101I-692-0263-36, Foto: o. Ang., 1944 Januar-Februar/ Licence CC-BY-SA 3.0*

Rubber boots, while extremely effective, are rarely seen in wartime photographs.

Troops wearing knee high rubber boots. *Bundesarchiv-Bild-101I-395-1513-02, Foto: Haustein. 1942 März-April/ Licence CC-BY-SA 3.0*

The M 1944 service shoes pictured in the wartime intelligence report were actually Italian boots.

Rubber boots were extremely effective but in short supply. *Bill Petz Collection*

Italian service shoes. *Helmut Weitze, Hamburg*

Experimental Mountain Boot with Replaceable Rubber Sole and Heel

Continental Army Sole Compound

	Face Stock	*Back Stock*
Buna S Defo 300	22.50	30.00
Buna SS	12.50	-
Sole Scrap Ground	3.00	5.00
Russ OK 3	33.25	15.00
Zinc Oxide	11.25	7.00
Cotton Fiber	5.00	20.00
TEG	-	13.00
Rosin	2.50	-
Naftolen	1.25	3.00
Mineral Oil	1.25	2.00
Montan Wax	3.50	3.00
Aldol	3.25	.70
Vulcazit AZ	1.00	.30
Sulfur	1.00	1.00

The experimental mountain boot with rubber sole, along with the formula for the rubber sole and heel.

The M 1944 Service Shoe. *Gerard Stezelberger of Relic Hunter Militaria*

Straw over shoes provided excellent protection against the cold. *The Collectors Guild*

The term "jackboot" is forever associated with the German soldier. *The Collectors Guild*

Dress shoes. *The Collectors Guild*

Leather high boots in wear.

Most of these soldiers are wearing dress shoes.

Low shoes gradually replaced the marching boot. *Michael Davis-VirtualGrenadier*

Personal gear and equipment, including a pair of low shoes. *Photo: National Archives and Record Administration (NARA)*

The distinctive sole of the mountain boots. *Photo: National Archives and Record Administration (NARA)*

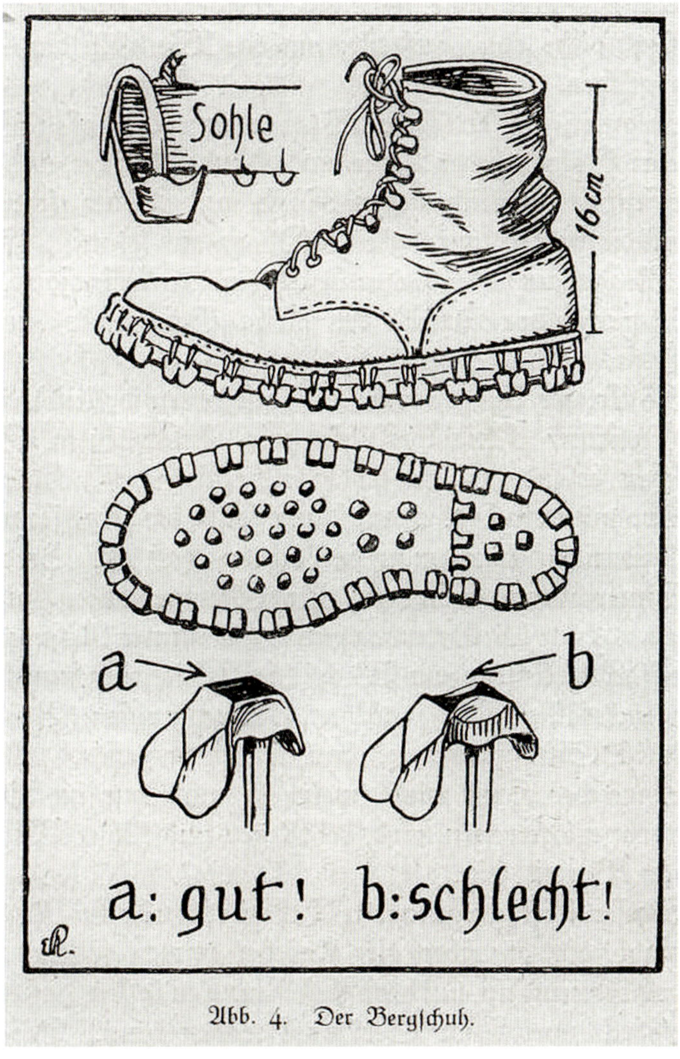

Abb. 4. Der Bergschuh.

The mountain boot as shown in a wartime regulation.

Mountain boots. *The Collectors Guild*

Hut shoes and climbing shoes for mountain personnel. *Gerard Stezelberger of Relic Hunter Militaria*

Sports shoes with smooth soles. *Gerard Stezelberger of Relic Hunter Militaria*

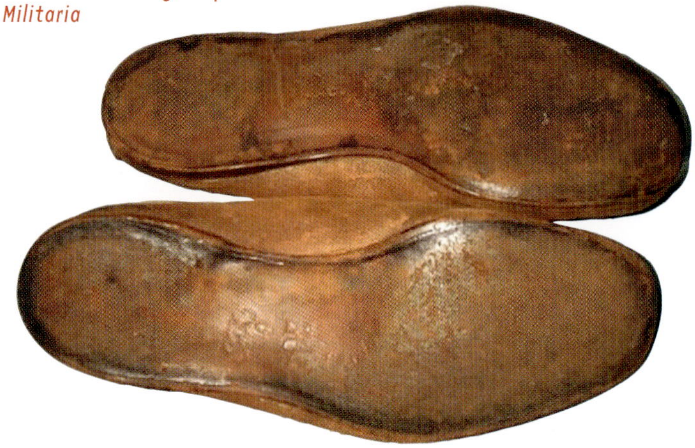

Wartime picture of the mountain troop climbing shoe.

Sports shoes were popular for wear during lulls in the action.

Tropical high boots for air force personnel. *The Collectors Guild*

Tropical high boots for SS personnel. *Michael Davis-VirtualGrenadier*

Army tropical high boots. *Michael Davis-VirtualGrenadier*

Tropical low shoes and high boots in wear.

Tropical low shoes for army personnel. *Michael Davis-VirtualGrenadier*

Front lacing boots for Paratroopers. *Michael Davis-VirtualGrenadier*

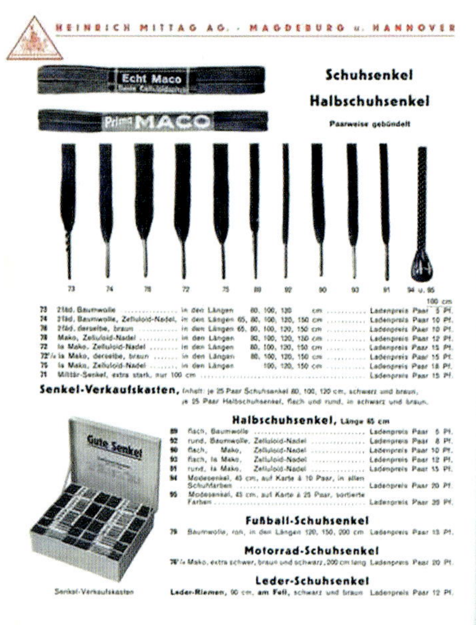

Wartime advertisement for shoe laces.

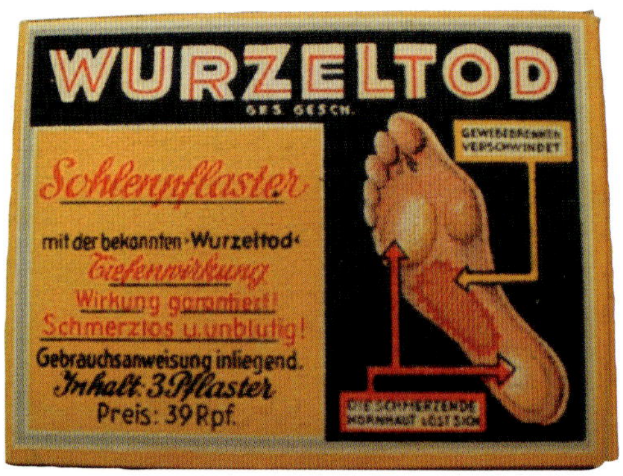

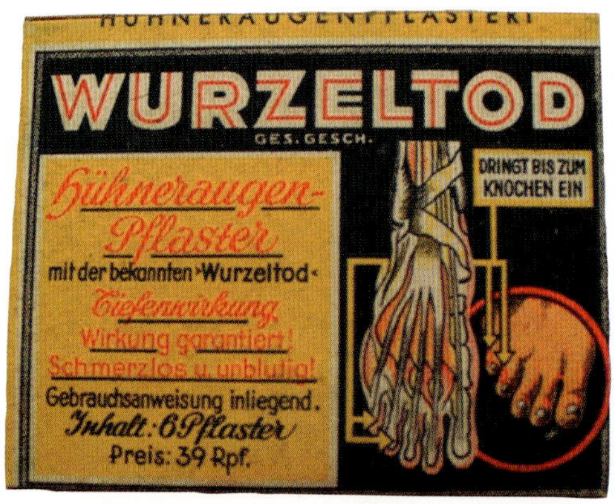

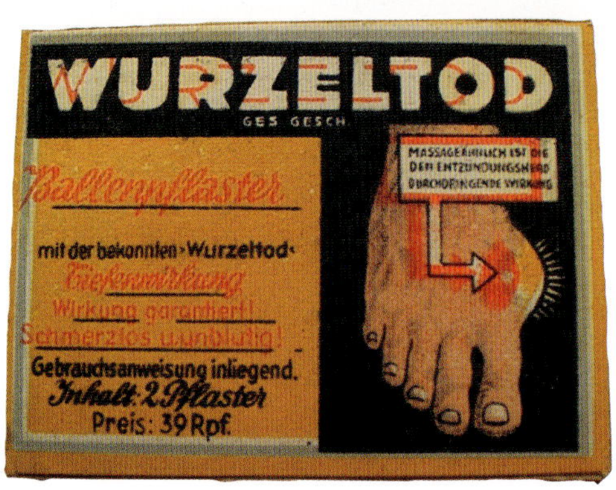

Three different types of foot care patches from Josef Lihl, Limbach, Sachsen. *Michel Verberkt Collection*

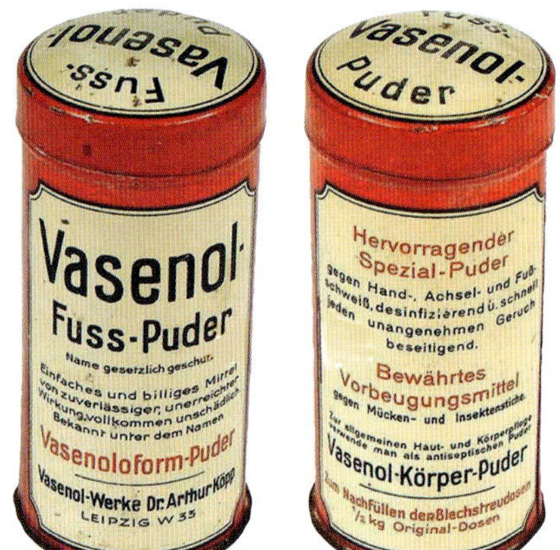

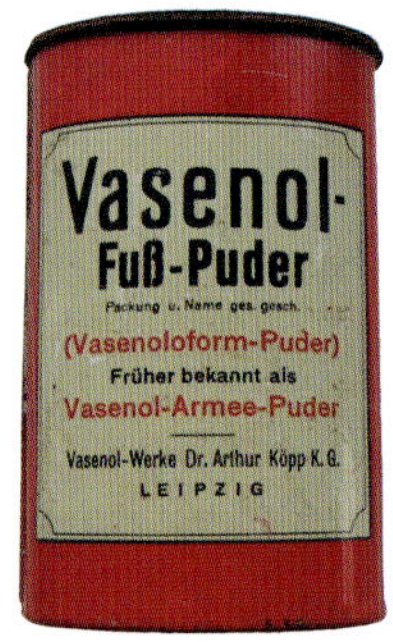

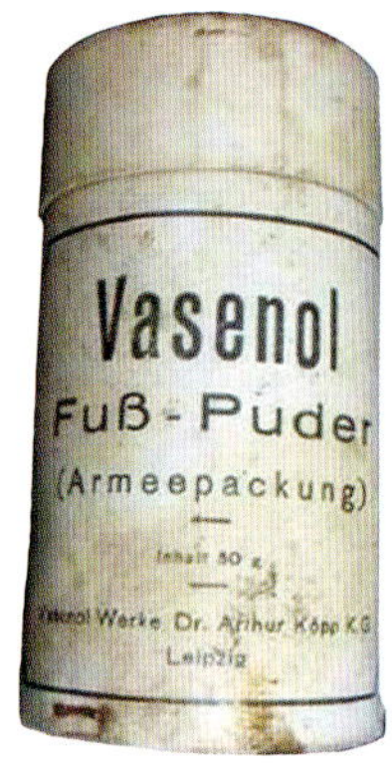

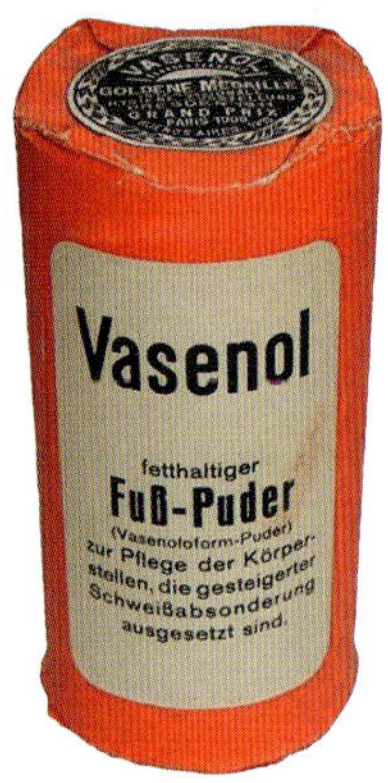

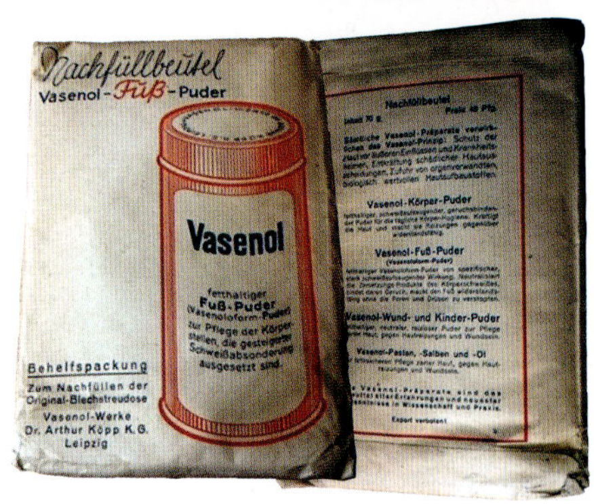

A variety of Vasenol brand foot powders.

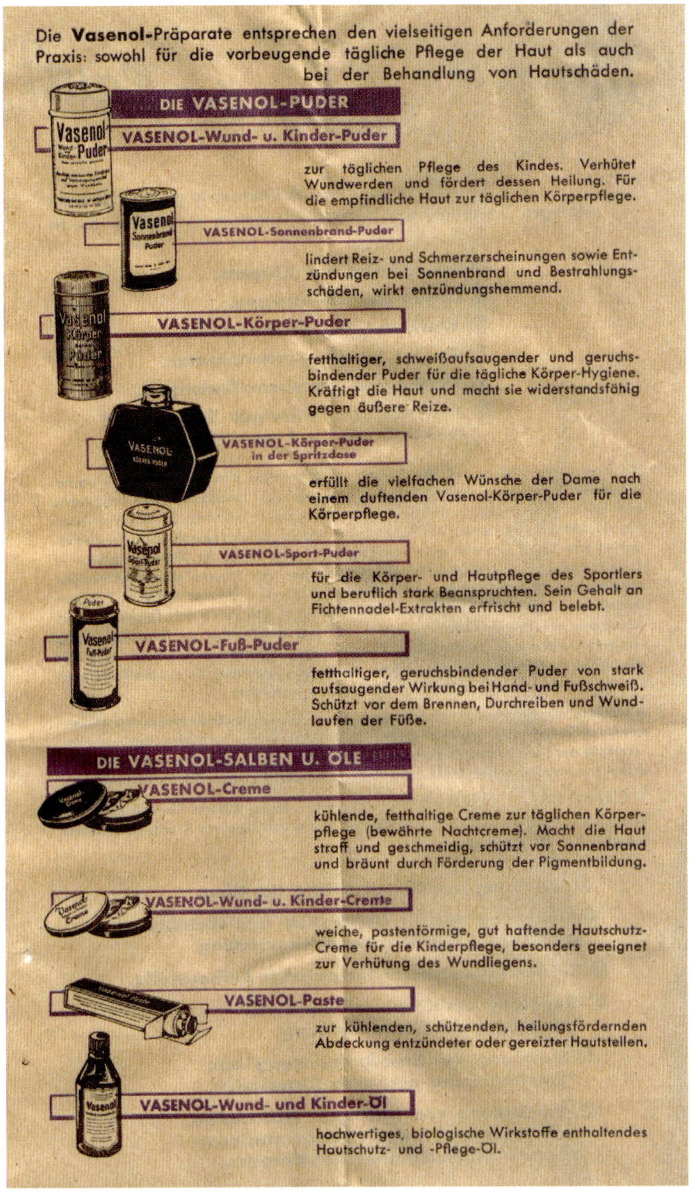

Die **Vasenol**-Präparate entsprechen den vielseitigen Anforderungen der Praxis: sowohl für die vorbeugende tägliche Pflege der Haut als auch bei der Behandlung von Hautschäden.

DIE VASENOL-PUDER

VASENOL-Wund- u. Kinder-Puder

zur täglichen Pflege des Kindes. Verhütet Wundwerden und fördert dessen Heilung. Für die empfindliche Haut zur täglichen Körperpflege.

VASENOL-Sonnenbrand-Puder

lindert Reiz- und Schmerzerscheinungen sowie Entzündungen bei Sonnenbrand und Bestrahlungsschäden, wirkt entzündungshemmend.

VASENOL-Körper-Puder

fetthaltiger, schweißaufsaugender und geruchsbindender Puder für die tägliche Körper-Hygiene. Kräftigt die Haut und macht sie widerstandsfähig gegen äußere Reize.

VASENOL-Körper-Puder in der Spritzdose

erfüllt die vielfachen Wünsche der Dame nach einem duftenden Vasenol-Körper-Puder für die Körperpflege.

VASENOL-Sport-Puder

für die Körper- und Hautpflege des Sportlers und beruflich stark Beanspruchten. Sein Gehalt an Fichtennadel-Extrakten erfrischt und belebt.

VASENOL-Fuß-Puder

fetthaltiger, geruchsbindender Puder von stark aufsaugender Wirkung bei Hand- und Fußschweiß. Schützt vor dem Brennen, Durchreiben und Wundlaufen der Füße.

DIE VASENOL-SALBEN U. ÖLE

VASENOL-Creme

kühlende, fetthaltige Creme zur täglichen Körperpflege (bewährte Nachtcreme). Macht die Haut straff und geschmeidig, schützt vor Sonnenbrand und bräunt durch Förderung der Pigmentbildung.

VASENOL-Wund- u. Kinder-Creme

weiche, pastenförmige, gut haftende Hautschutz-Creme für die Kinderpflege, besonders geeignet zur Verhütung des Wundliegens.

VASENOL-Paste

zur kühlenden, schützenden, heilungsfördernden Abdeckung entzündeter oder gereizter Hautstellen.

VASENOL-Wund- und Kinder-Öl

hochwertiges, biologische Wirkstoffe enthaltendes Hautschutz- und -Pflege-Öl.

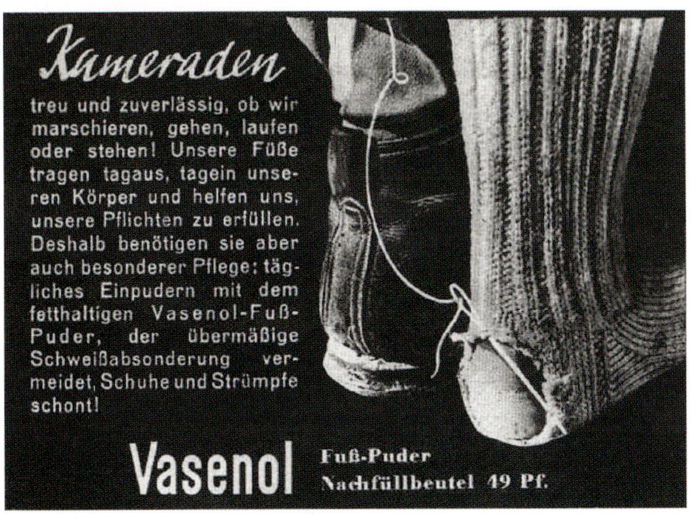

Period advertisements for Vasenol products.

Gerlachs foot powder. *www.raskantik.com*

Schweiss foot powder manufactured by the C. Viol chemical factory.

Eidechse brand foot cream.[1] *Bunkermilitaria.com*

Dialon brand foot and body powder.[2]

Vioform antiseptic powder.

Efasit brand foot cream.[3] *Frédéric Ruelle Collection*

MOVA brand foot powder. *Frédéric Ruelle Collection*

Foot powder manufactured for use in medical kits.

Army foot powder.[4] *OSTFRONT Militaria*

Milano brand foot powder.

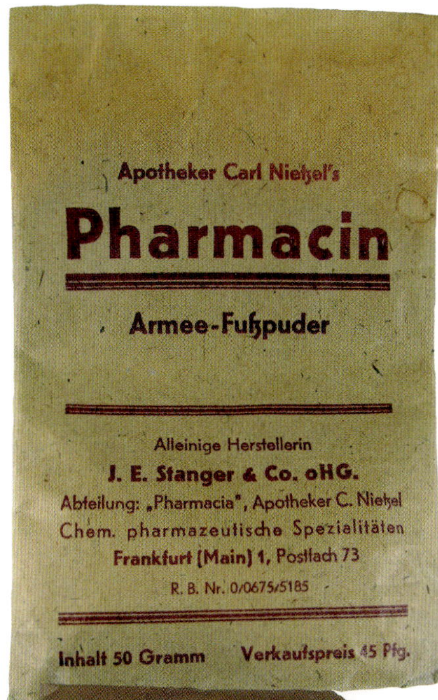

Note the RBN number on this package of foot powder.

Nivea brand foot powder.

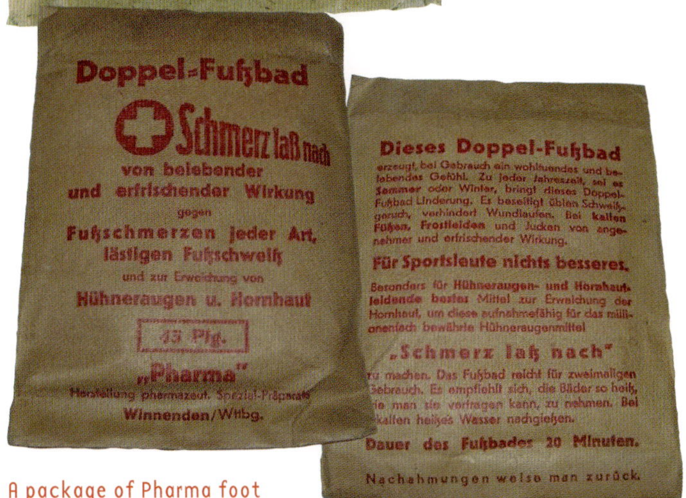

A package of Pharma foot bath solution. *Kevin Barrett Collection*

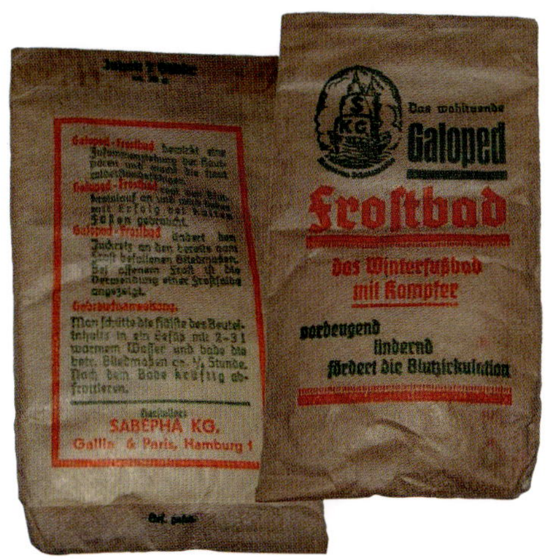

A package of Galoped foot bath solution.[5] *Kevin Barrett Collection*

Pudan foot powder. *OSTFRONT Militaria*

Foot care was critical to unit readiness.

Callous softner. *Bunkermilitaria.com*

Salizylsalbe for use on the feet. *Bunkermilitaria.com*

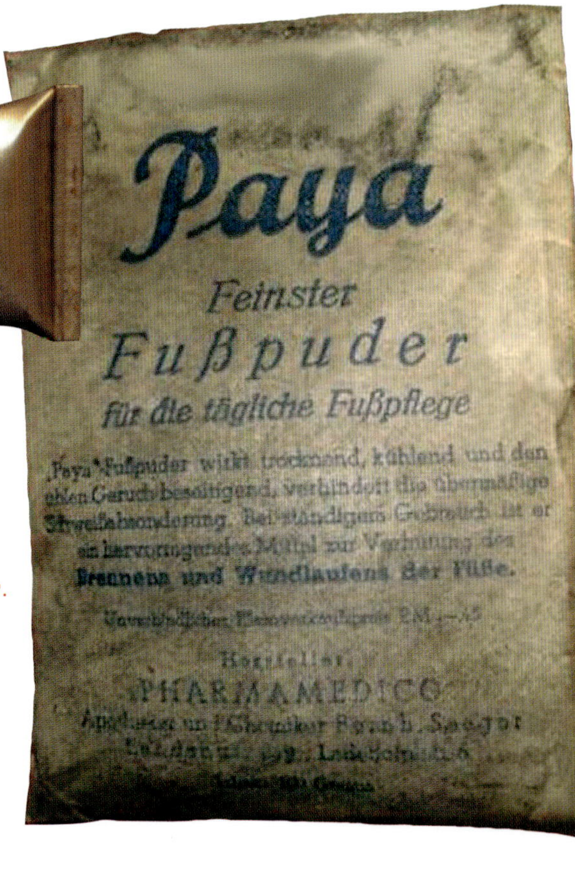

PAYA brand foot powder.

CHAPTER 4 ENDNOTES

1. No history was found on the firm, however, it is still in business as Eidechse Fußkosmetik GmbH, Großgmainer Str. 17, 83457 Bayerisch Gmain, Bayern, Germany.

2. In 1872, Karl Philipp Engelhard established the Fabrik Pharmazeutischer Präparate in Frankfurt a/m, Germany. By 1930, Dialon powder had gained worldwide popularity. The powder was sold in shakers with refill pouches also available. Dialon was exported to China and the USA. The firm was destroyed during the war. By 1949, the firm had resumed operations. It is still in business today. Here is a prewar advertisement.

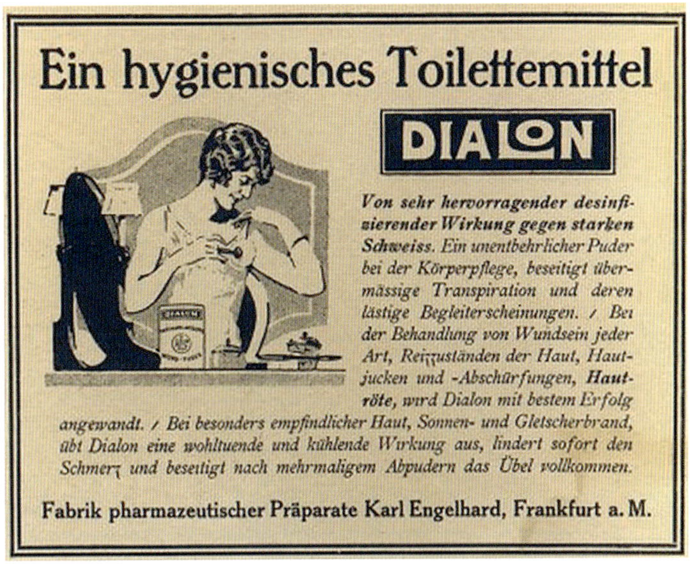

3. Gerhard F. Schmidt founded the TOGAL works in Munich, Germany, in 1914. By 1920, TOGAL products were available in thirty countries. Efasit was introduced in 1938. During the war, TOGAL-WERK AG was subjected to four aerial attacks that left the factory in ruins. The company is still in business. Here is a wartime advertisement.

4. No history was found on the firm Paul Schochert, Bischofswerda i. Sa. Here is the firm's listing in the 1929 Mosse Register of Firms.

Chem.-techn. Artikel. ×Schochert, Paul, ℱ 44, Ps 10509 Le. – ×Säurig, Alfred W., ℱ 318, Ps 35498 Le. u. 33100 Dr.

5. No history was found on the Sabepha KG firm. Here is the firm's listing in the 1929 Mosse Register of Firms.

Galliat & Paris s. Sabepha K.-G. Hmb 1 ✶24 70 52

CHAPTER 5
SHAVING

In the Wehrmacht, facial hair beyond a small, neatly trimmed mustache was against regulations, though such regulations were often relaxed under field conditions. The latter was particularly true in the Kriegsmarine (navy) and Gebirgsjäger (mountain troops). Growth of a full beard was the norm for U-Boat crews on active duty, though facial hair was expected to be shaved soon after reaching port.

Beyond the professional image a clean-shaven soldier portrayed, there were also real-world health and safety issues to consider. Lice, skin irritation, ringworm, etc., were issues to consider when growing a beard. A full beard could also prevent a gas mask from sealing properly.

There were hundreds if not thousands of firms that manufactured, distributed, and sold shaving gear. Most of the razor industry was concentrated in and around Solingen, home of the German steel industry.

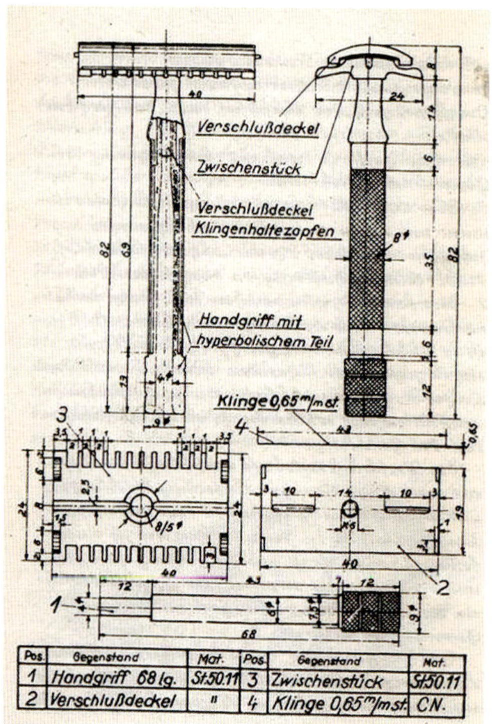

The Reichsheer published a manual on the razor.

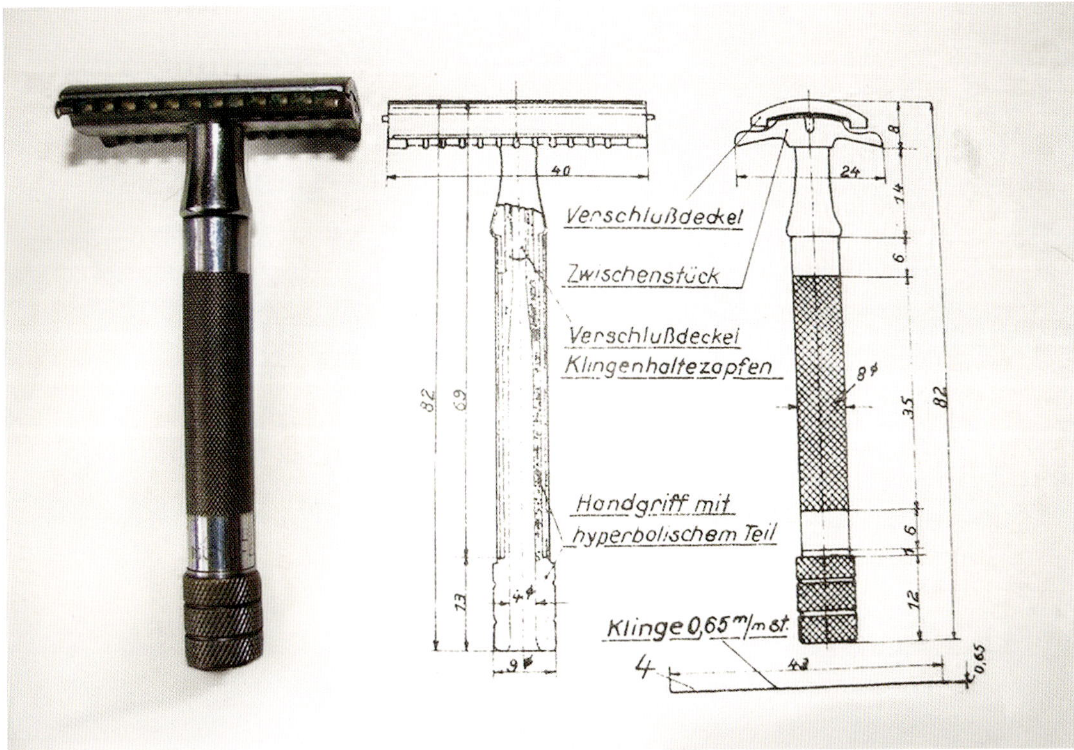

40
Verschlußdeckel
Zwischenstück
Verschlußdeckel
Klingenhaltezapfen
Handgriff mit
hyperbolischem Teil
Klinge 0,65 m/m st.
24
8
14
6
8⌀
35
82
69
6
12
13
4⌀
9⌀
42
0,65

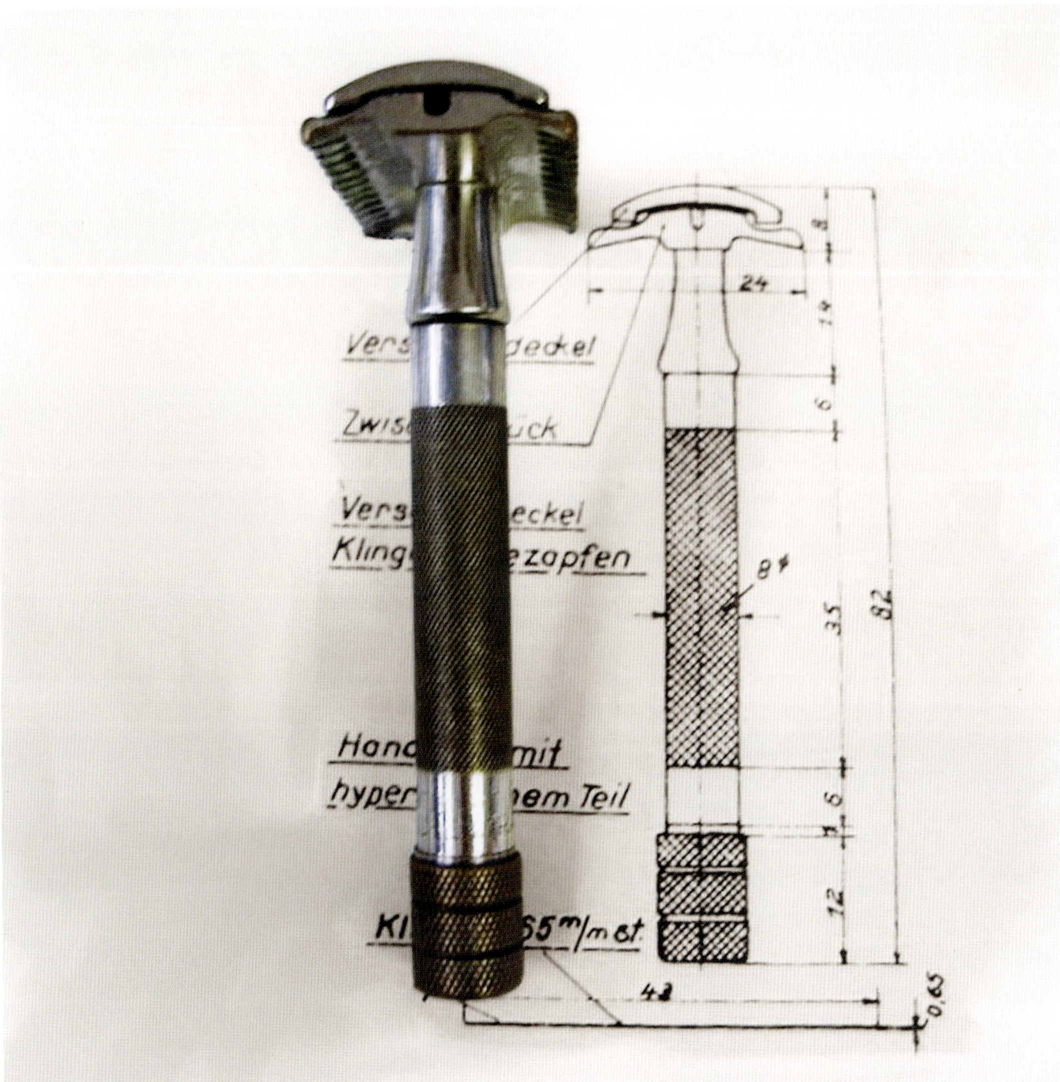

24
8
14
6
8⌀
35
82
6
12
42
0,65

Razor kit in a wooden box. *Chris Mason Collection*

Small razor kit in a leather case. *Bunkermilitaria.com*

MOHAG brand shaving kit.

A wide variety of razor kits were available. *Frédéric Ruelle Collection*

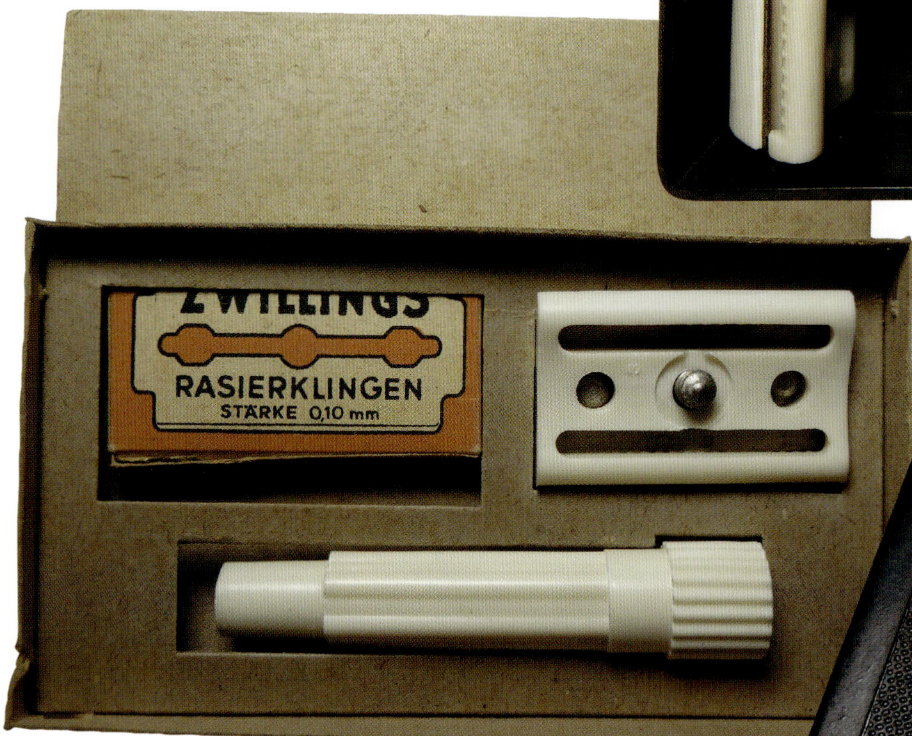

A wide variety of razor kits were available. *Frédéric Ruelle Collection*

A wide variety of razor kits were available. *Frédéric Ruelle Collection*

A wide variety of razor kits were available. *Frédéric Ruelle Collection*

Rotbart brand shaving kit. *Frédéric Ruelle Collection*

Razor carton marked "*Behelfspackung*," or auxiliary package. *Jim Kreunen of Militaria Plaza*

A small selection of razors in their original cartons. *Frédéric Ruelle Collection*

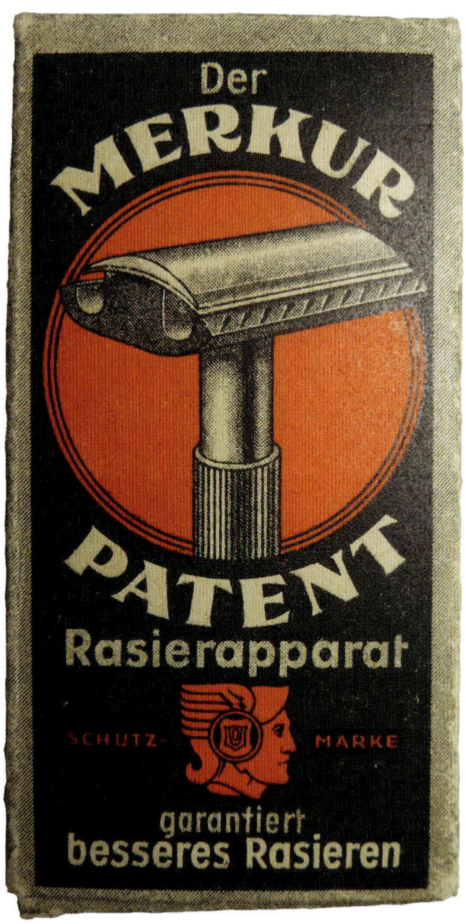

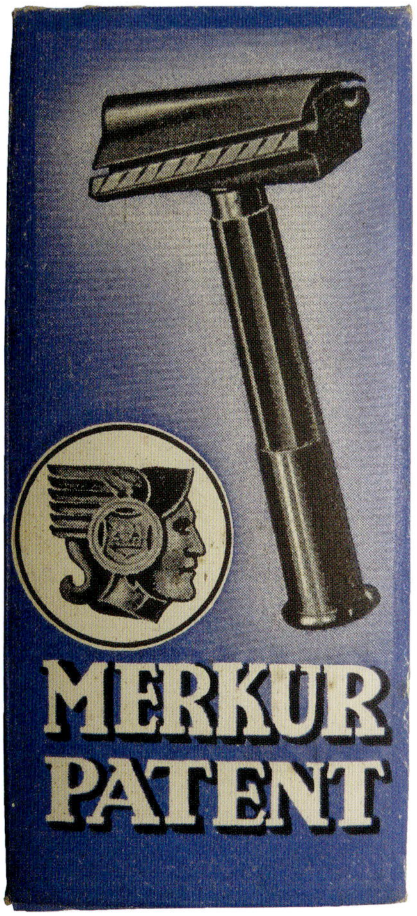

A small selection of razors in their original cartons. *Frédéric Ruelle Collection*

Rogerit and Tradition brand razors. *Bunkermilitaria.com*

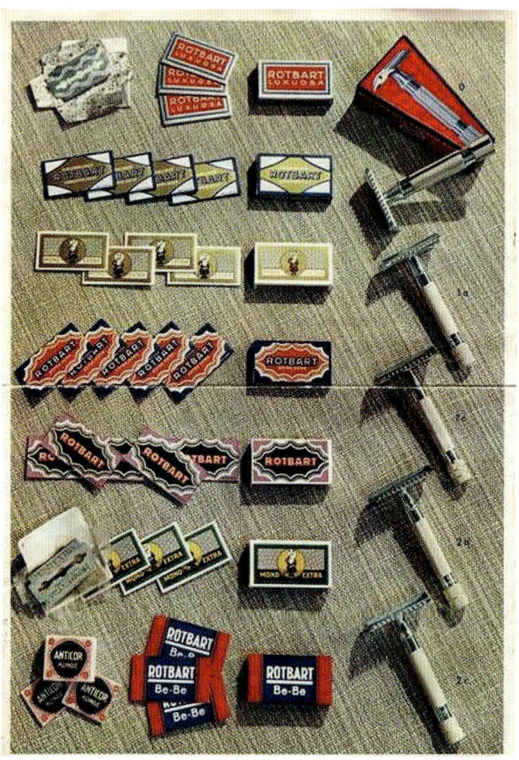

A few pages from a wartime Rotbart catalog. *OSTFRONT Militaria*

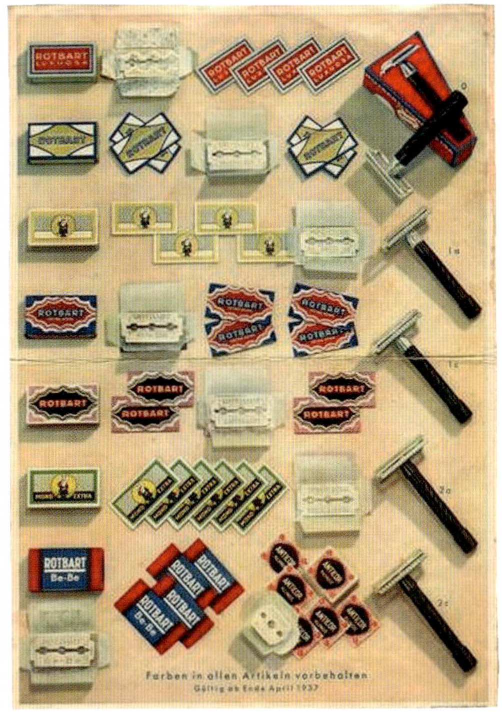

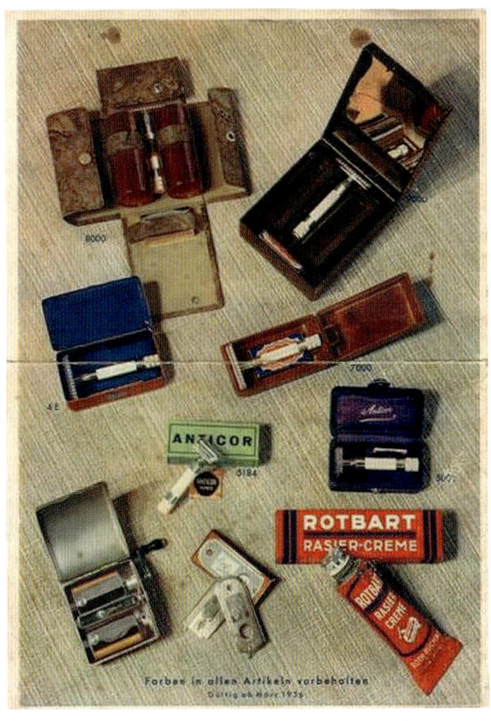

A few pages from a wartime Rotbart catalog. *OSTFRONT Militaria*

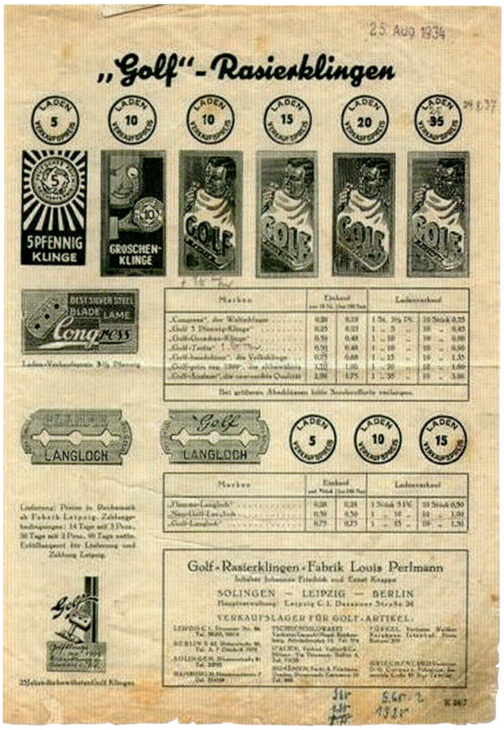

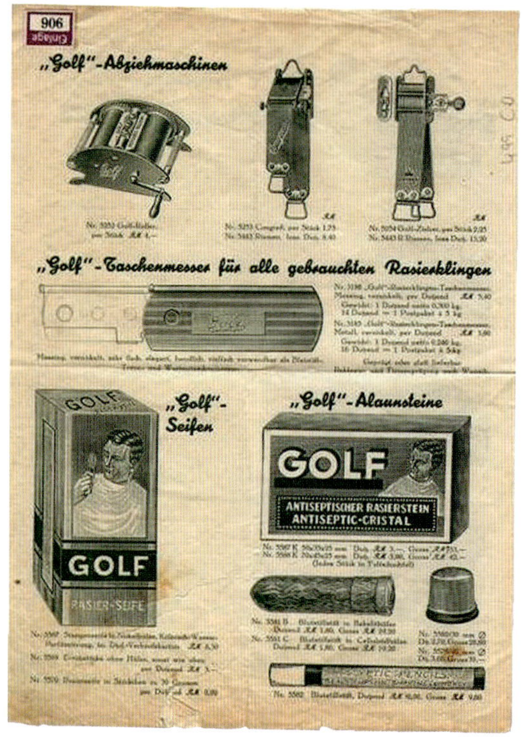

Advertisement for Golf brand shaving products.

Razors and blades are amongst the gifts shown here.

Electric razor shown with a wartime advertisement.

Shaving could be a challenge in a field environment. *Photos: US National Archives and Records Administration (NARA)*

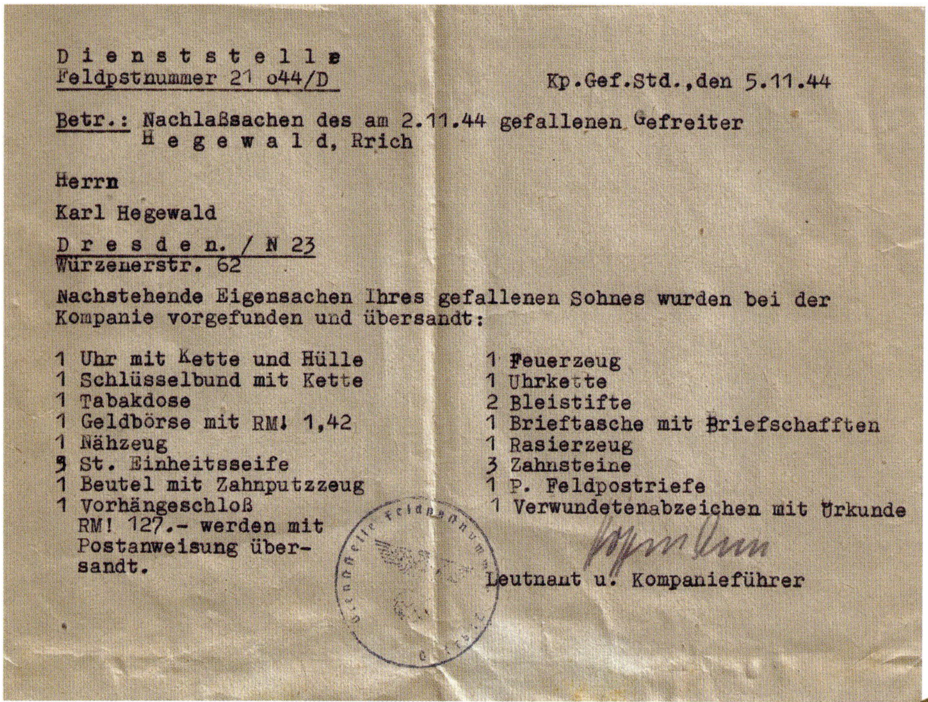

Dienststelle
Feldpstnummer 21 044/D

Kp.Gef.Std.,den 5.11.44

Betr.: Nachlaßsachen des am 2.11.44 gefallenen Gefreiter
H e g e w a l d, Erich

Herrn

Karl Hegewald

D r e s d e n. / N 23
Würzenerstr. 62

Nachstehende Eigensachen Ihres gefallenen Sohnes wurden bei der Kompanie vorgefunden und übersandt:

1 Uhr mit Kette und Hülle
1 Schlüsselbund mit Kette
1 Tabakdose
1 Geldbörse mit RM! 1,42
1 Nähzeug
5 St. Einheitsseife
1 Beutel mit Zahnputzzeug
1 Vorhängeschloß
RM! 127.- werden mit Postanweisung übersandt.

1 Feuerzeug
1 Uhrkette
2 Bleistifte
1 Brieftasche mit Briefschafften
1 Rasierzeug
3 Zahnsteine
1 P. Feldpostriefe
1 Verwundetenabzeichen mit Urkunde

Leutnant u. Kompanieführer

The grim reality of war. An inventory of a soldier's personal affects, including his shaving gear, sent from the unit commander to the family. *OSTFRONT Militaria*

Hundreds of different brands of razor blades were available on the commercial market.

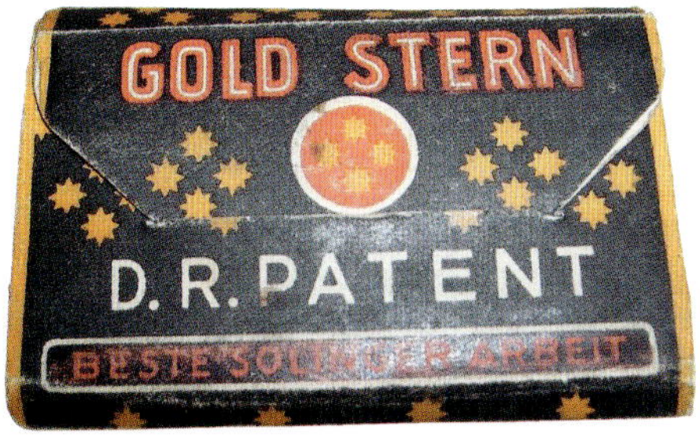
GOLD STERN
D.R. PATENT
BESTE SOLINGER ARBEIT

Hildo
HILDO SPECIAL
SPECIAL
SOLINGEN
HILDO SPECIAL

Blau-Jacke
hauchdünn
SOLINGEN
10 BLAU-JACKE
SOLINGEN
Blau-Jacke
SOLINGEN

SOLDATEN-FREUND
SOLDATEN-FREUND

G/0501

Birkendahl
MADE IN GERMANY
0,06 m/m
993 LUXUS
SOLINGEN

Herren-stolz
TRUMPF
15

S.A.

10
SPECIAL

ROBUR
GOLD
ROBUR
GOLD
0,10 mm

S.A. Klinge

Sonnal-Extra
NI-CPLATA
0,10 mm
ROTBART
Be-Be
SCHUTZ-MARKEN
EINGETR.
REG.D TRADE-MARKS
Etso
Privat
ETSO-PRIVAT
Boa
RAZOR BLADE
MADE IN GERMANY
BISMARCK
SCHUTZ
EINGETR.
MARKE
Adonis
"ADONIS"
RASIERKLINGEN BEFRIEDIGEN
DEN VERWÖHNTESTEN
SELBSTRASIERER
FERMARUD
rasiert gut
per 10 Stück
WEISS 0.45 RM
ROT 0.45
KUPFER 0.90
SILBER 0.90
GOLD 1.25
FERMARUD
Nur bei Ihrem Friseur zu haben
DIESEN KARTON
LEER
FÜR AUSSTELLZWECKE
VERWENDEN.
FERMARUD
rasiert gut
MULCUTO DIAMON
ZWEISCHNEIDER
D.R.P. № 640543
0,10 mm
FÜR DEN STÄRKSTEN BART
SOLINGEN
FERMARUD
Gold
FEINSTE QUALITÄTSARBEIT
FERMARUD
Gold
FEINSTE QUALITÄTSARBEIT

VOR DER RASUR
NACH DER RASUR
Vogel
Sehr sanft!
Für empfindliche Haut

Vogel

BISMARCK
Senior

GOLD-EXTRA
SCHWEDENSTAHL
0.08
mm

MOND-
EXTRA

MULCUTO DIAMON
MULCUTO
ZWEISCHNEIDER
D. R. P. No. 640543
VORRASUR
MULCUTO DIAMON
ZWEISCHNEIDER
NACHRASUR
1
2
3
0,10
mm

Jowika
Solingen
113

Sonnal
HP

SONNAL
Brillant

Apollo brand razors. *Michel Verberkt Collection*

Wartime advertisement for razors and razor blades.

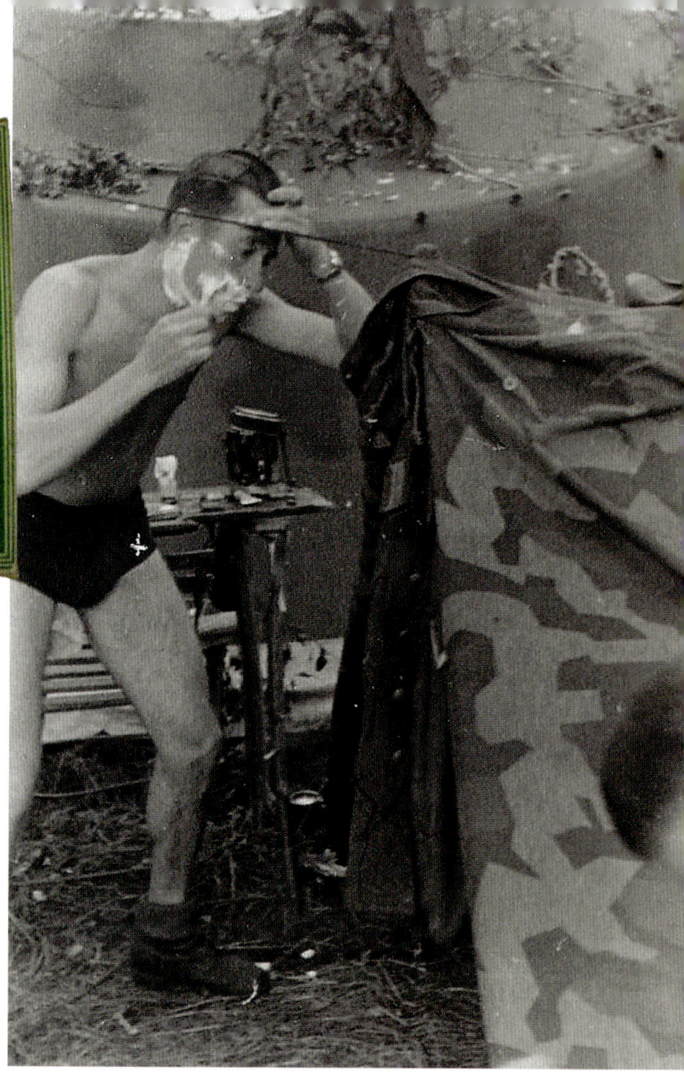

Shaving on a daily basis required a lot of discipline in the field. *OSTFRONT Militaria*

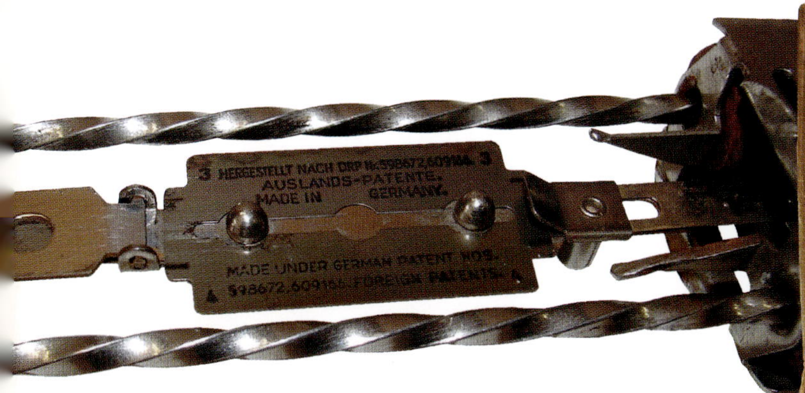

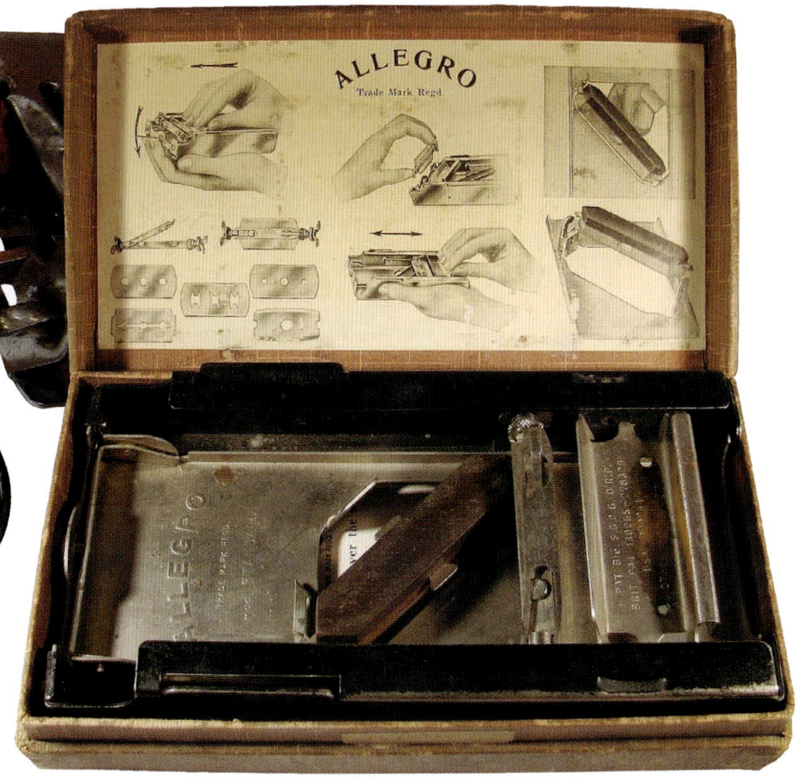

A number of ingenious products were manufactured to sharpen razor blades.

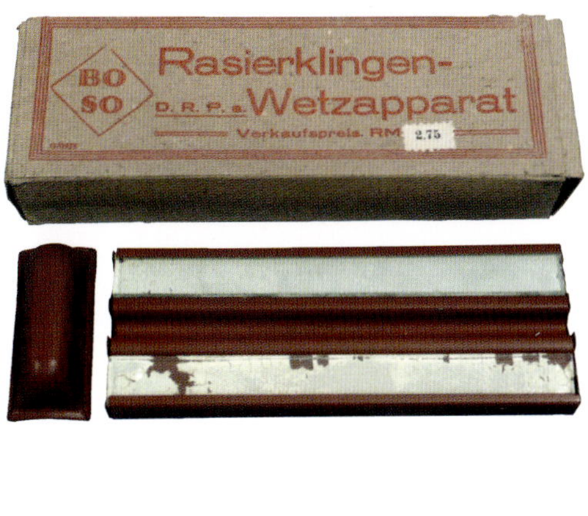

BOSO, Brico, and Gebruder Schmidt razor sharpeners. *Michel Verberkt Collection and Bunker Militaria*

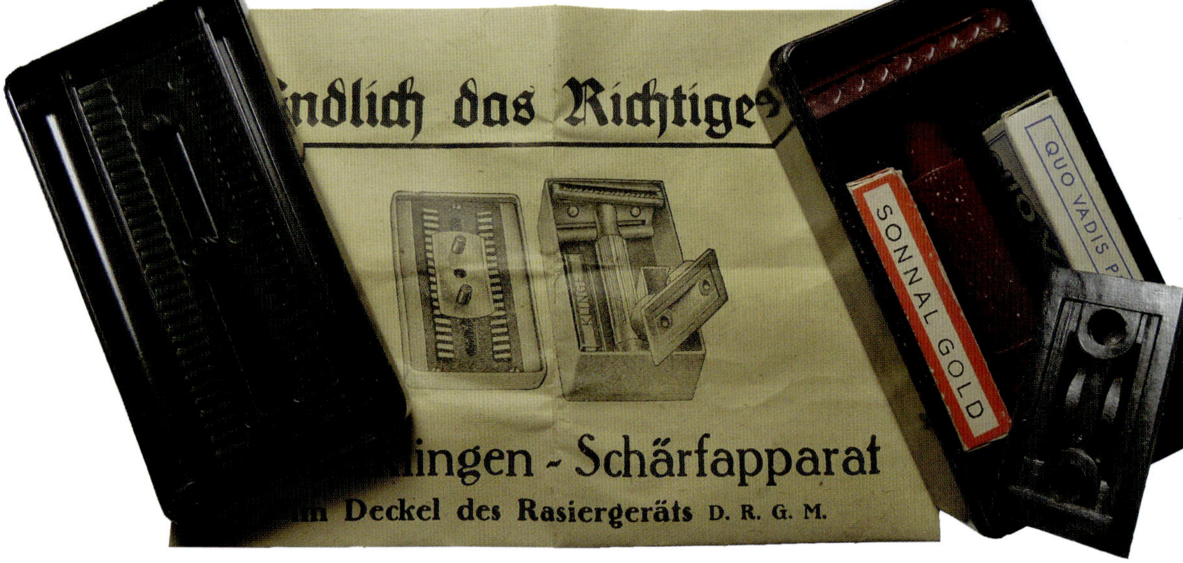

A razor sharpener was built into the cover of this razor kit. *Frédéric Ruelle Collection*

Straight razor manufactured by J.A. Henckels.

Straight razor from an unknown manufacturer. *Bunkermilitaria.com*

Puma brand straight razor. *Frédéric Ruelle Collection*

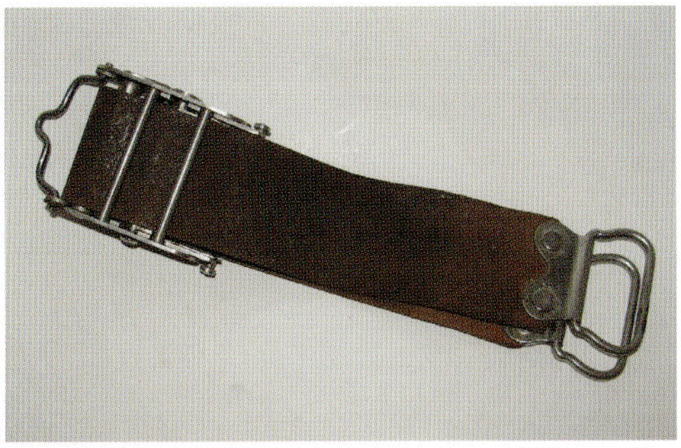

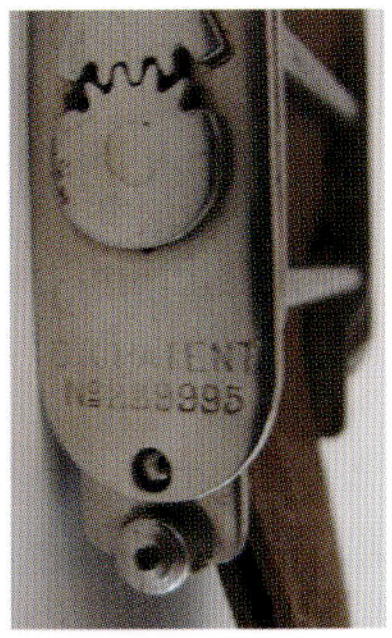

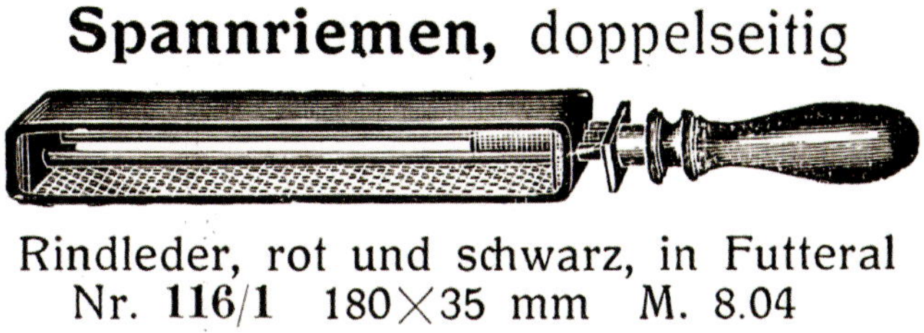

Two types of straight razor sharpeners along with period advertisements of similar products.

Soldiers taking advantage of some down time to take care of personal business.

A straight razor sharpener marked as army property. *Bunkermilitaria.com*

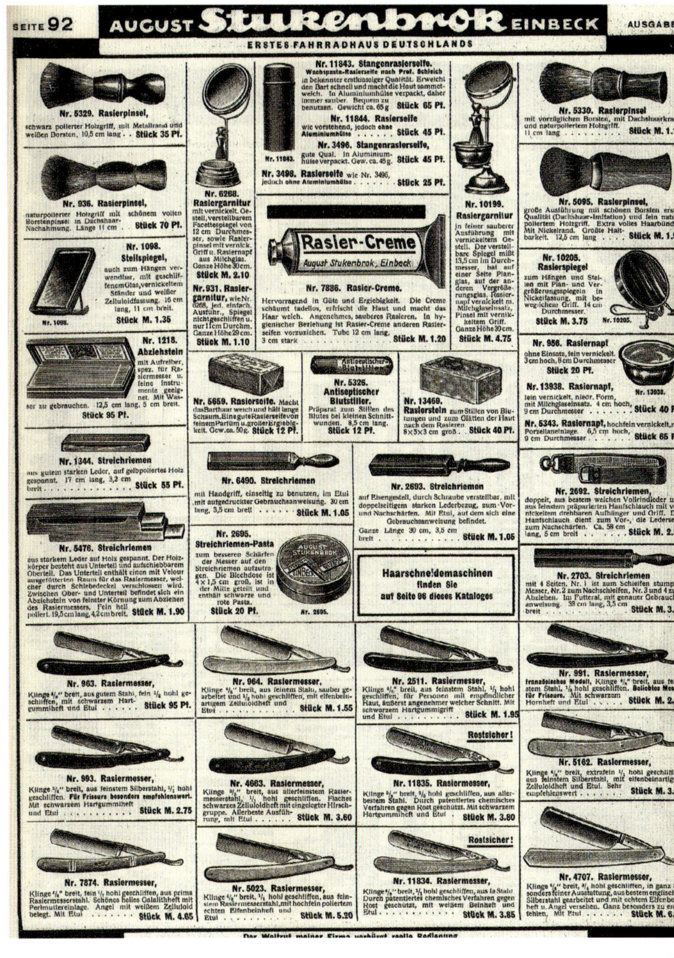

SEITE 92 AUGUST Stukenbrok EINBECK AUSGABE

ERSTES FAHRRADHAUS DEUTSCHLANDS

Nr. 5329. Rasierpinsel, schwarz polierter Holzgriff, mit Metallrand und weißen Borsten, 10,5 cm lang . . **Stück 35 Pf.**

Nr. 936. Rasierpinsel, naturpolierter Holzgriff mit schönem vollen Borstenpinsel in Dachshaar-Nachahmung. Länge 11 cm . . **Stück 70 Pf.**

Nr. 1098. Stellspiegel, auch zum Hängen verwendbar, mit geschliffenem Glas, vernickeltem Ständer und weißer Zelluloidfassung. 16 cm lang, 11 cm breit. **Stück M. 1.35**

Nr. 1218. Abziehstein mit Aufreiber, spez. für Rasiermesser u. feine Instrumente geeignet. Mit Wasser zu gebrauchen. 12,5 cm lang, 5 cm breit. **Stück 95 Pf.**

Nr. 6268. Rasiergarnitur mit vernickelt. Gestell, verstellbarem Facettespiegel von 12 cm Durchmesser, sowie Rasierpinsel mit vernick. Griff u. Rasiernapf aus Milchglas. Ganze Höhe 30 cm. **Stück M. 2.10**

Nr. 931. Rasiergarnitur, wie Nr. 6268, jed. einfach. Ausführ., Spiegel nicht geschliffen u. nur 11 cm Durchm. Ganze Höhe 29 cm. **Stück M. 1.10**

Nr. 11843. Stangenrasierseife. Wachspasta-Rasierseife nach Prof. Schleich in bekannter erstklassiger Qualität. Erweicht den Bart schnell und macht die Haut sammetweich. In Aluminiumhülse verpackt, daher immer sauber. Bequem zu benutzen. Gewicht ca. 65 g **Stück 65 Pf.**

Nr. 11844. Rasierseife wie vorstehend, jedoch ohne Aluminiumhülse . . . . . . **Stück 45 Pf.**

Nr. 3496. Stangenrasierseife, gute Qual. In Aluminiumhülse verpackt. Gew. ca. 45 g. **Stück 45 Pf.**

Nr. 3498. Rasierseife wie Nr. 3496, jedoch ohne Aluminiumhülse . . . . **Stück 25 Pf.**

Rasier-Creme August Stukenbrok, Einbeck

Nr. 7886. Rasier-Creme. Hervorragend in Güte und Ergiebigkeit. Die Creme schäumt tadellos, erfrischt die Haut und macht das Haar weich. Angenehmes, sauberes Rasieren. In hygienischer Beziehung ist Rasier-Creme anderen Rasierseifen vorzuziehen. Tube 12 cm lang, 3 cm stark . . . . **Stück M. 1.20**

Nr. 10199. Rasiergarnitur in feiner sauberer Ausführung mit vernickeltem Gestell. Der verstellbare Spiegel mißt 13,5 cm im Durchmesser, hat auf einer Seite Planglas, auf der anderen Vergrößerungsglas. Rasiernapf vernickelt m. Milchglaseinsatz, Pinsel mit vernikkeltem Griff. Ganze Höhe 39 cm. **Stück M. 4.75**

Nr. 5330. Rasierpinsel mit vorzüglichen Borsten, mit Dachshaarkranz und naturpoliertem Holzgriff. 11 cm lang . . . . **Stück M. 1.10**

Nr. 5095. Rasierpinsel, große Ausführung mit schönen Borsten erster Qualität (Dachshaar-Imitation) und fein naturpoliertem Holzgriff. Extra volles Haarbündel. Mit Nickelrand. Große Haltbarkeit. 12,5 cm lang . . . . **Stück M. 1.95**

Nr. 10205. Rasierspiegel zum Hängen und Stellen mit Plan- und Vergrößerungsspiegeln in Nickelfassung, mit beweglichem Griff. 14 cm Durchmesser. **Stück M. 3.75**

Nr. 956. Rasiernapf ohne Einsatz, fein vernickelt. 3 cm hoch, 8 cm Durchmesser **Stück 20 Pf.**

Nr. 13938. Rasiernapf, fein vernickelt, niedr. Form, mit Milchglaseinsatz. 4 cm hoch, 9 cm Durchmesser . . . . **Stück 40 Pf.**

Nr. 5343. Rasiernapf, hochfein vernickelt, mit Porzellaneinlage. 6,5 cm hoch, 9 cm Durchmesser . . . . . . **Stück 65 Pf.**

Nr. 5659. Rasierseife. Macht das Barthaar weich und hält lange Schaum. Eine gute Rasierseife von feinem Parfüm u. großer Ergiebigkeit. Gew. ca. 50 g. **Stück 12 Pf.**

Nr. 5326. Antiseptischer Blutstiller. Präparat zum Stillen des Blutes bei kleinen Schnittwunden. 8,5 cm lang. **Stück 12 Pf.**

Nr. 13469. Rasierstein zum Stillen von Blutungen und zum Glätten der Haut nach dem Rasieren 8×5×3 cm groß . . **Stück 40 Pf.**

Nr. 1344. Streichriemen aus gutem starken Leder, auf gelbpoliertes Holz gespannt. 17 cm lang, 3,2 cm breit . . . . **Stück 55 Pf.**

Nr. 5476. Streichriemen aus starkem Leder auf Holz gespannt. Der Holzkörper besteht aus Unterteil und aufschiebbarem Oberteil. Das Unterteil enthält einen mit Velour ausgefütterten Raum für das Rasiermesser, welcher durch Schiebedeckel verschlossen wird. Zwischen Ober- und Unterteil befindet sich ein Abziehstein von feinster Körnung zum Abziehen des Rasiermessers. Fein hell poliert. 19,5 cm lang, 4,2 cm breit. **Stück M. 1.90**

Nr. 6490. Streichriemen mit Handgriff, einseitig zu benutzen, im Etui mit aufgedruckter Gebrauchsanweisung. 30 cm lang, 3,5 cm breit . . . . . . **Stück M. 1.05**

Nr. 2695. Streichriemen-Pasta zum besseren Schärfen der Messer auf den Streichriemen aufzutragen. Die Blechdose ist 4×1,5 cm groß, ist in der Mitte geteilt und enthält schwarze und rote Pasta. **Stück 20 Pf.**

Nr. 2693. Streichriemen auf Eisengestell, durch Schraube verstellbar, mit doppelseitigem starken Lederbezug, zum Vor- und Nachschärfen. Mit Etui, auf dem sich eine Gebrauchsanweisung befindet. Ganze Länge 30 cm, 3,5 cm breit . . . . **Stück M. 1.05**

Haarschneidemaschinen finden Sie auf Seite 96 dieses Kataloges

Nr. 2692. Streichriemen, doppelt, aus bestem weichen Vollrindleder und aus feinstem präparierten Hanfschlauch mit vernickeltem drehbaren Aufhänger und Griff. Der Hanfschlauch dient zum Vor-, die Lederseite zum Nachschärfen. Ca. 58 cm lang, 5 cm breit . . . . . . **Stück M. 2.85**

Nr. 2703. Streichriemen mit 4 Seiten. Nr. 1 ist zum Schleifen stumpfer Messer, Nr. 2 zum Nachschleifen, Nr. 3 und 4 zum Abziehen. Im Futteral, mit genauer Gebrauchsanweisung. 38 cm lang, 3,5 cm breit . . . . **Stück M. 3.75**

Nr. 963. Rasiermesser, Klinge 4/8" breit, aus gutem Stahl, fein 1/2 hohl geschliffen, mit schwarzem Hartgummiheft und Etui . . . . . . **Stück 95 Pf.**

Nr. 964. Rasiermesser, Klinge 4/8" breit, aus feinem Stahl, sauber gearbeitet und 1/2 hohl geschliffen, mit elfenbeinartigem Zelluloidheft und Etui . . . . **Stück M. 1.55**

Nr. 2511. Rasiermesser, Klinge 4/8" breit, aus feinstem Stahl, 1/1 hohl geschliffen, für Personen mit empfindlicher Haut, äußerst angenehmer weicher Schnitt. Mit schwarzem Hartgummigriff und Etui . . . . **Stück M. 1.95**

Nr. 991. Rasiermesser, französisches Modell, Klinge 4/8" breit, aus feinstem Stahl, 1/2 hohl geschliffen. **Beliebtes Messer für Friseure.** Mit schwarzem Hornheft und Etui . . . . . **Stück M. 2.55**

Nr. 993. Rasiermesser, Klinge 5/8" breit, aus feinstem Silberstahl, 1/1 hohl geschliffen. **Für Friseure besonders empfehlenswert.** Mit schwarzem Hartgummiheft und Etui . . . . **Stück M. 2.75**

Nr. 4663. Rasiermesser, Klinge 5/8" breit, aus allerfeinstem Rasiermesserstahl, 1/1 hohl geschliffen. Flaches schwarzes Zelluloidheft mit eingelegter Hirschgruppe. Allerbeste Ausführung, mit Etui . . . . . . **Stück M. 3.60**

Rostsicher!

Nr. 11835. Rasiermesser, Klinge 5/8" breit, 1/2 hohl geschliffen, aus allerbestem Stahl. Durch patentiertes chemisches Verfahren gegen Rost geschützt. Mit schwarzem Hartgummiheft und Etui . **Stück M. 3.80**

Nr. 5162. Rasiermesser, Klinge 4/8" breit, extrafein 1/1 hohl geschliffen aus feinstem Silberstahl, mit elfenbeinartigem Zelluloidheft und Etui. Sehr empfehlenswert . . . . **Stück M. 3.15**

Nr. 7874. Rasiermesser, Klinge 4/8" breit, fein 1/1 hohl geschliffen, aus prima Rasiermesserstahl. Schönes helles Galalithheft mit Perlmuttereinlage. Angel mit weißem Zelluloid belegt. Mit Etui . . . . **Stück M. 4.65**

Nr. 5023. Rasiermesser, Klinge 4/8" breit, 1/1 hohl geschliffen, aus feinstem Rasiermesserstahl, mit hochfein poliertem echten Elfenbeinheft und Etui . . . . **Stück M. 5.20**

Rostsicher!

Nr. 11834. Rasiermesser, Klinge 4/8" breit, 1/1 hohl geschliffen, aus Ia Stahl. Durch patentiertes chemisches Verfahren gegen Rost geschützt, mit weißem Beinheft und Etui . . . . **Stück M. 3.85**

Nr. 4707. Rasiermesser, Klinge 4/8" breit, 3/4 hohl geschliffen, in ganz besonders feiner Ausstattung, aus bestem englischen Silberstahl gearbeitet und mit echtem Elfenbeinheft u. Angel versehen. Ganz besonders zu empfehlen. Mit Etui . . . . . . **Stück M. 6.65**

Der Weltruf meiner Firma verbürgt reelle Bedienung

Period catalog showing a selection of shaving products.

A few examples of mirrors that were available.

A nice shaving station.

Sarg brand razor soap.

A small can of Waldheimer brand razor soap.

Palmolive brand razor soap. *OSTFRONT Militaria*

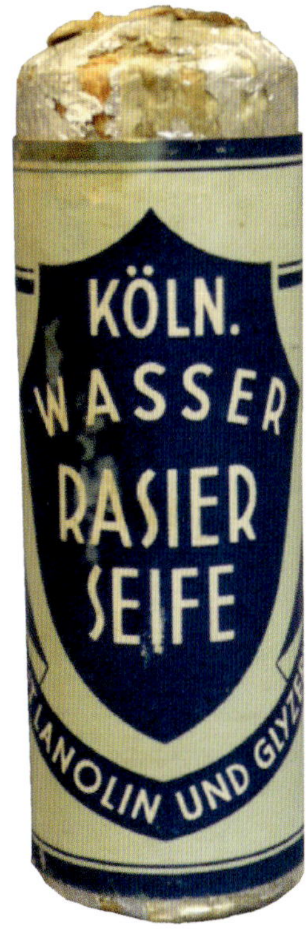

Razor soaps and creams were packaged in different ways. *Bunkermilitaria.com*

Razor brushes.
Frédéric Ruelle Collection

Simi brand aftershave.
Frédéric Ruelle Collection

Septic pencil.
Bunkermilitaria.com

Shaving cloth.

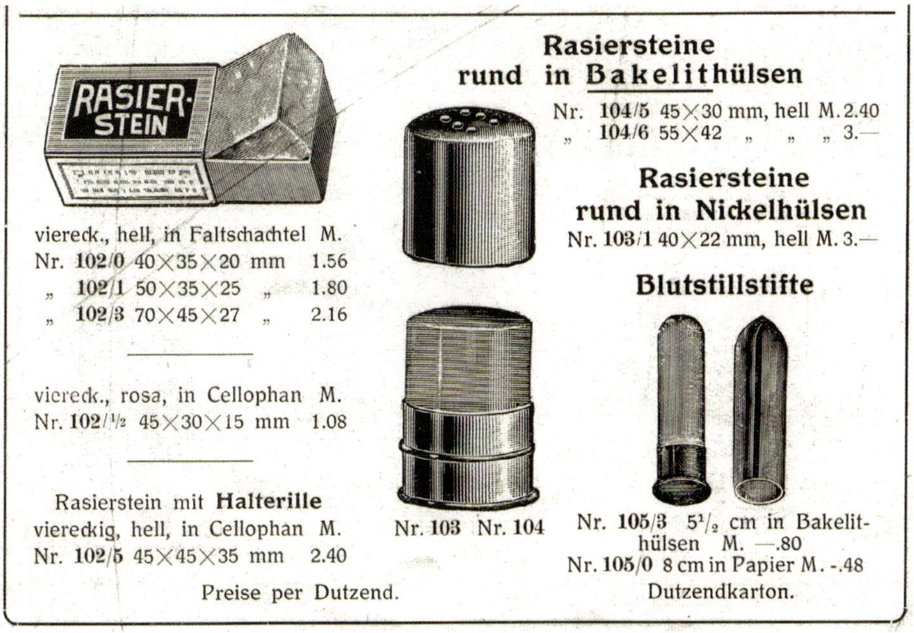

Advertisement for a sharpening stone and septic stick.

Teamwork.

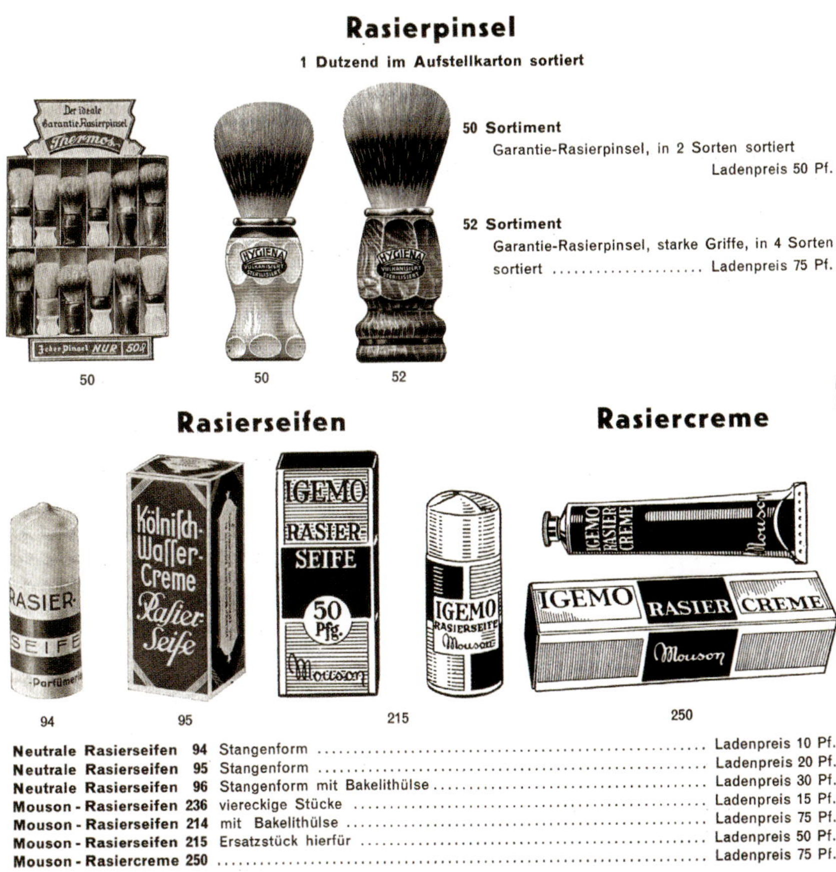

Advertisement for shaving brush, razor soap, and shaving cream.

A can of razor strap paste.
Bunkermilitaria.com

CHAPTER 6
HAIR CARE

Most armies of WWII published regulations establishing specific grooming standards for their soldiers. Safety, uniformity, and projecting a professional image are some of the basic reasons why grooming standards were established. Beyond projecting a professional image, poor grooming practices can lead to health issues that could impact unit readiness. Lice were the scourge of the German soldier. Humans are host to three different kinds of lice: head lice, body lice, and pubic lice. Head lice are extremely contagious and can be spread from person to person by sharing brushes, hats, etc., despite the cleanliness of the person. These lice do not spread disease and are generally more of a nuisance than anything. Head lice infestations can be controlled with lice combs, medicated shampoos, etc. Pubic lice are spread through sexual activity and present no health dangers except itching. These lice are controlled in the same manner as head lice (see chapter 8).

German regulations dictated hair was shaved from the neck and tapered up to the top above the ears all the way around. The hair was usually long on top and combed and slicked back from the forehead. If parted, the part was very high on the head. Pomade was very popular for slicking back the top of the hair.

The comb or brush was essential to good hair care. Allied intelligence personnel conducted an investigation into the comb industry with their findings published in the report *German Comb Industry*. After the war, Allied investigators visited thirty firms that manufactured combs and produced raw materials, as well as those manufacturing the tools and dies. The general impression of the investigators was that German production methods were similar to those used by the British. The German comb industry was subject to limitations caused by the war and in particular, the production of vulcanite combs appears to have ceased in 1940; the production of saw cut combs from celluloid and cellulose acetate sheet was dependent on existing stocks or the available limited supplies of these materials.

The following materials and factories were mentioned in the intelligence report on combs. Obviously other materials and factories were involved in the manufacture of combs.

a. Vulcanite is a hard rubber produced by vulcanization. Various qualities of rubber to include Buna were used to manufacture combs. Factories using this material were-Continental Gummi-Werke, A.G. Hannover: New York Hamburger Gummi-Waaren Co, Maurien Strasse 19, Hamburg: Bolta-Werke, G.M.B.H. Aussere Sulzbacherstrasse 164, Hamburg: Rheinische Gummi and Celluloid Fabrik, Gummi Strasse, Mannheim-Neckerau.

b. Celluloid, Cellulose Acetate, Cellon or Zellon is a mixture of cellulose acetate and camphor. It is soluble in acetone. Cellulose acetate had many wartime uses: photography film, cellophane, eyeglass frames, combs, electrical insulators in lacquer form, gas masks, transparent face shields, jewelry, as well use as a synthetic fiber. Factories using this material were Rheinische Kammfabrik, St. Tonis, Nr. Krefeld: August Wulf: Ernst Kuster: Knigge and Lindhoff: Breiter and Koch: Hormann and Co.: Hattendorf and Held: Wilhelm Meyer and Co.: Gustav Konig: Paul Rosbach, Bad Salzuflen: Rheinische Gummi and Celluloid Fabrik, Gummi Strasse, Mannheim-Neckerau: Schwabische Celluloiwaarenfabrik, Mengen, Wurttemberg: Oscar Schenck, Nacf. Mengen, Wurttemberg.

c. Polystyrene is a strong plastic that can be injected, extruded or blow molded. I. G. Farben began manufacturing polystyrene in Ludwigshafen, Germany, around 1931, hoping it would be a suitable replacement for die-cast zinc. Success was achieved when they developed a reactor vessel that extruded polystyrene through a heated tube and cutter, producing polystyrene in pellet form. Polystyrene was also known as Trolitul. Some of the factories which used Polystyrene were-Rheinische Kammfabrik, St. Tonis, and Nr. Krefeld, using Polystyrene supplied by Dynamit A.G.

d. Polyvinyl chloride, commonly abbreviated PVC, is one of the most widely produced plastics in today's world. It was created by the German chemist Eugen Baumann in 1872, but never patented until 1913 when German Friedrich Klatte invented a new method for the polymerization of vinyl chloride using sunlight. PVC is durable, cheap, and easily worked. It can be made softer and more flexible by the addition of plasticizers. In this form, it is used in clothing and upholstery, electrical cable insulation, inflatable products, and many applications in which it replaces rubber. No specific factories were mentioned.

e. Astralon, or an equivalent material was not used in Britain during the war. It is a co-polymer of 80 parts Vinyl Chloride and 20 parts Acrylic Resin. Dynamit A.G. manufactured several grades of Vinyl Chloride interpolymers, of which Astralon is the unplasticised sheeting. This material was tried out by several German Comb manufacturers, with varying success. It is regarded as a non flammable Celluloid substitute and said to combine toughness with flexibility. It is said not to absorb moisture and to be heat resisting to 80 degrees Celsius. Although Polystyrene (Trolitul) powder is most widely used for German Molded Comb production, Polyamide (Nylon type) molding powders were used experimentally. This powder is made in three grades A-B-C. Igamid A is harder than B, and has a higher melting point, about 215 degrees Celcius. Igamid 6A is flexible and leather like. Igamid A is said to be most suitable for Combs. Buchholz and Company Lauterbach, Wurttemberg used Astralon.

f. Horn consists of keratin and includes solid keratin from other parts of animals, such as hoofs. Horn may be used as a material in tools, furniture and decoration, among others. Horn is somewhat thermoplastic and was used for many purposes where plastic would now be used. Factories using this material were-Arnold and Co., Lauterbach, Wurttemberg: Jacob Denzel, Calw, Wurttemberg.

g. Plexiglass (Perspex type sheet) Poly(methyl methacrylate) (PMMA) is a transparent thermoplastic, often used as a light or shatter-resistant alternative to glass. It is sometimes called acrylic glass. Chemically, it is the synthetic polymer of methyl methacrylate. The material was developed in 1928 in various laboratories, and was first brought to market in 1933 by Rohm and Haas Company, under the trademark Plexiglas. It has since been sold under many different names including Lucite and Perspex. The Buchholz and Company Factory, Lauterbach, Wurttemberg manufactured combs using Plexiglas.

h. Casein is the name for a family of related phosphoprotein proteins commonly found in milk. Some of the earliest plastics were based on casein. In particular, galalith was well-known for use in buttons. Fiber can be made from extruded casein. Lanital, a fabric made from casein fiber products, was particularly popular in Italy during the 1930s. Factories using this material were-Jacob Denzel, Calw, Wurttemberg: Celler Knopf Fabrik, Sienecke and Co., Alte Grenzestrasse 31, Celle: International Galalith Co., Hamburg was the principle manufacturer of Casein sheets for the Comb industry before the war.

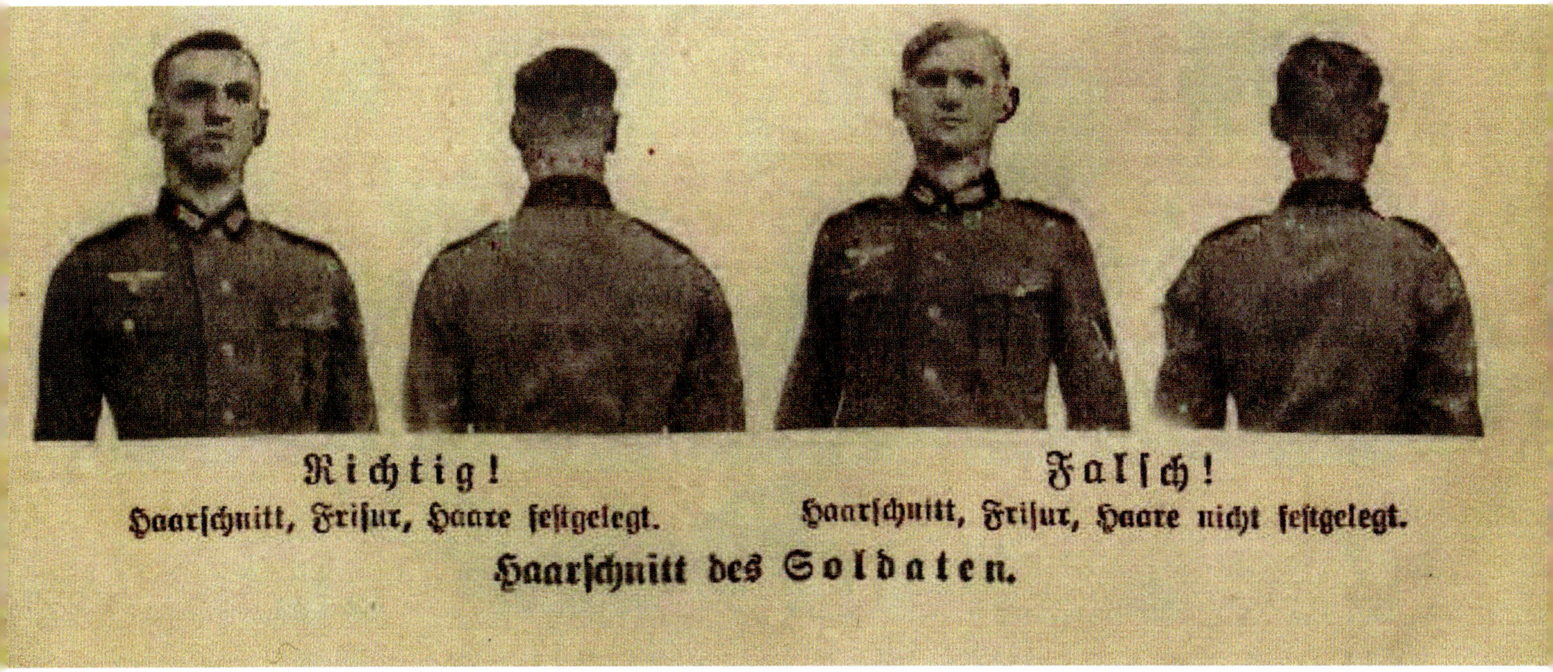

The regulation style of haircut is shown on the left.

High and tight! *Bundesarchiv-Bild-101I-104-1095-17 Foto: Kessler, Rudolph 1943/ Licence CC-BY-SA 3.0*

Two types of portable grooming kits. *OSTFRONT Militaria*

Rasier- und Toilettegarnituren in Rindledertaschen.

Wichtig! In alle Hülsen passen Normalstücke der Markenrasierseifen. Eine Hülse enthält 1 Stück Ia. Stangenseife, die andere 1 Garantiepinsel; die kleine 1 Alaunstein.

Nickelhülsen sind aus Messing.

Rasierapparate sind Messing verchromt, kurze Verschraubung; lange Verschraubung (Mehrpreis 20 Pfg. Stück) muss extra vorgeschrieben werden.

geschlossen 5×9 cm
Nr. 1110/11 B M. -.90
Bakelitfüllung
Nr. 1110/11 M M. 1.-
Nickelfüllung

geschl. 5×9½ cm
Nr. 1110/10 M. -.95

geschl. 9½×10 cm
Nr. 1110/12 M. 2.15
Nickelfüllung

geschloss. 13×10 cm
Nr. 1110/13½ M. 2.85
Nickelfüllung

geschlossen 11×8½ cm
Nr. 1110/16 M. 2.30
Nickelfüllung

geschlossen 11×10½ cm
Nr. 1110/18 M. 2.65
Bakelitfüll., Metallapparat

geschlossen 19×11 cm
Nr. 1110/15 M. 3.60

geschlossen 17×11 cm
Nr. 1110/14 M. 3.60
Nickelfüllung

geschlossen 22×11 cm
Nr. 1110/17 M. 4.75
Nickelfüllung.

Preise per Stück.

geschlossen 11½×9 cm
Nr. 1110/20 M. 3.75
Nickelfüllung

geschlossen 16×12 cm
Nr. 1110/27 M. 4.50
Bakelitfüll., Metallapparat

— 6 —

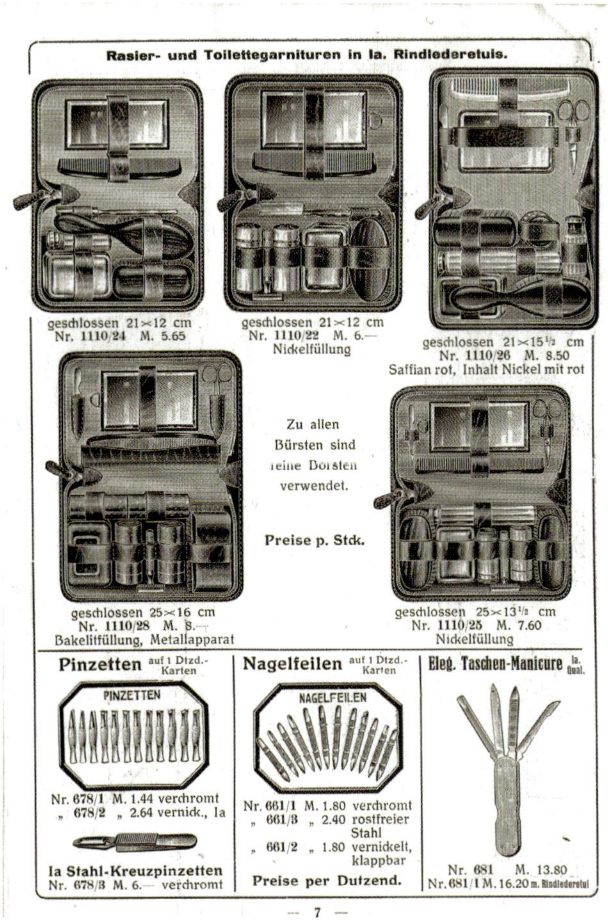

Rasier- und Toilettegarnituren in Ia. Rindlederetuis.

geschlossen 21×12 cm
Nr. 1110/24 M. 5.65

geschlossen 21×12 cm
Nr. 1110/22 M. 6.—
Nickelfüllung

geschlossen 21×15½ cm
Nr. 1110/26 M. 8.50
Saffian rot, Inhalt Nickel mit rot

Zu allen Bürsten sind reine Borsten verwendet.

Preise p. Stck.

geschlossen 25×16 cm
Nr. 1110/28 M. 8.—
Bakelitfüllung, Metallapparat

geschlossen 25×13½ cm
Nr. 1110/25 M. 7.60
Nickelfüllung

Pinzetten auf 1 Dtzd.-Karten

PINZETTEN

Nr. 678/1 M. 1.44 verchromt
„ 678/2 „ 2.64 vernick., Ia

Ia Stahl-Kreuzpinzetten
Nr. 678/3 M. 6.— verchromt

Nagelfeilen auf 1 Dtzd.-Karten

NAGELFEILEN

Nr. 661/1 M. 1.80 verchromt
„ 661/3 „ 2.40 rostfreier Stahl
„ 661/2 „ 1.80 vernickelt, klappbar

Preise per Dutzend.

Eleg. Taschen-Manicure Ia. Qual.

Nr. 681 M. 13.80
Nr. 681/1 M. 16.20 m. Rindlederetui

— 7 —

A sampling of grooming kits found in a wartime catalog.

A couple of hard rubber combs from the New York Hamburger Gummi-Waaren Compagnie.[1]
The Collectors Guild

Comb manufactured from plastic or celluloid.

Aluminum comb.

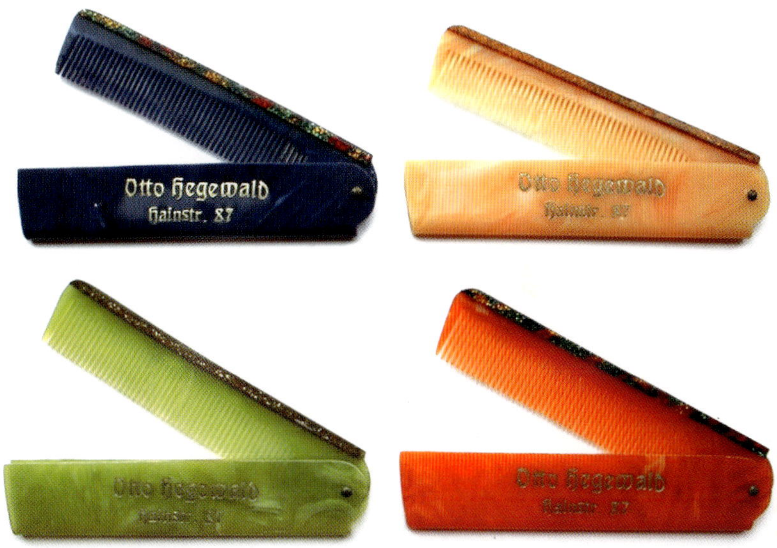

Several different colors of combs from the same manufacturer.
Michel Verberkt Collection

Kämme und Haarschmuck

Nr. 36610. Bester schwarzer Staubkamm a. Ia. Hartgummi. Länge ca. 8 cm........ 19 Pf.

Nr. 36611. Feiner schwarzer Taschenfrisierkamm aus Kunsthorn. Länge ca. 10 cm. 12 Pf.

Nr. 36612. Hübscher schwarzer Taschenkamm aus Hartgummi. Länge ca. 11 cm........ 19 Pf.

Nr. 36613. Bubikopfkamm aus Hartgummi, bequem in der Handtasche zu tragen. Länge ca. 13 cm........ 19 Pf.

Nr. 36614. Fein polierter Frisierkamm aus Kunsthorn, blond. Länge 18½ cm .... 30 Pf.

Nr. 36615. Derselbe Kamm in weiß .... 30 Pf.

Nr. 36616. Prima Frisierkamm, schwarz, aus Kunsthorn. Länge ca. 18½ cm .... 30 Pf.

Nr. 36617. Handlicher Bubikopfkamm aus schwarzem Hartgummi. Länge ca. 17½ cm .... 35 Pf.

Nr. 36618. Prima Schildpatt-Frisierkamm aus farbigem Hartgummi. Länge ca. 17 cm. . 58 Pf.

Nr. 36619. Prima schwarzer, starker Gummikamm. Länge ca. 20 cm .... 50 Pf.

Nr. 36620. Vorzüglicher schwarzer Herrenfrisierkamm a. Hartgummi. Länge ca. 18 cm .... 24 Pf.

Nr. 36621. Apart. Taschenkamm mit Silberverzierung. Hülse aus Perlmutter-Imitation. Länge des Kammes ca. 10 cm ...... 90 Pf.

Nr. 36622. Maniküre-Etui aus rotem Saffianleder, 5 teilig. Mk. 2.10

Nr. 36623. Schildpattfarbiger Taschenkamm. Praktisch und bequem. Länge mit Griff ca. 19 cm. 50 Pf.

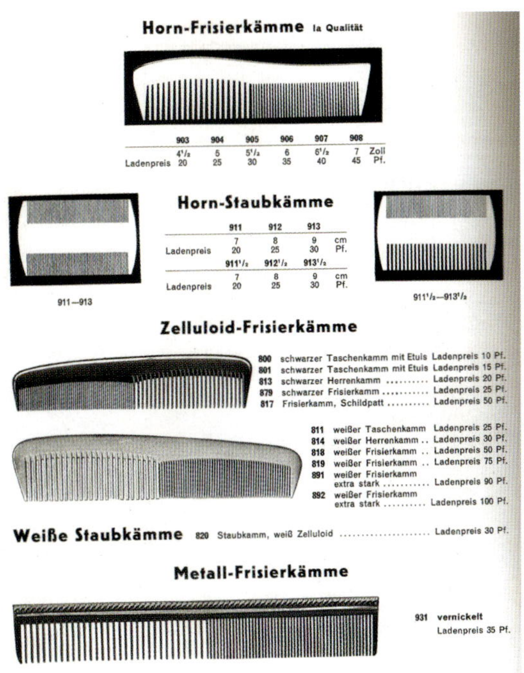

Horn-Frisierkämme Ia Qualität

	903	904	905	906	907	908	
	4½	5	5½	6	6½	7	Zoll
Ladenpreis	20	25	30	35	40	45	Pf.

Horn-Staubkämme

	911	912	913	
	7	8	9	cm
Ladenpreis	20	25	30	Pf.
	911½	912½	913½	
	7	8	9	cm
Ladenpreis	20	25	30	Pf.

911—913

911½—913½

Zelluloid-Frisierkämme

800 schwarzer Taschenkamm mit Etuis Ladenpreis 10 Pf.
801 schwarzer Taschenkamm mit Etuis Ladenpreis 15 Pf.
813 schwarzer Herrenkamm .... Ladenpreis 20 Pf.
879 schwarzer Frisierkamm .... Ladenpreis 25 Pf.
817 Frisierkamm, Schildpatt .... Ladenpreis 50 Pf.

811 weißer Taschenkamm Ladenpreis 25 Pf.
814 weißer Herrenkamm .. Ladenpreis 30 Pf.
818 weißer Frisierkamm .. Ladenpreis 50 Pf.
819 weißer Frisierkamm .. Ladenpreis 75 Pf.
891 weißer Frisierkamm extra stark .... Ladenpreis 90 Pf.
892 weißer Frisierkamm extra stark .... Ladenpreis 100 Pf.

Weiße Staubkämme

820 Staubkamm, weiß Zelluloid .... Ladenpreis 30 Pf.

Metall-Frisierkämme

931 vernickelt
Ladenpreis 35 Pf.

A selection of period comb advertisements showing the wide variety of materials used.

A selection of hair products from Dr. Dralle.

Trilysin brand hair tonic.[2]

A bottle of Auxol hair tonic along with a wartime advertisement.

Schwarzkopf brand shampoo.[3] *OSTFRONT Militaria*

SANO shampoo from France.

4711 brand shampoo. *OSTFRONT Militaria*

Shampoo manufactured by Ernst Walter.

Palmolive brand shampoo.[4] *OSTFRONT Militaria*

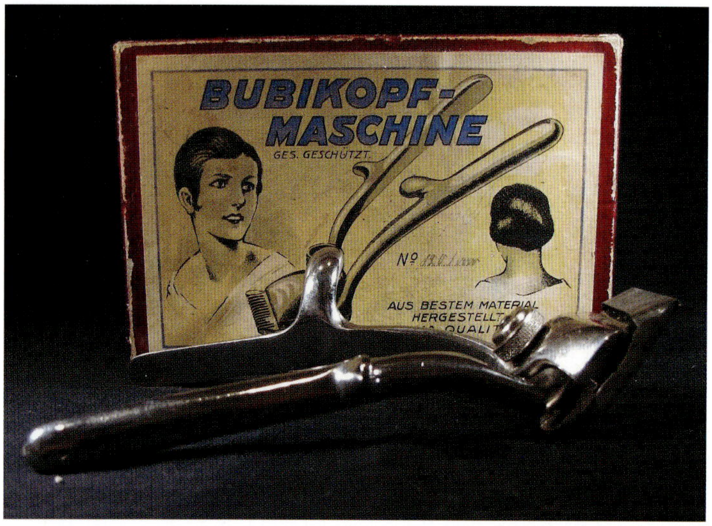

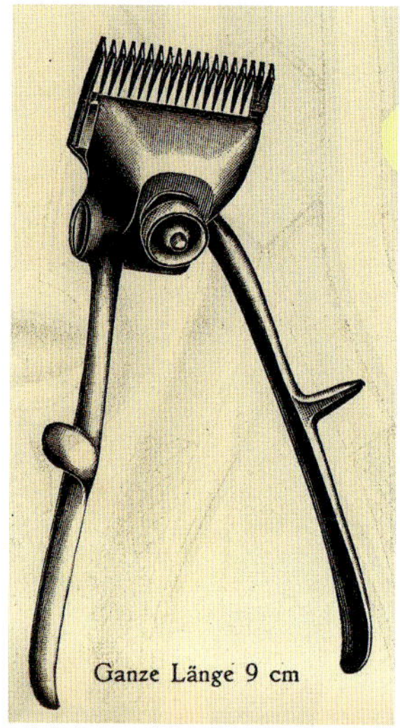

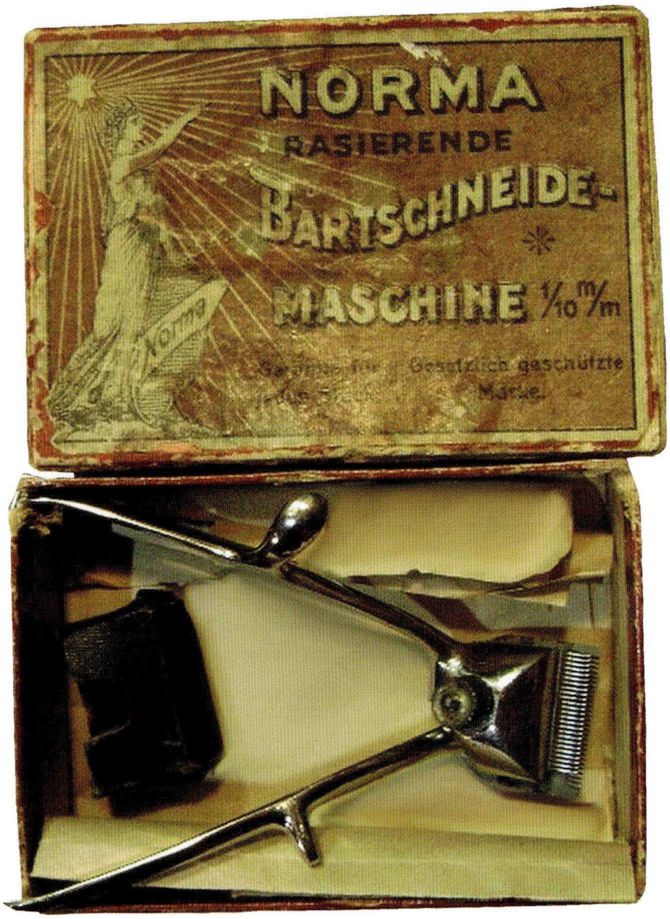

A selection of hair clippers. *Michel Verberkt Collection*

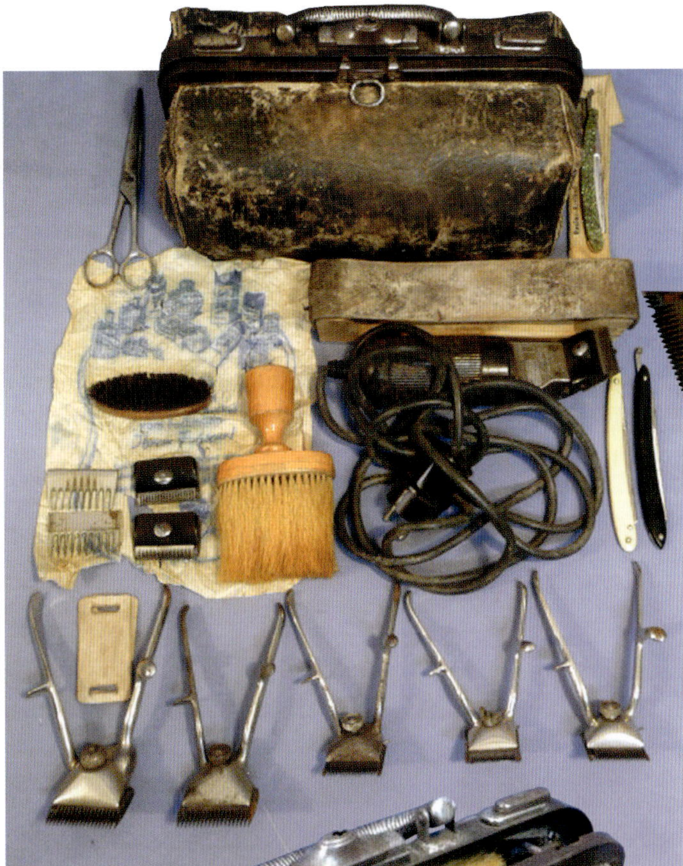

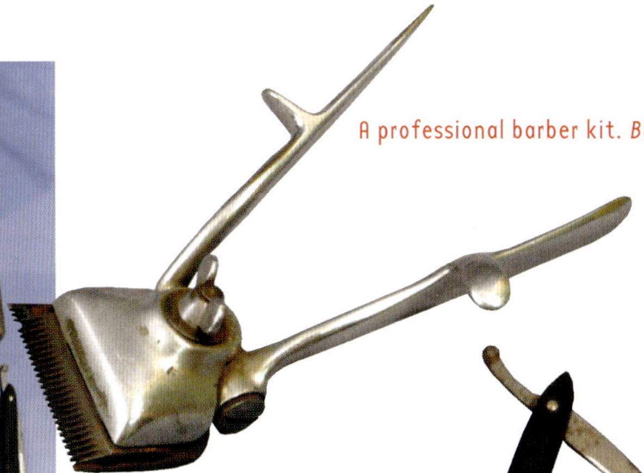

A professional barber kit. *Bunkermilitaria.com*

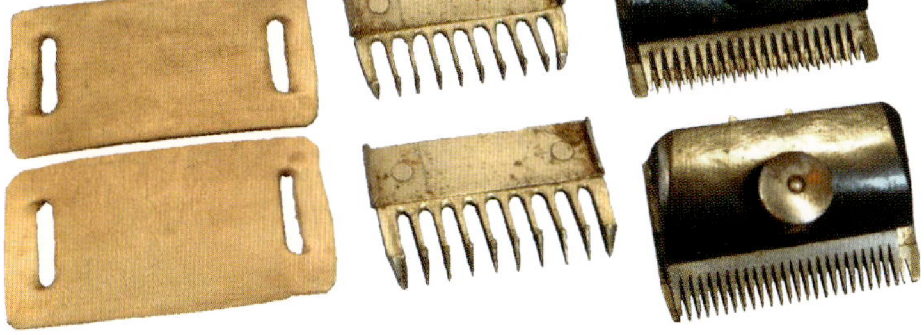

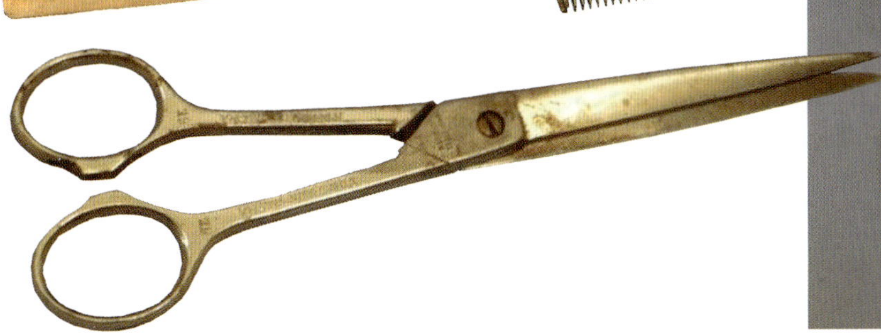

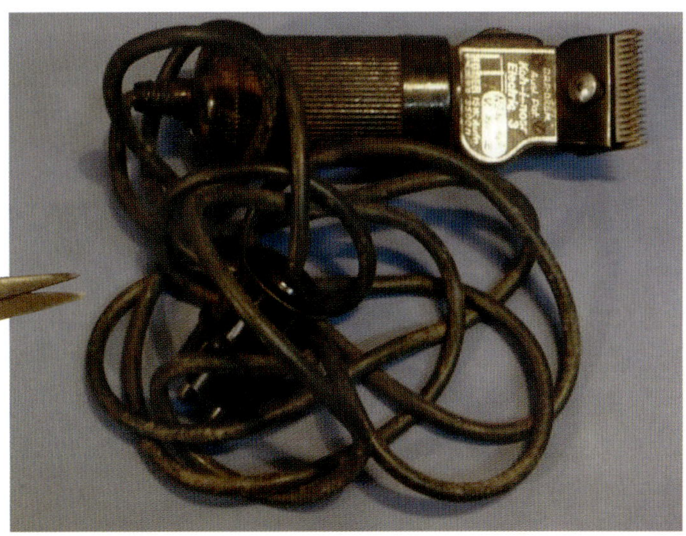

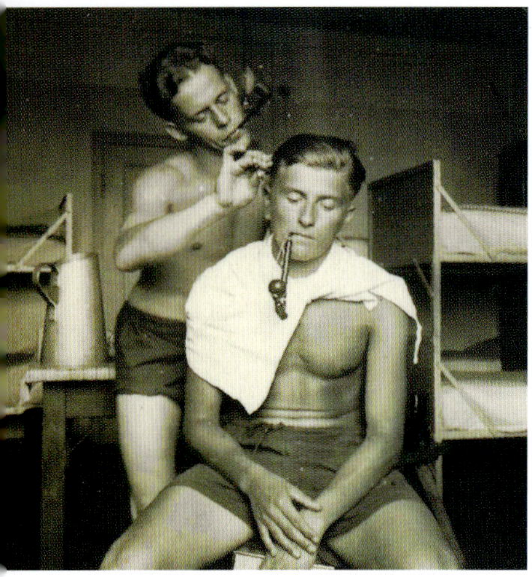

A trip to the barber was a pleasant experience.

Nivea brand hair lotion.

Looking good! *Bundesarchiv Bild 101I-394-1459-21, Foto: WandererApril 1942/ Licence CC-BY-SA 3.0*

Fox brand hair cream.[5]
www.raskantik.com

This catalog advertised hair clippers.

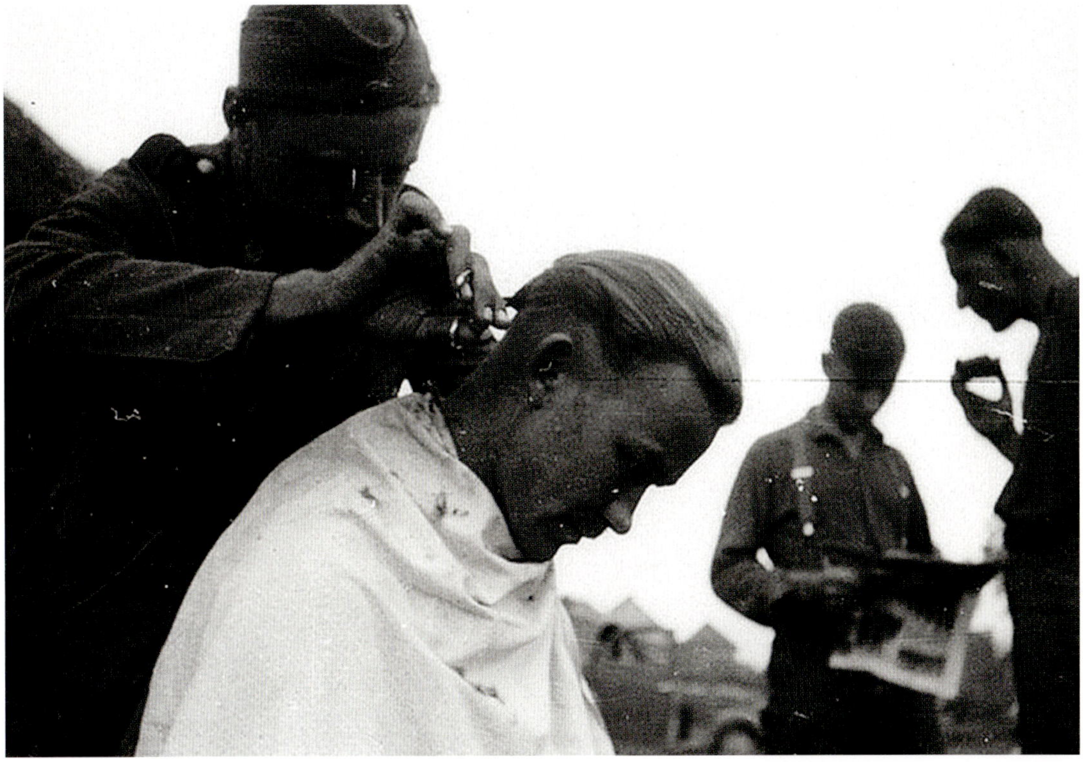

SS personnel getting a haircut. *Photos: US National Archives and Records Administration (NARA)*

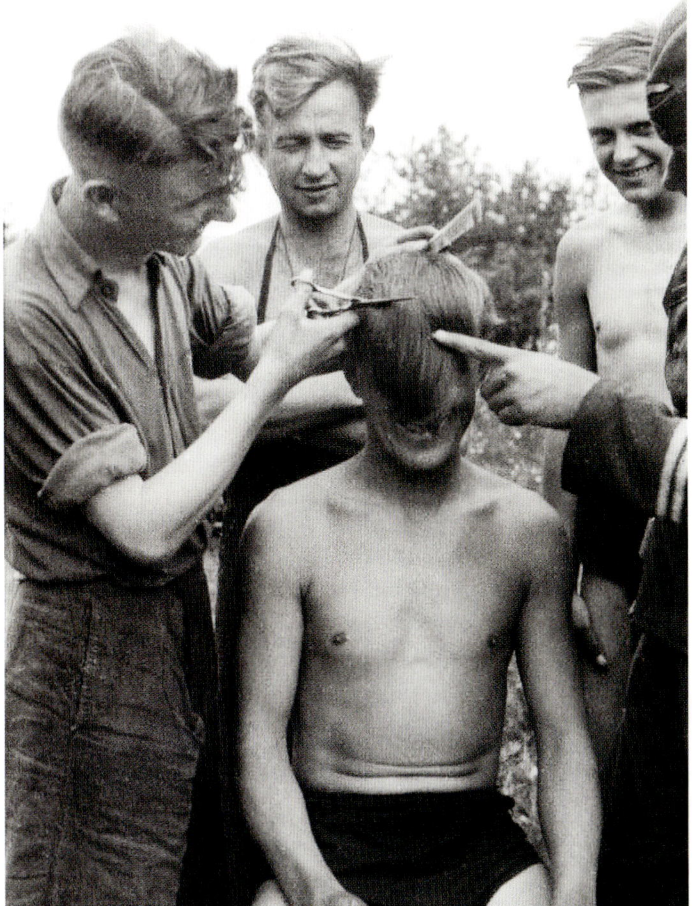

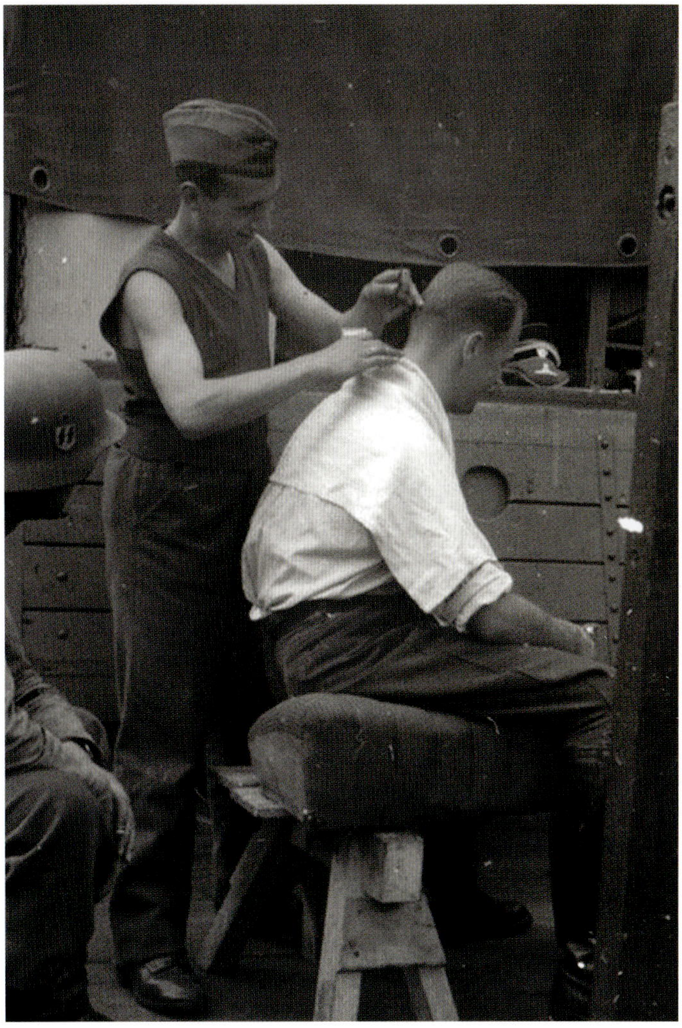

CHAPTER 6 ENDNOTES

1. The New York Hamburger Gummi-Waaren Compagnie was founded in 1870. It relocated to Lüneburg in 2009. Here is their address in the 1941 Hamburg phone book.

New-York Hamburger Gummi-Waaren-Compagnie, Hmb 33 *23 12 51

2. No history was found on the firm that manufactured Trilysin hair care products. Here is a wartime advertisement.

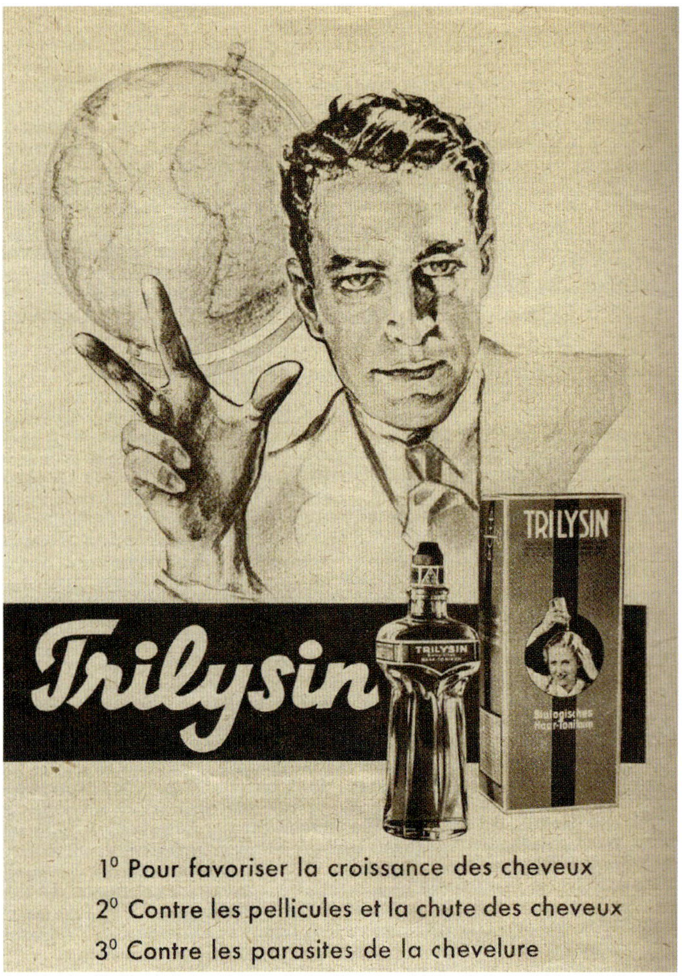

3. The firm Heinz Schwarzkopf Chem. Fabrik, Berlin, Germany, was founded in 1898. In 1927, the company introduced the first liquid shampoo on the market. The company is still in business. Here is a prewar advertisement.

4. Around 1900, the B.J. Johnson Company, Milwaukee, Wisconsin, USA, started making a soap entirely of palm and olive oil. The soap was so popular that the company was renamed Palmolive after it. It became the world's best-selling soap. A Missouri-based soap manufacturer named Peet Brothers merged with Palmolive to become Palmolive-Peet. In 1928, Palmolive-Peet bought the Colgate Company to create the Colgate-Palmolive-Peet Company. In 1953, "Peet" was dropped from the title, leaving only "Colgate-Palmolive Company," the current name.

5. No history was found on Fox Werk, Wien, Austria. Here is the firm's listing in the 1943 Wien phone book.

Fox-Werk Fabrik Chemischer Produkte Eugen Woska Wien-Atzgersdorf (XXV) Wiener Str 95 R 3 45 75

CHAPTER 7
FIRST AID

Every soldier had a basic knowledge of first aid, such as treating minor cuts, headaches, etc. As a member of the military, the soldier was given additional instruction on how to identify and treat certain types of ailments and wounds associated with combat or other military duties. Standard over-the-counter drugs and other first aid items were available at the Kantine, from home, or from the local economy. Small pocket first aid kits were widely available and proved useful for taking care of minor ailments. As can be guessed, the focus is on those things that the soldier could do himself to keep healthy. Some of the items pictured are clearly issue medical items that were sometimes dispensed to soldiers or were similar to commercial items that a soldier might have access to.

In *German Clothing, Equipment and Rations* the authors examined the care of the German soldier in cold climates:

a. Frostbite: As might be expected, the Germans felt that the chief means of preventing frostbite was instructing the men in how to take care of themselves in cold weather. Aside from prevention by using clothing and equipment properly the Germans felt that much frostbite of exposed portions of the skin, such as the face, and to a certain extent, the hands could be somewhat avoided by using Anti Frostbite Salve. It was of no use on the feet. General Wischhusen and the Surgeon of the 1st German Army said that the benefit was gained from the insulation given by the grease and not from any chemical action. Any clean grease, he felt would have been equally effective. Chemically the salve is simply petrolatum with about 10% ammonium sulfoicthyolic acid. The use of alcohol was theoretically frowned on by the medical officers because of the lowering of resistance to the cold, but some was permitted because of the beneficial effect on morale was thought to offset the harmful effects. The best treatment of frostbite had not been decided on by the Germans, notwithstanding their long experience on the Eastern Front. Rubbing of slight cases was considered advisable. At the beginning of the war, severe cases were warmed slowly but recently quick thawing in rooms above normal temperatures and alternate hot and cold baths were gaining favor.

b. Evacuation of the Wounded in Winter: A considerable amount of paper clothing, especially trouser legs, sleeves and vests and paper sleeping bags were captured from the Germans. These, it was definitely stated, were intended only for use in the evacuation of casualties in the winter. They were not a substitute for wool clothing, blankets, etc. but were considered superior to them for evacuations. This point was emphasized by the Chief Surgeon of the Commander in Chief of the West, General Huabenreisser, the Surgeon of the First German Army, General Wischhusen, and the Surgeon of the 6th German Air Force, Co1onel Micholowsky. The paper was excellent insulation and kept the men very warm. It was disposable. It was sterile and acted when necessary as a blood blotter. The wounds were bandaged with thicker bandages than normal. Then chemical heating pads which became warm when water is added were put in and the patient was wrapped in paper clothing and paper sleeping bags. Finally woolen blankets were wrapped around the whole.

Leaflets like "Injuries from the Cold" were provided to each soldier to be pasted into his paybook.

***INSTRUCTION SHEET 153*, TO BE PLACED IN THE POCKET OF THE PAYBOOK OR PASTED IN. WRITTEN AUGUST 1942**

INJURIES FROM THE COLD: RECOGNITION, PREVENTION, FIRST AID

The cold is an invisible, treacherous enemy because freezing occurs without being noticed, without any warning pain. You must remember the danger and keep a close watch on yourself. Take particular care of ears, nose, fingers and toes.

Affected parts look pale or white and are numb. Great cold makes you tired and exhausted. Men who go to sleep may freeze the whole surface of the body and die because their whole body temperature drops too low.

Most freezing can be avoided. This requires acclimatization first and secondly knowledge of the danger, that is to say experience.

Acclimatization is accomplished by getting the skin used to the cold. Wash yourself in ice cold water, rub your skin with snow, and then carefully dry yourself off. Use windless sunny days in the winter to do calisthenics and run with a bare upper half of your body. Get your skin used to a quick change to temperatures between hot and cold; hot showers, hot steam showers, cold showers, and thumping massage.

Protect yourself from dampness on your skin and dampness in your underclothing, stockings, and gloves. Moist skin freezes. Don't pick up snow with your bare hands. The snow melts and you freeze. Keep from sweating. If this should happen, keep moving. As a sentry or outpost stand first on one foot then on the other. As a driver, keep moving your toes, stamp your heels. Bend, stretch, open and clinch your fists; keep moving your face muscles. All this can protect you from freezing to death even in extreme cold and wind.

Try to have a thermos of hot tea or coffee with you.

Beware of alcohol. It is a false friend: It works the same way as thrusting your hands into warm water when the temperature is below freezing and it is windy. Afterwards you freeze more easily. Use alcohol only after you get back into a warm place.

Look out for shrunken or small clothing. It cuts off the circulation of the blood. Shoes and gloves must be larger than needed. Mittens are better than gloves.

Felt, paper, and straw are a good protection against the cold. Leather is not good, except when it is lined with fur. Felt boots are better than fur boots. In a sharp wind, fur caps and face masks are needed.

Don't touch metal with bare skin (glasses, frames, zippers, binoculars, weapon parts, equipment parts.) Don't wear rings on your fingers in the cold.

Rub all exposed skin as well as fingers and feet with frost protective cream. The skin must be dry before applying.

Avoid exposing your skin to gasoline, rapid evaporation will cause immediate freezing.

When freezing threatens, use ration heating fuel (and chemical heating pads).

After stopping in the open, change socks (and shoes) immediately. When movement resumes, take off all extra clothing. Sweating is very harmful in the winter.

The first aid for freezing is simple. If spots are pale and numb, rub the skin and kneed the affected area until warmth, feeling and color return. (Author's note: US policy was not to rub or massage the affected area.) Do this immediately, even in the open, without losing the time that would be needed to get into a house or to find a trained medical soldier. You can do that next. Massage from the healthy toward the affected parts and remove or loosen all binding clothing. Start by using one hand and then the other to the affected parts from freezing. Keep your comrades from going to sleep outside because of the cold and shake them when they stop caring. If freezing men are woken, they often get into a state of excitement. If they fall asleep again they endanger their lives.

If parts of the body are frozen stiff, be careful about giving first aid so that you will not break up tissues in the fingers, toes, and ears. Take soldiers who are frozen solid into cold rooms, kneed their skin with cold, moist cloths until they thaw out. Then let them move their extremities themselves and let them breathe deeply. Then give them warm drinks when they can hold the cup themselves and swallow. Give them warm sugar water, coffee, or fruit juice with a little alcohol added. In bad cases send immediately for a doctor even if the case seems hopeless.

And last but not least remember that most frostbite and trench foot is avoidable by taking the proper precautions against the cold, by being observant and quickly administering first aid when required.

A variety of salves and creams were used to help combat frostbite.

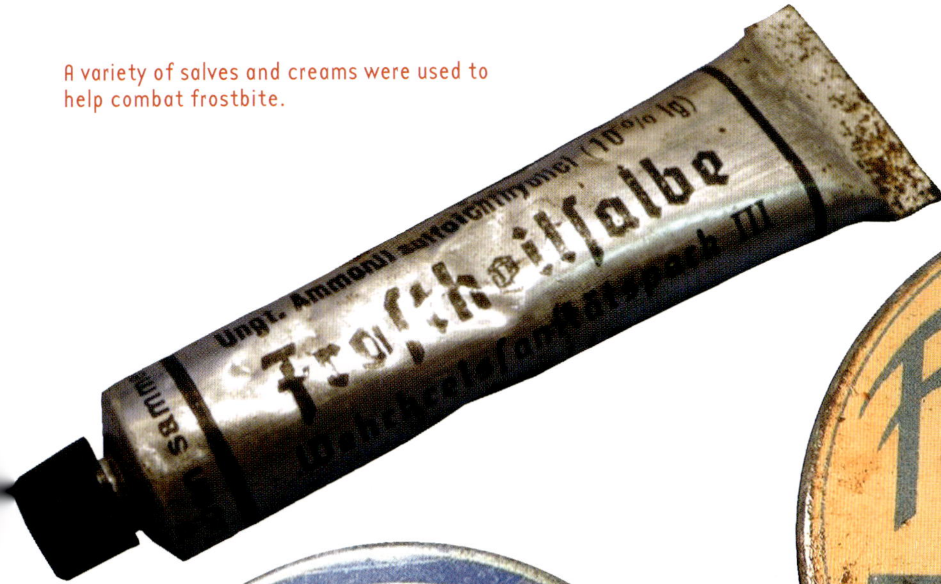

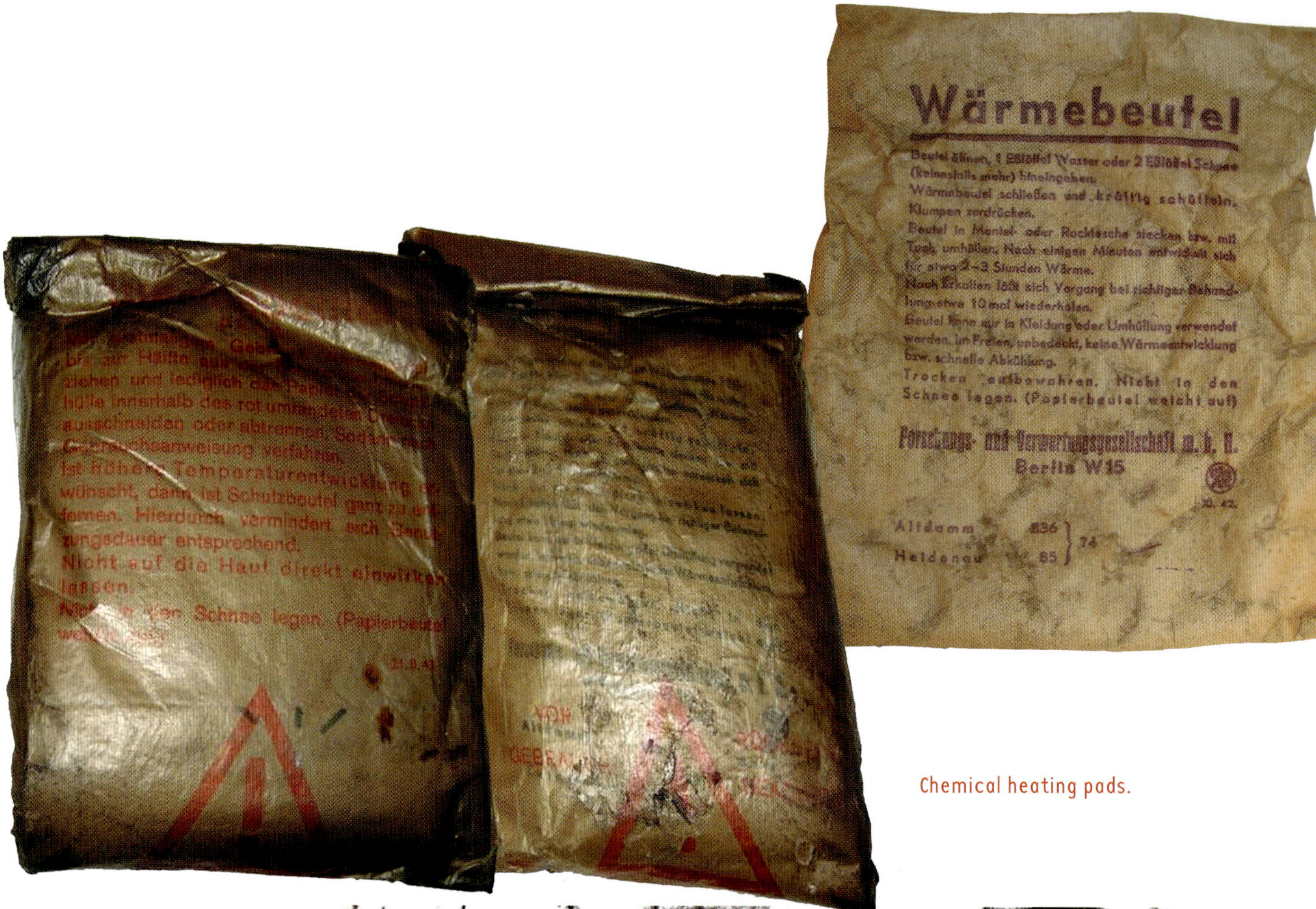

Chemical heating pads.

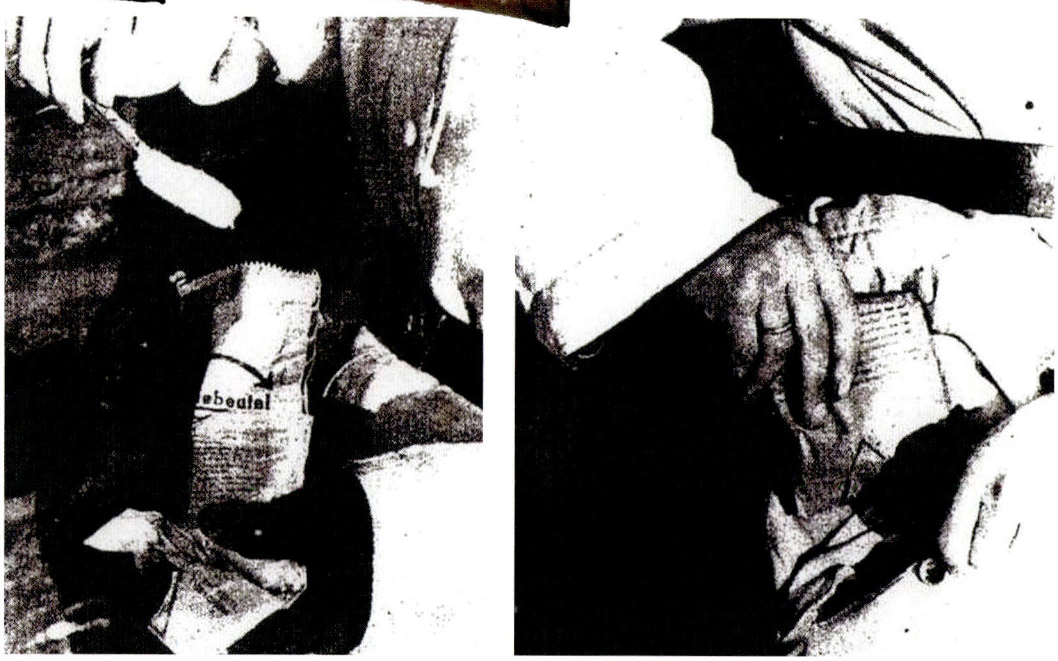

German Chemical Heating Pads. (Left) Heated with 2 spoonsful of snow. (Right) Slipped into the pocket to keep the fingers warm.

Berliner Illustriete Zeitung, Feb 18, '43

Nr. 13571.
Leibwärmer,
rein Messing, hochglanzpoliert. Mit 2 Ringen und geschnittener Messingverschraubung. Ein Durchrosten ist unmöglich, da aus reinem Messing gefertigt. 28 cm lang . . . . **Stück M. 3.60**

Nr. 13572. Leibwärmer wie Nr. 13571, jedoch in guter Weißblech-Ausführung, 30 cm lang . . . . **Stück M. 1.05**

Hot water bottles.

Nice picture of personal items sent to a soldier, including frostbite salve and a hot water bottle.

Marfanil-Prontalbin powder was used to prevent infections.

Small, pocket first aid kits. *Ed Stroh Collection*

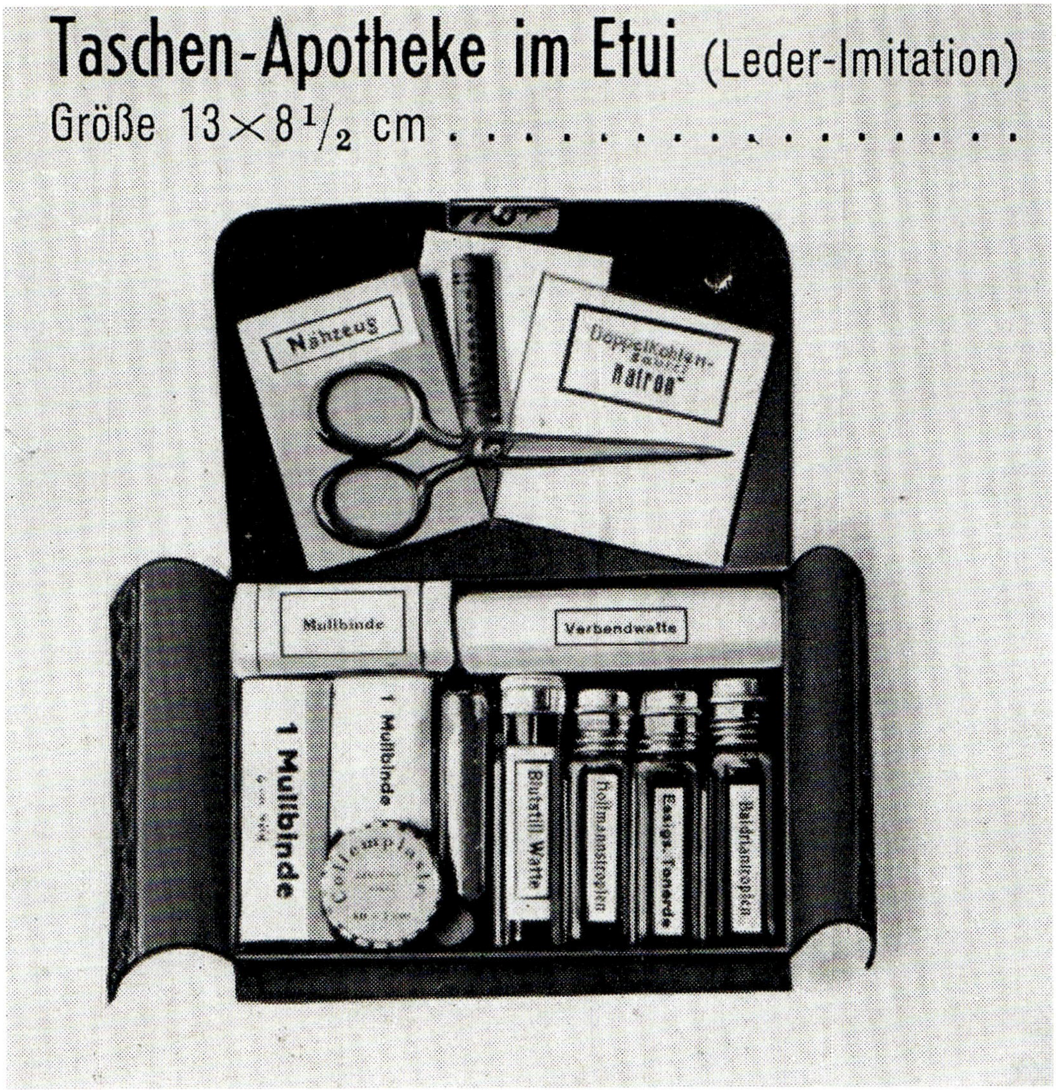

Wartime advertisements for pocket first aid kits.

First aid station. *Bundesarchiv-Bild-101I-100-0755-11, Foto: Kumme, 1942*

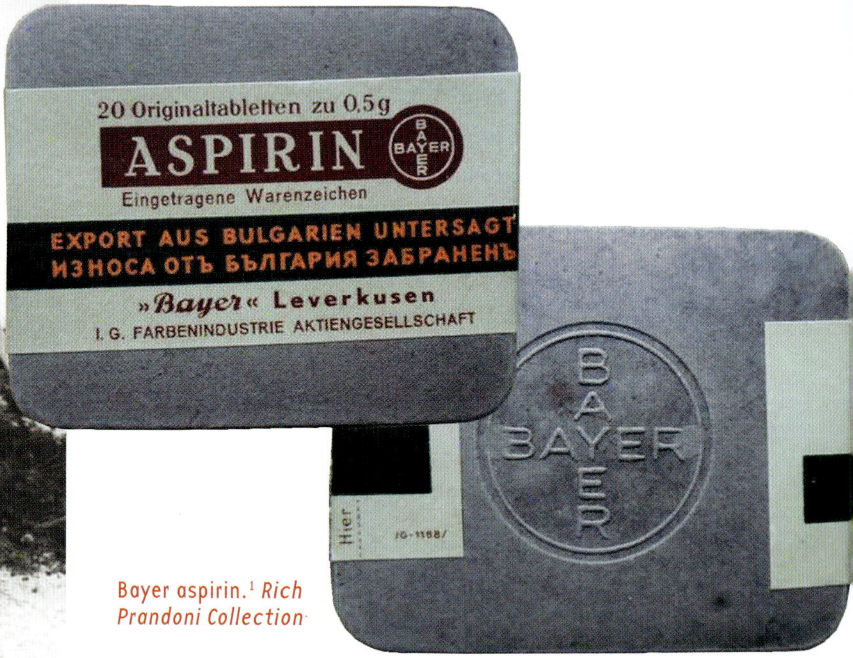

Bayer aspirin.[1] *Rich Prandoni Collection*

A medical kit with contents.

Powder to help alleviate headaches, fever, etc.

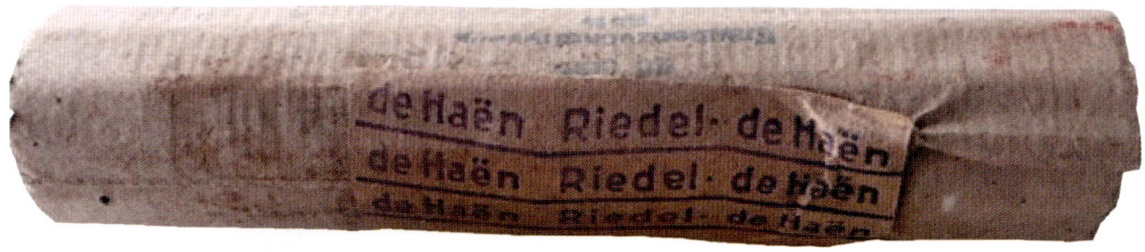

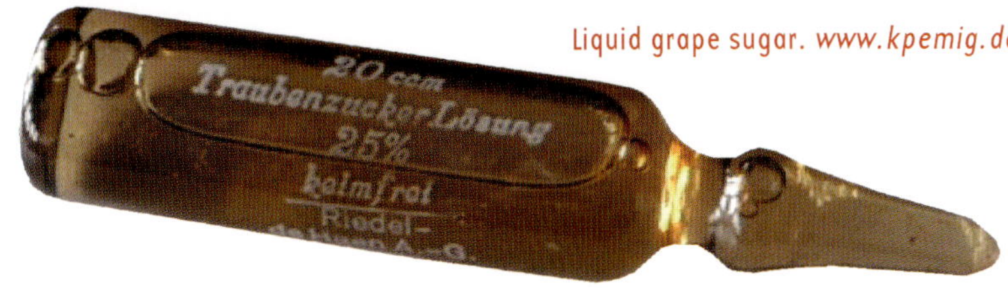

Liquid grape sugar. *www.kpemig.de*

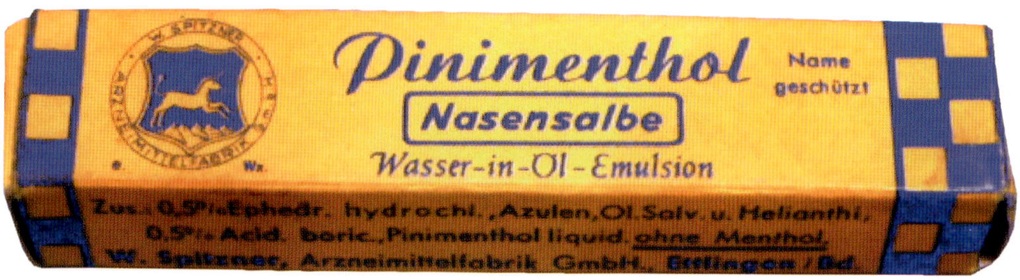

Nose ointment.

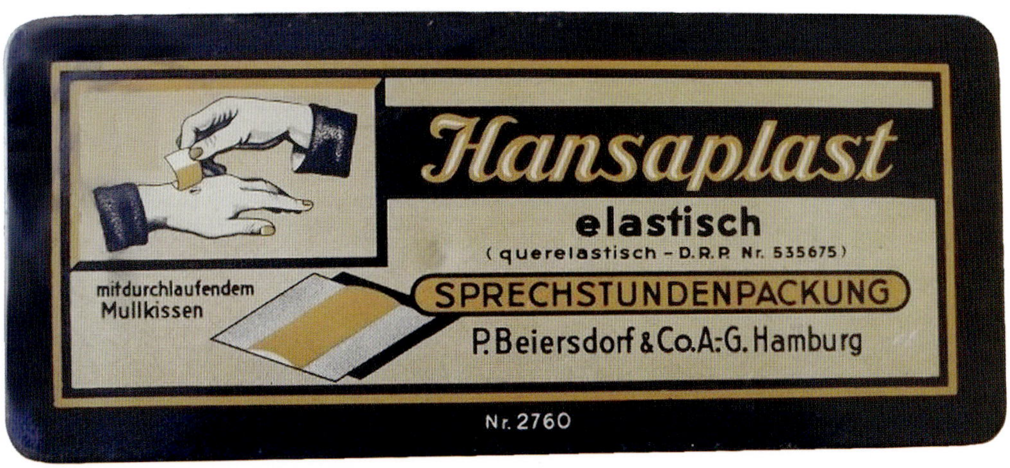

Adhesive bandages.

A variety of pills and tablets used to combat various illnesses. *Bunkermilitaria.com*

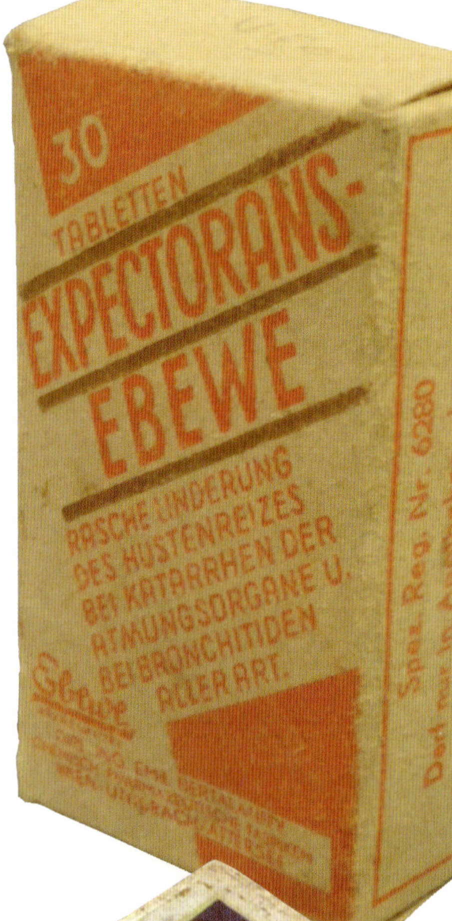

A variety of pills and tablets used to combat various illnesses. *Bunkermilitaria.com*

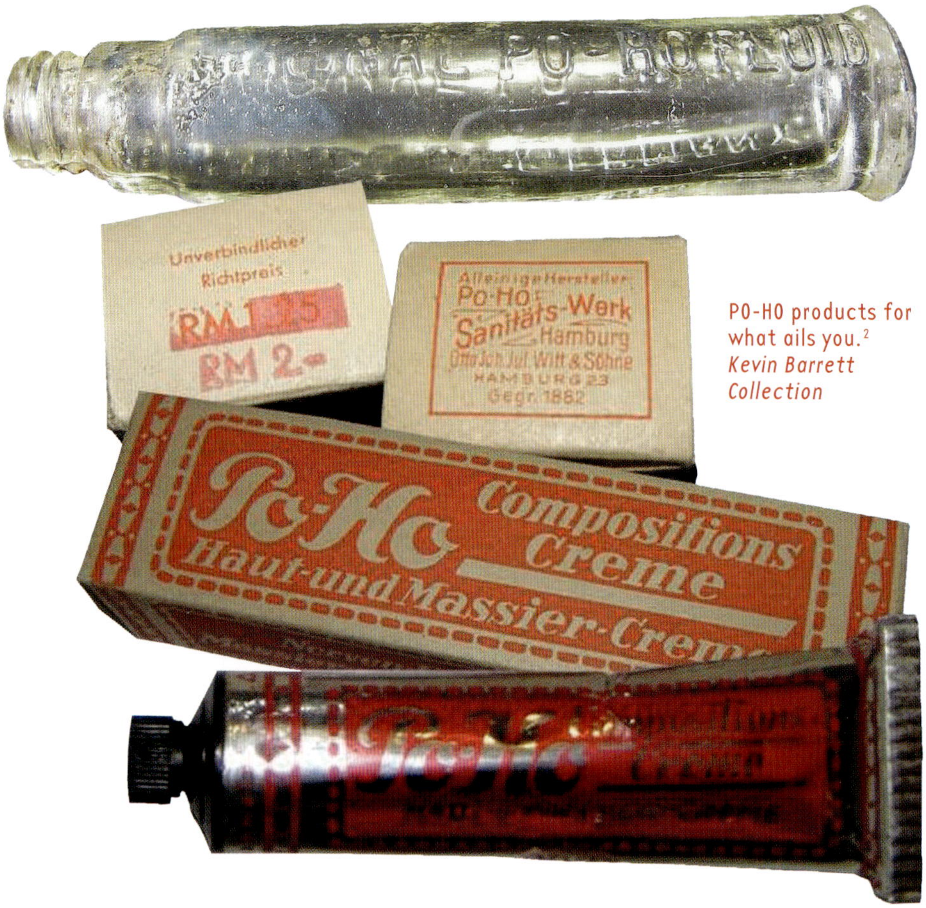

PO-HO products for what ails you.[2] *Kevin Barrett Collection*

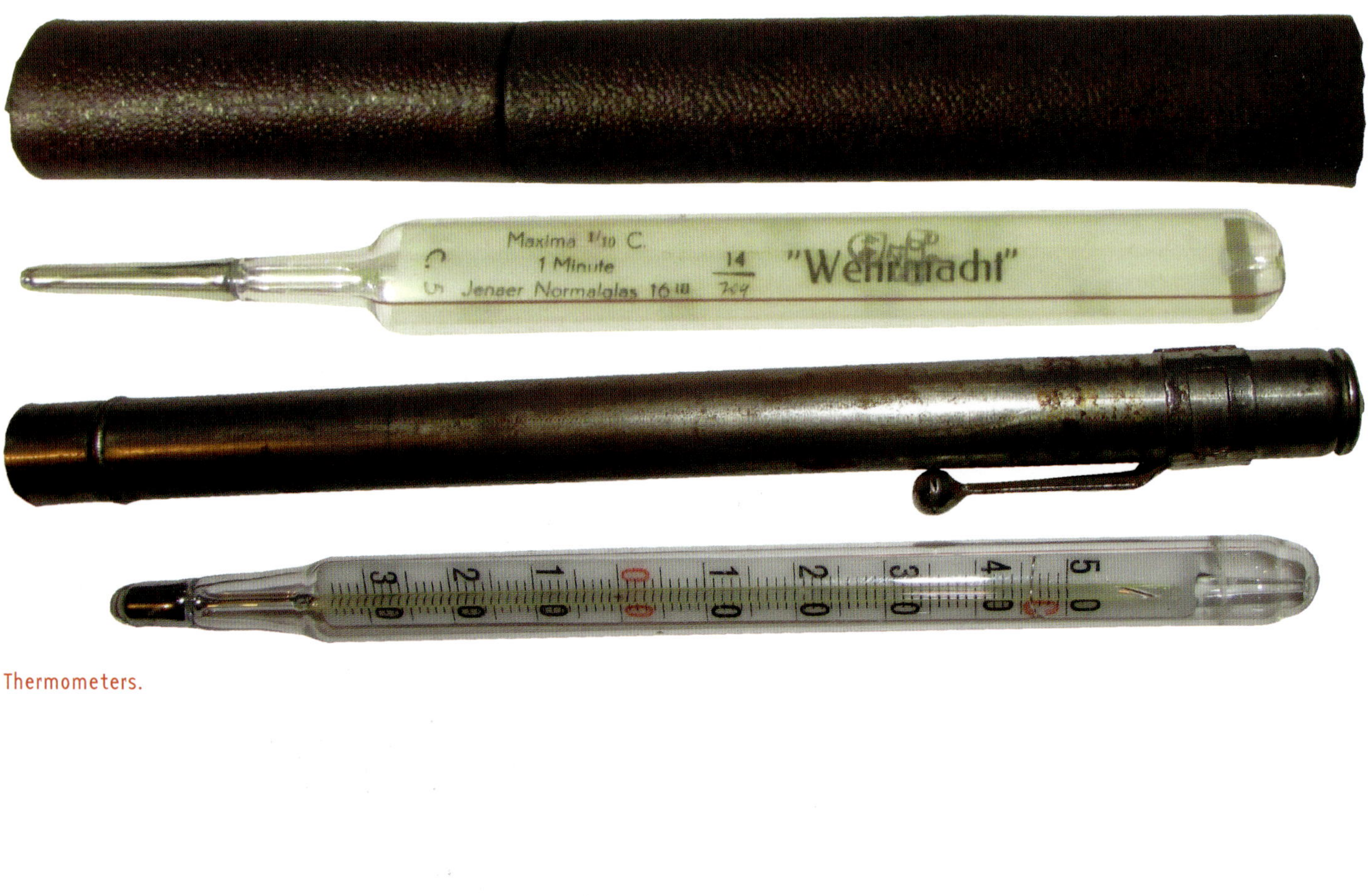

Thermometers.

Large mosquito net and frame used to construct a tent. *www.kpemig.de*

The good life!

This style of netting was popular in areas where mosquitoes, flies, and other insects were a problem.

Mosquito netting in use. *Photos: National Archives and Records Administration (NARA)*

Insect repellents were used to repel mosquitoes and flies.[3]

Flypaper.

The definition of a condom is a barrier device most commonly used during sexual intercourse to reduce the probability of pregnancy and spreading sexually transmitted diseases. Because condoms are waterproof, elastic, and durable, they are also used in a variety of secondary applications, like waterproofing personal items or equipment. Presently condoms are most often made from latex, but some are made from other materials, such as polyurethane or lamb intestine.

The rubber vulcanization process that gave rubber its elasticity was patented by Goodyear in 1844. The first rubber condom was produced in 1855. Latex—rubber suspended in water—was invented in 1920. Latex condoms were stronger and thinner than rubber condoms and had a shelf life of five years (compared to three months for rubber). Most armies provided condoms to their troops—even in Germany, which outlawed all civilian use of condoms in 1941.

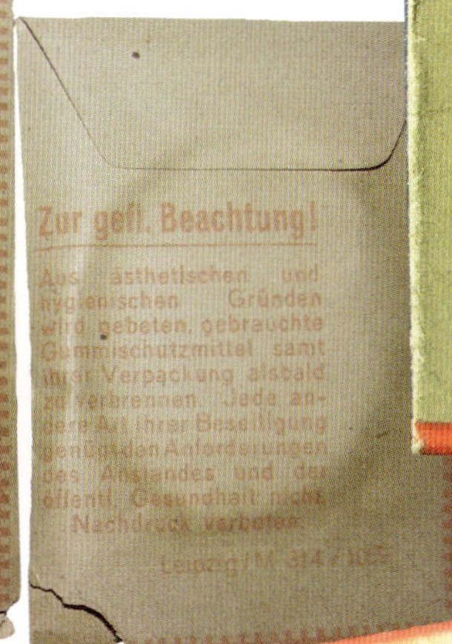

These Sanex brand condoms were specifically manufactured for the military.[4]

Venus brand condoms.

Sanitor brand condoms.

Odilei brand condoms.[6] *Frédéric Ruelle Collection*

Blausiegel brand condoms.[5]

Miguin brand condoms.[7]

Parisi brand condoms.

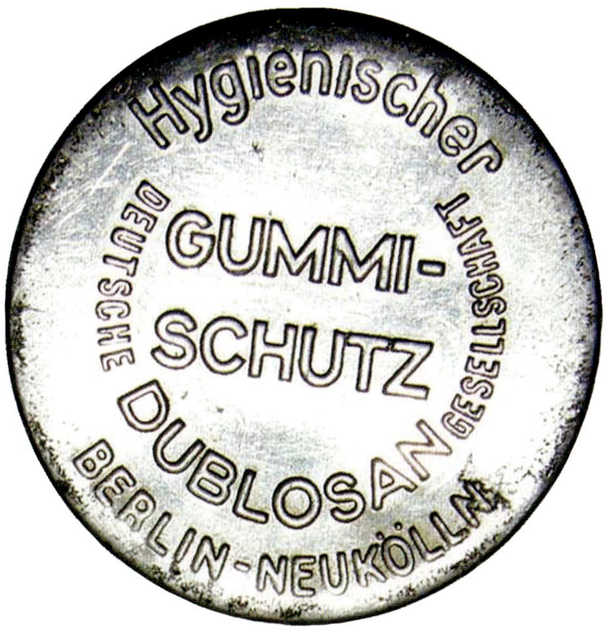

Dublosan condoms packed in aluminum containers.[8]

Eukal brand condoms.

Jodex condoms along with their paper insert. *Kevin Barrett Collection*

Reproductions of this style of condom are so good that it is almost impossible to determine fake from real. *Ed Stroh Collection*

In 2005, an article was published in the German magazine *Der Speigel* titled "The Nazi Death Machine: Hitler's Drugged Soldiers" by Andreas Ulrich, translated from the German by Christopher Sultan. The subject was the use of methamphetamines—specifically Pervitin—by the German military. The article gave the impression that the German soldier went into battle high on drugs or alcohol. Here are a few of the statements made in the article.

a) Many of the Wehrmacht's soldiers were high on Pervitin when they went into battle, especially against Poland and France - in a Blitzkrieg fueled by speed…The military leadership liberally dispensed such stimulants, but also alcohol and opiates, as long as it believed drugging and intoxicating troops could help it achieve victory over the Allies.
b) During the short period between April and July of 1940, more than 35 million tablets of Pervitin and Isophan (a slightly modified version produced by the Knoll pharmaceutical company) were shipped to the German army and air force.
c) Although Pervitin was classified as a restricted substance on July 1, 1941, under the Opium Law; ten million tablets were shipped to troops that same year.

I do not dispute that Pervitan was issued to the German soldier, but wonder if the author might have sensationalized the story just a bit. The article did not state how much or how often the German soldier was administered Pervitin. I took the quantities of Pervitin cited in the article at face value and compared them to German troop strength to figure out how many doses the German soldier was given. I made the following assumptions in order to arrive at my conclusions:

a) I assumed the quantity thirty-five million tablets (17.5 million doses) delivered in 1940 were all distributed and consumed by the military for the French 1940 campaign. I also treated the total quantity as Pervitan.
b) I assumed the quantity ten million tablets (five million doses) delivered in 1941 were all distributed and consumed by the military by the end of December 1941, in support of the Russian campaign (June 22, 1941 to December 31, 1941).
c) Two tablets totaling six milligrams is considered one dose. (Author's note: This is a fact.)
d) I assumed that only combat troops were administered the drug.

Utilizing data from W. Victor Madeja's work *Hitler's Dying Ground: Disintegration of the German Armed Forces in World War 2*, I calculated the total number of combat personnel involved in selected campaigns to estimate how much Pervitan was administered to soldiers.

At the start of the France 1940 campaign, the total strength of the Wehrmacht was 6.1 million personnel. I used a tooth (combat troops) to tail (support troops) ratio of 5:1; for every combat soldier there were five in support. Using that ratio, I determined that 1,006,500 personnel were actually available for combat functions. Of the total of 160 divisions in the military inventory, only 137 (86%) took part in the French campaign, so I estimated that 865,590 personnel were actually involved in a combat role and administered the 17.5 million doses of Pervitan over a forty-day period. In simple terms, each soldier was administered twenty doses over the course of the campaign, or one dose every other day. (Author's note: During my research I discovered there were many different methods used to calculate the tooth to tail ratio. The 5:1 ratio appears to be the one most widely accepted, especially for the first half of the war.)

At the start of the Russian 1941 campaign, the total strength of the Wehrmacht was 7.2 million personnel. Again, I applied a tooth to tail ratio of 5:1. Using that ratio, I determined that 1,188,000 personnel were actually available for combat functions. Of the total 209 divisions in the military inventory, only 150 (72%) took part in the Russian campaign, so I estimated that 855,360 personnel were actually involved in a combat role and administered the five million doses of Pervitan over a six-month period. In simple terms, each soldier was administered six doses over a six-month period or one dose per month.

Now just how dangerous was Pervitan? It was introduced in 1938 as an over-the-counter drug and in 1941 was classified as a restricted drug. As my unscientific analysis shows, there was a significant decline in Pervitan use between the French campaign and the first six months of the attack on Russia. This was due to stricter medical standards being adopted before the drug could be administered. Could the stricter standards be due to excessive use during the French campaign, perhaps? So were the dosages given to the German soldier excessive? Was the German practice of using stimulants different from what the combatants of other nations were doing? To the last question, both the United States and British military administered Benzedrine to their troops.

The answer to the first question is found in an article titled "The Effects of Analeptics on the Fatigued Subject" by D.P. Cuthbertson and J.A.C. Knox. This study was dated 1 August 1946, but was actually an update to a study on Pervitan undertaken in 1942 at the request of the British Military Personnel Research Committee of the Medical Research Council. The study set out to determine several points, the most important being: "Did analeptics increase the output of work of fatigued men and if so what dosage was required?" Several points made in the article are reproduced here:

a) Symptoms following 10 mg methedrine (Pervitan). The symptoms arising from this dosage were, on the whole, very mild.
b) 10mg methedrine (Pervitan), or 15mg Benzedrine, was found to be safe and effective dose under the conditions described, but 20mg methedrine (Pervitan), or 30mg Benzedrine, was an overdose for most subjects.

   Apart from the occasional development of slight headache, muzziness and nausea, 10mg methedrine (Pervitan) would seem to be a safe and effective dose under the conditions described in the present paper.
c) With regard to the possible uses of analeptics in war it seems clear that these drugs should not be given indiscriminately to large numbers of men because of the wide individual variations in response. Euphoria, noisiness or lack of judgment in even a few sensitive individuals might well upset an entire operation. On the other hand, it is probable that the use of analeptics in emergencies by individuals or by small groups of men, whose reactions to the drug are already known, may sometimes be justified.

So if the findings of the above study are correct, the German dose of six milligrams was well below what the study deemed to be a safe dosage of ten milligrams. From available evidence, it appears the Germans became concerned about the effects of Pervitan after the French 1940 campaign and directed its use be supervised by medical personnel. While I certainly do not condone the use of drugs, it is apparent Germany's policies were in line with the other major combatants that used stimulants during WWII. While Pervitan was administered to the German soldier, caffeine was the overwhelming stimulant of choice for the German military. It was widely dispensed in the form of chocolates like Scho-ka-kola.

To conclude the discussion on Pervitan, I defer to several Allied intelligence reports on its use. While the findings in the *Der Speigel* magazine article might be shocking to the modern audience, the benefits of using stimulants during the war (if properly administered) outweighed its dangers. The following article titled "Stimulants for Members of the German Luftwaffe, Tactical and Technical Trends," No. 5, August 13, 1942, reported:

> A firm in Brussels is reported to be the distributor of the stimulant called "Pervitin" (see page 19, Tactical and Technical Trends, No. 4), (Author's note: Not found) used by members of the German Luftwaffe. It is prepared in the form of a pellet or pill. The manufacturer is Temmlerwerke of Berlin. The following ingredients are used in its manufacture: phenyl, methylaminopropane hydrochloric, Saccharin lactis, and Amylum.
>
> COMMENT: In this country, "Pervitin" is believed to be similar in chemical structure to our drug Benzedrine. The British consider Benzedrine and also Methedrine to be helpful in temporarily increasing physical vigor, relieving fatigue and preventing sleep.

The following article titled "Memorandum on the Use of Benzedrine and Methedrine in War, Tactical and Technical Trends," No. 11, November 5, 1942, reported:

> Benzedrine (also called Amphetamine) and Methedrine (German equivalent Pervitin) are substances belonging to the group called analeptics (restoratives). For practical purposes the actions of these drugs are the same, but 1 dose of Methedrine is as potent as 1 1/2 doses of Benzedrine, weight for weight. Their chief action is to stimulate the higher activities of the brain, showing itself especially in decreased sensations of tiredness and fatigue, and in a disinclination and inability to sleep. The administration of Benzedrine does not increase the mental or physical efficiency of a man who is not tired, and Benzedrine should not be taken with this object.
>
> Mention may be made here of the trend of German reports on the use of analeptics. In the latter half of 1941, these reports were enthusiastic, but toward the end of the year warnings commenced to appear, and in the early months of 1942 reports tended to be definitely against their use except under rigid control. The substance in use was Pervitin.
>
> The effect of these substances on troops has now been studied in the laboratory and in the field, and the following conclusions have been drawn by British medical authorities.
>
> a) The valuable effect of Benzedrine to individuals engaged in war operations is to reduce the desire for sleep, and the fatigue which results in loss of efficiency and makes difficult the continuation of essential duties.
>
> b) Circumstances may thus arise in which the administration of Benzedrine may be advantageous for skilled personnel when they are severely fatigued and unable to continue at a reasonable level of efficiency without an additional stimulus. Where "Benzedrine" is written, "Methedrine in equivalent dosage" may be substituted except where this is obviously inappropriate. The use of Benzedrine should be confined to emergencies or crises, and it should not be taken regularly. The decision to give Benzedrine must only be made in circumstances when there is reasonable expectation that the emergency will be at an end within 12 hours.
>
> c) No person whose duties involve the making of difficult decisions, should be permitted to take Benzedrine in a crisis unless he has tested his reactions to it previously.
>
> d) Benzedrine must not be given indiscriminately to large bodies of troops.
>
> e) A single dose should not exceed 10 milligrams. A dose of 5 mg may be repeated once or even twice at intervals of 4 to 6 hours. If an individual is of the opinion that a dose of 10 mg does not produce appreciable effects upon him, the use of the drug should be given up.
>
> f) The administration of Benzedrine should be under the control of a medical officer.

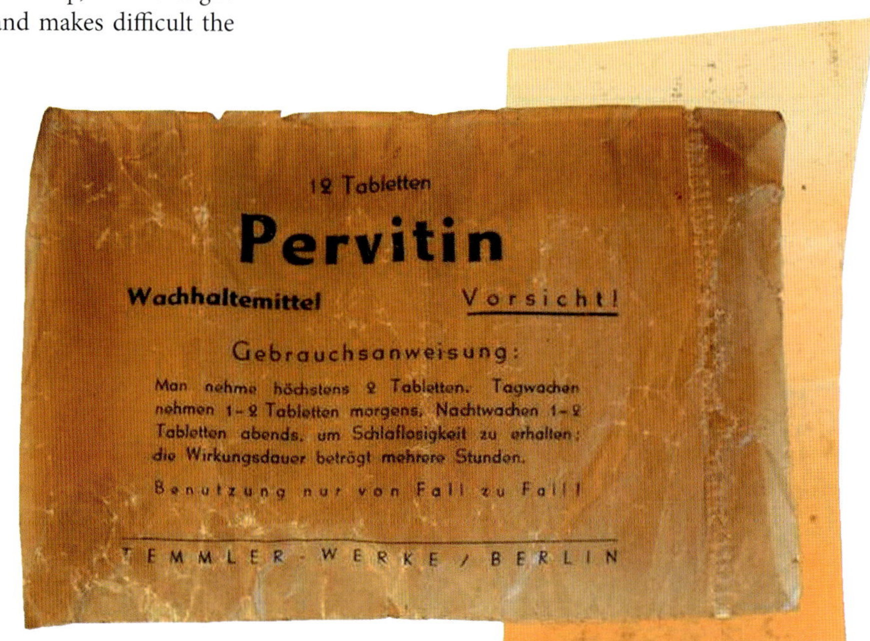

Pervitin.[9] *Ed Stroh Collection*

CHAPTER 7 ENDNOTES

1. The general partnership "Friedr. Bayer et comp." was founded August 1, 1863, in Barmen, Germany, by dye salesman Friedrich Bayer and master dyer Johann Friedrich Weskott. Bayer's research efforts gave rise to numerous intermediates, dyes, and pharmaceuticals, including the "drug of the century" Aspirin®, which was launched in 1899. Leverkusen became the company's headquarters in 1912. In the mid-1920s, Bayer transferred its assets to I.G. Farbenindustrie AG (I.G.) and was deleted from the commercial register as a company. The Bayer tradition lived on in I.G.'s Lower Rhine operating consortium, which consisted of the Leverkusen, Dormagen, and Elberfeld sites, as well as the Uerdingen site. Leverkusen became the headquarters for the I.G.'s pharmaceutical sales association and the Bayer Cross was used as the trademark for all of I.G.'s pharmaceutical products. Bayer is still a household word. Here is a wartime advertisement.

2. The PO-HO Sanitäts Werk, Hamburg, Germany, was founded in 1882. It is unknown if the firm survived the war. Here is a prewar brochure.

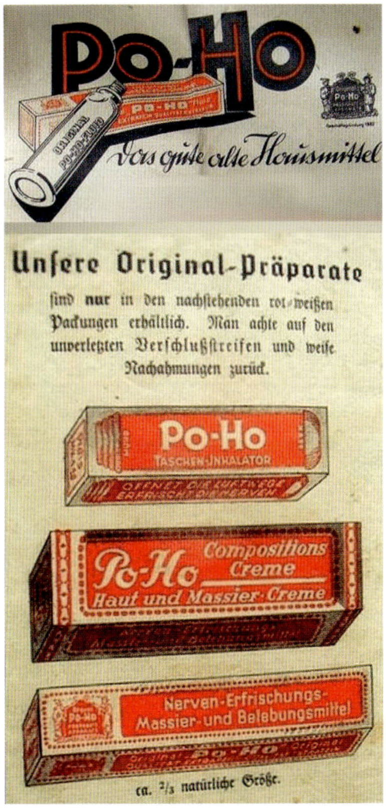

3. Schering AG, Berlin, Germany, was a research-centered German pharmaceutical company founded in 1851 by Ernst Christian Friedrich Schering. It merged with Bayer's pharma sector in December 2006. Here is their listing in the 1941 Berlin phone book.

Schering A.G. + Hauptverwaltung Bln N 65 Müllerstr 170-172 Abt. Chemie u. Werk Bln
∗ 46 00 12

4. The Vulkan Gummiwarenfabrik Weiss & Baessler A.G., Leipzig, Germany, was founded in 1886. The Sanex brand name was registered in 1932. As a shell company, it moved to Cologne in 1959. We believe the Sanex brand name may still be in use. Here is a prewar advertisement.

5. The firm of Emil Richter und Käufer, Erfurt, Germany, was founded in 1928. The Blausiegel brand was introduced in 1934. The company moved from East Germany to Bielefeld in 1948/49. The Blausiegel brand is still being manufactured.

6. I was unable to find a history for the Otto Dillner factory in Leipzig, Germany. The only thing I know for sure is it was operating in the early 1900s and there was no reference to it after the war. The term ODILEI is derived from select letters from Otto DILLNER and Leipzig. In the 1940s, the firm produced condoms for the Wehrmacht. Here is their listing in the 1929 Mosse Register of Firms.

Dillner GmbH, Otto, ℋ 60352 u. 60577, Gummiwarenfabr. – O 28, Torgauer Str. 30. Ps 3943, Bk Comm.- u. Privatbk., TA Neverrip.

7. I believe that Miguin condoms were manufactured by the Mitteldeutsche Gummi- und Guttapercha-Gesellschaft MIGUIN Edelmuth & Co., Frankfurt an der Oder, Germany. I could not locate anything else on the firm.

8. No history was found on the Deutsche Dublosan Gesellschaft. Here is their listing in the 1941 Berlin phone book.

Deutsche Dublosan GmbH. +
Nkln Mittelbuschweg 6. 7
✱ 62 43 01

9. The Temmler Werke GmbH was founded in Detmold, Germany, in 1917. A subsidiary was established in Berlin shortly after. Preparations for the treatment of respiratory diseases were the hallmark of Temmler Pharma. By 1933, the company, with expanded production facilities, was concentrated around the Berlin area. In 1938, a Temmler chemist in Berlin synthesized Pervitin, which was manufactured and publicly sold as a stimulant and drug for psychiatry. In 1945, the facility in East Berlin was occupied and disassembled. The company was completely reassembled in Hamburg. In 1960, the whole company transferred from Hamburg to Marburg. Here is a wartime advertisement.

Temmler Werke Vereinigte Chemische Fabriken Hermann Temmler Inh. Theodor H. Temmler Johtal Am Flugpl 6
✱ 63 22 81
Nach 6. Nachtruf (63 18 21)
+ Prok. Preß 50 14 24
+ Prok. Ley 63 16 82

CHAPTER 8
KEEPING THE UNIFORM CLEAN

The German soldier was responsible for the care and cleaning of his uniform and other issue equipment. A basic knowledge of sewing was certainly a plus for any soldier. In the field, large repairs to the uniform or leather equipment were turned over to the unit's cobblers or tailors. Unserviceable items were turned in and exchanged through the supply system. Washing the uniform was also an individual responsibility. In the winter this was a challenge, unless the soldier had some way of drying the uniform. Certain items like the reversible winter over garment were extremely difficult to dry. Some soldiers resorted to whitewashing the white side of the uniform to keep its camouflage advantage.

In *German Clothing, Equipment and Rations* the authors provided the following comments on the care and cleaning of uniforms:

a. General: According to U. S. Army standards, very little was done for the German soldier to enable him to keep himself and his clothing clean in the field. With certain exceptions noted below, it was up to the soldier to bathe himself and to wash his own clothing with the limited amount of poor grade soap he was issued. Each man received only one 3 oz. cake of toilet soap and one three oz. cake of laundry soap per month. He also received a 1 oz. piece of shaving soap every three months. As a consequence, the troops often became infested with lice and body crawling insects and some typhus epidemics broke out. Colonel Michelowsky, Chief Surgeon of the 6th Air Force, explained that out of 4,000 of his men recently examined, 60 were lousy, although after the cessation of hostilities, it should have been easier to cut down on infestation.

b. Fumigation: Each medical company had a Nissen fumigation trailer, which deloused the clothing by means of steam and hot air. As the clothing was being fumigated, the men were given showers. Regular portable shower units were, however, usually not available, as these units were part of the equipment of the decontamination companies and so were rarely forward of the Army (Armee) area. Therefore, the medical soldiers had to improvise showers in most cases. These were made from materials at hand according to suggested plans. All men in the line were periodically deloused as they returned to a rest or reserve area. On the return trip from the East, there were several set points where the trains stopped and everyone was deloused. Problems arose, however, during the early years of the war because the men sometimes became badly infested between delousing. It was especially serious on the Eastern Front in the winter, for the men did not have a second complete set of clothing to use during the fumigation. Consequently, a better method had to be devised; the solution seemed to be impregnating the clothing with anti-louse preparations.

c. Anti Louse Preparations: The first type of anti louse preparation used was called 'Russla' but this proved to be comparatively ineffective. This was followed by 'Delicia' which smelled so bad that the troops wouldn't use it. 'Lauseto' was not in production long enough to determine whether or not it was really more effective. It was introduced in December 1944 and was not broadly distributed. The Germans had not used DDT powder. Generalstabarzt (Major General of the Medical Corps) Haubenreisser, Chief Surgeon of the commander in chief of the West, said that 'Delicia' was supposed to last for three weeks, provided the impregnated clothing was not boiled. He provided samples of the 'Delicia' and 'Lauseto' as well as the authorized instructions for both. (Author's note: Instructions for the use of lice preparations are provided below).

d. Laundries: There were no mobile field laundries. No special equipment except for sterilization was issued to hospitals where laundering was usually done by local people, hospital personnel etc. At some semi permanent Luftwaffe establishment's local labor was gathered to furnish laundry service.

e. Fumigation, Delousing, Showers, Laundries, Etc. The American Infantryman is able to keep cleaner under combat conditions than the German soldier. Sterilization and Bath units' have operated so far forward that they were still under enemy artillery fire. In many places these units cooperated with mobile field laundries in setting up the 'clothing exchange system,' which was put into operation under the direction of Brigadier General Joseph Sullivan, Quartermaster of the Fifth Army. Soldiers just out of the line removed and turned in all clothing which could be laundered as they went to their shower baths. After they had bathed, they received a complete set of clean clothing without delay. They never saw their dirty clothing again, which was removed to a laundry and issued clean to some other similarly sized soldier a few days later. In this way, the individual was frequently able to get himself and his clothing clean. The German soldier was able to get his clothing sterilized only in rare instances. Usually he had to bathe himself as best he could. The German Army had no mobile laundries. The soldier had to wash his own clothing by hand if the opportunity arose. The results achieved by the two armies were very different, not only from the standpoint of comfort but also from that of health. It was not unusual for the German soldier to become lousy and some typhus epidemics broke out. The American soldier on the other hand was almost completely free from infestation. The anti louse preparation used by the two armies were very different too. American DDT powder has received a deservedly high reputation, but the German preparations were not so effective. The ineffective Russla powder was replaced by Delicia, but the smell of this was so offensive that it was rarely used. Lauseto was introduced only in late 1944 and so it was impossible to give an accurate judgment on its qualities since it had not yet been widely distributed at the end of the war.

INSTRUCTIONS ON THE DELICIA PACKAGE READ AS FOLLOWS:

Delicia Louse preparation
Fabric Impregnation Material
A new kind of impregnation material for clothing which will kill all body crawling insects such as clothing, felt and head lice, flea, ticks, and mites along with their larvae and nits. Delicia protects you against reinfestation. Delicia louse preparation should be dissolved in water and when it becomes milky white should be used to impregnate fabrics, wash rooms, or delouse animals. As soon as it is dry, it begins to kill the insects.

Large Over-package for 10 men
Ernst Freyberg, chemical Factory Delitia in Delizsch
Special Vermin preparations since 1817

The following is a translation of the instructions issued by the German Surgeon General on the use of Delicia:

INSTRUCTIONS FOR THE USE OF DELICIA

Delicia louse preparation may be used in varying strengths. People with tender skin should use a "weak" solution. The "strong" solution should be used only for impregnating handkerchiefs and clothes.

Strength Table for a normal package:

AMOUNT OF WATER PER PACKAGE	STRENGTH	USE
1 Liter	weak	For impregnating clothing for 2 men
2 Liters	normal	For impregnating clothing for one man
1 Liter	strong	For impregnating clothes, handkerchiefs

After the water has been measured out, the contents of the package will be placed into it and stirred thoroughly. It is ready for use in thirty minutes and is not effective sooner. Do not use it sooner.

To Prevent Clothes Lice: Swish dry inner clothing (shirt, drawers, socks, and sweater) around in the Delicia solution, wring it out slightly, and let it dry in the open air at a moderate (room) temperature. Use the rest of the solution to brush onto blankets, bedding, and the insides of the uniform. Places particularly subject to infestation (seams, collars of jackets, waist bands of trousers, suspenders, etc.) should be well moistened. After treatment, the clothes should be thoroughly dried and then may be worn continuously for a long time.

To delouse leather goods or shoes, stuff in the impregnated old rags. After the rags have dried, stuff them into and wrap them around the arteries, then store them for about ten hours in a fairly hot place (about 86 degrees F) near a stove.

"Delicia" was unpopular because of its smell, which became even more objectionable when the wearer got warm. Furthermore, it lasted only three weeks before the impregnation had to be repeated. Consequently, "Lauseto" was developed. "Lauseto" was said by both General Haubenreisser and Colonel Michelowsky to last on clothing in use about three months—unless the clothing was boiled—and on stored clothing for one year. General Wischhusen, Surgeon of the 1st German Army, said that he believed it was less fast than previously believed; he thought it could be washed out even in warm water. The following are the German Surgeon General's instructions for impregnating clothing using "Lauseto":

The white side of this camouflaged parka was whitewashed.

INSTRUCTIONS FOR USE OF LAUSETO

The following solutions are to be poured into an empty container (pail or tub):

a. For clothes that will be worn immediately, use 100 grams (7 teaspoons full) of Lauseto to make a 1% solution.
b. For clothes that will be stored, use 250 grams (1 drinking cup) to make a 2.5% solution. To this Lauseto, add 10 liters (1 pail full) of water slowly while stirring continuously in order to make an emulsion. This emulsion is sufficient for impregnating 5 men's clothing. (Five each of the following: shirts, belly bands, drawers, socks or foot wraps (pairs) and sweaters.) These articles of clothing should be thoroughly dried and then placed in the emulsion and kneaded until thoroughly wet, probably for 15 minutes. Then they should be wrung out over the pail carefully to prevent injuring them and dried in the open air. In the winter, they should be dried indoors in a heated room.

In order to make the effect of the impregnation last for three months (under a) or for a year (under b), the clothing must not be boiled after treatment. After boiling, retreatment is necessary.

Both preparations were often mixed in drums into which the men dipped their own clothing. The medics supervised this.

Lice combs.

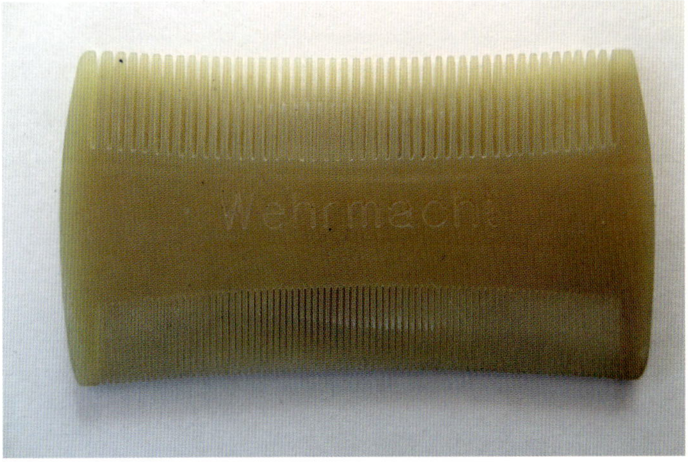

Russla louse powder was generally ineffective.[1]
Ed Stroh Collection

Delicia powder was unpopular because of its foul odor.[2]
OSTFRONT Militaria

Another lice powder produced by Delitia. Could this be Lauseto? *OSTFRONT Militaria*

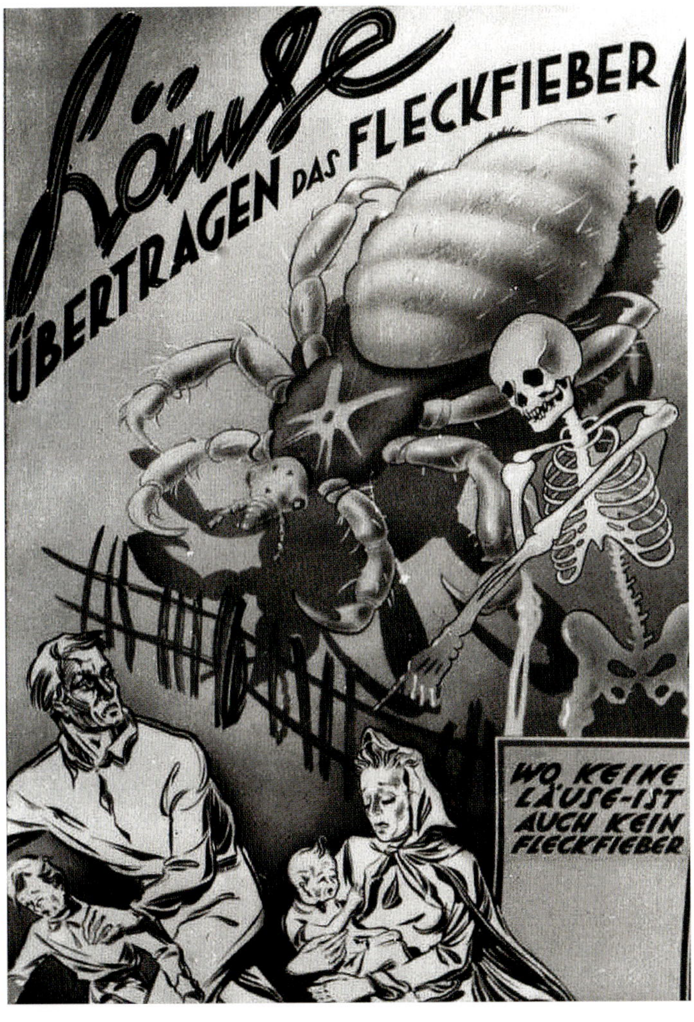

This poster shows the danger of lice. *Photo: US National Archives and Records Administration (NARA)*

Follow the sign to the delousing station.

Hand sprayer for insecticides. *Ron Richter Collection*

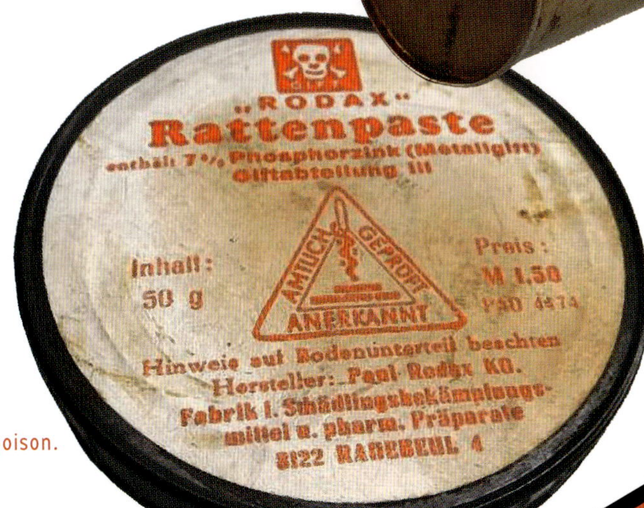

"RODA" rat poison.

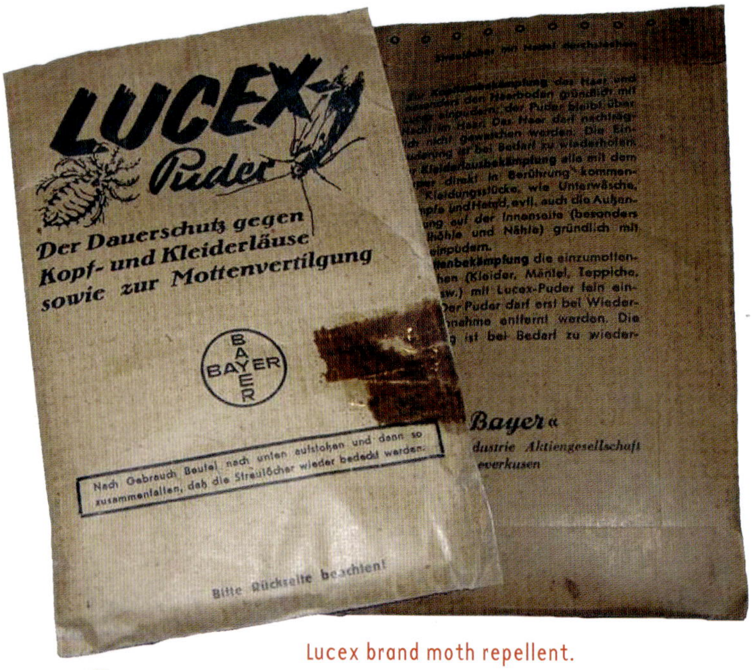

Lucex brand moth repellent.

These young ladies are placing a suit into a mothproof bag.

MOTT-EX moth repellent.[3]

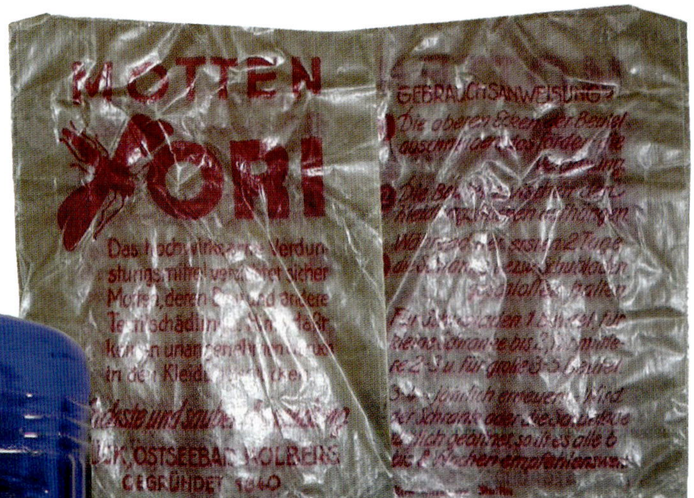

Motten ORI moth repellent was manufactured by the same firm that produced AoK cosmetics.

Tala moth repellent manufactured by Jan Vlasák chemical work, Königgrätz. *Michel Verberkt Collection*

Illo brand moth repellent.

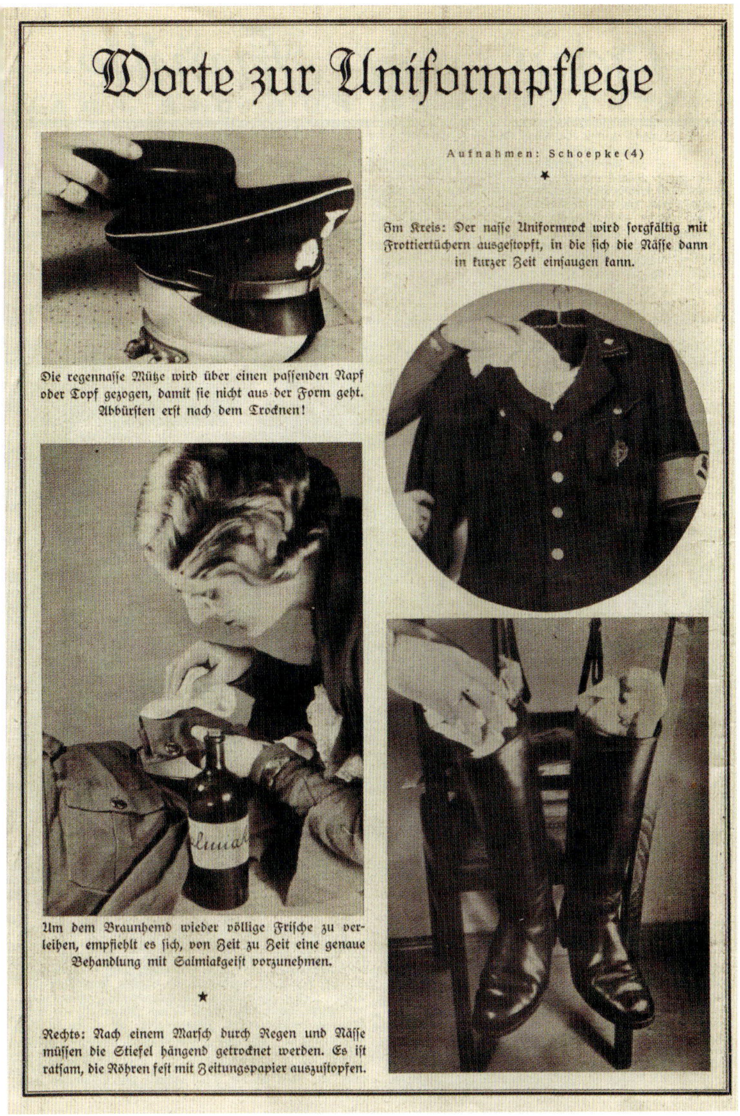

Worte zur Uniformpflege

Aufnahmen: Schoepke (4)

★

Im Kreis: Der nasse Uniformrock wird sorgfältig mit Frottiertüchern ausgestopft, in die sich die Nässe dann in kurzer Zeit einsaugen kann.

Die regennasse Mütze wird über einen passenden Napf oder Topf gezogen, damit sie nicht aus der Form geht. Abbürsten erst nach dem Trocknen!

Um dem Braunhemd wieder völlige Frische zu verleihen, empfiehlt es sich, von Zeit zu Zeit eine genaue Behandlung mit Salmiakgeist vorzunehmen.

★

Rechts: Nach einem Marsch durch Regen und Nässe müssen die Stiefel hängend getrocknet werden. Es ist ratsam, die Röhren fest mit Zeitungspapier auszustopfen.

Wartime article on uniform care.

This product was used to make clothing, shelter halves, etc. water repellent.

Cleaning wipes.

Soap was an essential ingredient for keeping the body, clothing, work areas, etc., clean. Allied intelligence personnel investigated the soap industry at the end of the war. The following reports were used in the preparation of this chapter: *Synthetic Detergents and Related Surface Active Agents in Germany*, *Synthetic Detergents and Washing Agents*, and *The German Soap Industry*. In chemistry, soap is a salt of a fatty acid. Soaps are mainly used as surfactants for washing, bathing, and cleaning. Surfactants are compounds that lower the surface tension of a liquid, the interfacial tension between two liquids, or that between a liquid and a solid.

The objectives of the investigations were to evaluate the efficiency of German synthetic detergents, obtain information on German research and development trends, and to obtain specific process information. A good portion of these reports read like a chemistry book, so unfortunately, it is necessary to talk a little chemistry to tell the story of Germany's wartime synthetic detergent industry.

Types of soap produced in prewar Germany were generally of a higher quality than wartime products. As shortages of materials occurred quality was continually reduced, until a government controlled program was put in effect in 1939. The government established specifications for a limited number of standardized products. Brand names were abolished and each manufacturer produced the standard item under an individual RIF (Reichstelle fur Industrielle Fettversorgung). The agency continued to control formulae and to set production quotas for the individual plants during the war. Rationing went into effect several years before the war, but became more restrictive once the war began.

Except for the development of synthetic detergents into household products and the development of several new types of detergents, there were very few new developments during the war. Technical developments appear to have been concentrated in efforts to extend soap and soap products by substitution of available synthetics, use of increased amounts of alkalis, and the addition of inert fillers like kaolin, chalk, marble dust, etc. No household laundry soap was produced during the war, as general scrubbing and washing operations were carried out by the use of alkalis and washing powders containing low soap or detergent content. It appears no special or unusual products were developed for the Wehrmacht. Information developed in conducting the interviews showed the Wehrmacht was seriously short of all soap and detergent products and facilities for using them.

The Germans developed a variety of synthetic detergents prior to and during the war, primarily from alternative available raw materials. Some were superior to previous types for special uses, but none surpassed Gardinol (a mixture of the sodium salts of sulfated fatty alcohols made by reducing the mixed fatty acids of coconut oil, cottonseed oil, or fish oils) and Igepon for general utility.

The fundamental reason Germany developed a variety of detergent classes was to obtain products that would perform better than soap, particularly in hard water and under neutral or acid conditions. Towards that goal, the Germans developed the following classes or groups of detergents:

a. Alkyl Sulfates: Organic esters of sulfuric acid created by sulfation of a fatty alcohol chain that vary according to the number of carbons in that hydrocarbon chain. It was a good detergent for white wash and fine wash.
b. Igepon types: detergents based on natural oils and fats or on synthetic fatty acids.
c. Medialans: Medialan A is similar to soap in many of its properties, but is resistant to water hardness up to 270 ppm as Calcium Carbonate. Although it was not advertised for its softening properties, it was recognized by its customers as a good softening agent for rayon and stable fiber. It was claimed to be the best skin detergent.
d. Polyethylene Oxide Types: The synthetic detergents of this class were made by condensation of ethylene oxide with fatty alcohols or alkyl phenols. It was a good detergent for wool.
e. Alkyl Sulfonates: the outstanding product in this class were Mersolats, which were not considered good detergents.
f. Alkyl Aryl Sulfonates: the outstanding detergent in this class was called Igepal NA and was considered a good detergent.
g. Lamepons: the main advantage of Lamepons are in wool washing and hair washing.

The German soldier (officer and enlisted) received the same soap as civilians. No products comparable to the bar soaps provided to the US armed forces—which contained a large proportion of synthetics—were produced in Germany.

During WWI, the Germans suffered from a fat shortage that stimulated research on soap substitutes. As a result of their research, a fatty alcohol sulfonate detergent like Gardinol was developed. These detergents were excellent, but were expensive to produce and did not work well in acidy solutions.

Extensive research into synthetic detergents was initiated in 1925, after the consolidation of the large dye factories belonging to I.G. Farben was completed. This resulted in the development of Igepons and Igepals based on the condensation of ethylene oxide first with fatty acids and alcohols and later with alkyl phenols and napthtols.

The various raw materials, fatty acid chlorides from all sorts of natural fats for the Igepons, and the oxygenated products with which ethylene oxide would be condensed made it possible to produce a range of synthetic detergents suitable for a variety of purposes. I.G. Farben dominated the synthetic detergent field and other large soap manufacturers worked closely with them, especially during the war, but did not develop any non-soap detergents of their own.

The Germans developed the Fischer-Tropsch process, which is a set of chemical reactions that converts a mixture of carbon monoxide and hydrogen into liquid hydrocarbons. The large-scale production of synthetic hydrocarbons from coal provided a cheap and abundant supply of petroleum substitutes from which it was possible to prepare synthetic detergents, along with numerous other products.

German practices in washing clothes and dishes in the household were distinctly different from American practices. These differences had an influence on the types of washing compounds produced and on the use of synthetic detergents in such products. In Germany, they spoke of three types of washing in the household or in the laundry: Feinwasche (fine washing), Bundwasche (bundle washing), and Weisswasche (white washing).

Before the war fine washing—done in cold or at the most a lukewarm solution—used a number of products like Lux flakes—a pure soap containing about 30% coconut oil—and products based solely on synthetic detergents of Igepon T, or the fatty alcohol sulphate type. Sunlicht Gesellschaft marketed a fine wash powder called Fex based on Igepon T. During the war, Igepon practically disappeared, along with Lux flakes.

White washing of cottons in laundries was done at very high temperatures (60-80°C, or 140-176°F), and at home the clothes were boiled for half an hour or more. Bundle washing (i.e., assorted clothes other than whites) was done at slightly lower temperatures, and in the home the re-use of the washing solution from the white wash was commonly recommended at 60-70°C (140-158°F). The washing powders sold for this type of washing contained a large proportion of soda ash, usually with other alkalis. The prewar washing powder of this type made by both Henkel and Sunlicht for the retail trade contained about 33% anhydrous soap, i.e., soap that does not contain water.

The washing of dishes at home in Germany was commonly done with an alkaline washing compound containing no soap or a synthetic detergent of any kind, hence producing no foam in the dishpan. This long established practice was explained as due to the very hard water in Germany.

Fats became so scarce in Germany during the war that synthetic detergents had to be used to provide the civilian population with washing compounds. As the war progressed, the use of synthetic detergents had to be stretched further and further. By the war's end, the civilian ration of washing products had reached a low of fifty grams per person per month of fine wash powder and 250 grams per person per month of washing powder, chiefly soda ash. The soap ration amounted to not over forty grams of fat per person per month of very poor quality soap.

Interrogation of all soap makers, as well as German soldiers, indicated there were not any special detergents with or without synthetics produced for the Wehrmacht. The German military received the same kind of soaps that were available to civilians. In the early war years, the army was perhaps better supplied in the quantity of such items as floating soap, shaving soap, and laundry soap than the civilian population. As the war progressed, even the military was impacted by shortages. The issue of soap dropped from one fifty-gram bar per man per week to one bar per month or longer. There were no special detergents for washing mess kits or clothing, merely a bar of "Kern-Seife"—a piece of unfilled laundry soap made perhaps with synthetic fatty acids as natural fats became more scarce. No soap in bar form containing synthetic detergent appears ever to have been made or even attempted in Germany.

There was a belief that synthetic detergents should be used in washing powders to augment the civilian soap ration. Since washing powders were not well adapted for general military issue the German soldier was not issued them. The development of special soaps or detergents in bar form and in flake or powder form for toilet use and laundering or general purpose cleaning in any kind of hard water—particularly sea water—was never a problem in Germany.

For washing wool, the Germans claimed Leonil O was best, followed by the purely synthetic fat free Leonil FFO. Igepon T was also highly rated. The best product for cleaning cellulose fibers was Alipal D.

The following is a list of all known wartime products produced by Sunlicht Gesellschaft A.G., Mannheim/Rheinau. Most of the company records were destroyed during the war so most of the information was based on memory.

a. Toilet Soaps: A variety of products under various names were produced. These soaps were manufactured to a limited extent for special purposes until 1942. The weights of the soaps were 88 grams, 100 grams, 120 grams, 125 grams, and 200 grams.
b. Shaving Soaps: The fatty acid percentage of the finished product was approximately 85%. The net weight was 45 grams.
c. Fex: It was based on a synthetic detergent that contained Igepon and was used mainly for washing wool, silk, rayon, and other fine fabrics. The net weight was 100 grams.
d. Washing Powders: Products of different compositions were produced. The net filling weights per package were 250 grams and 500 grams.
e. Bleaching Soda: The net filling weight per package was 250 grams.
f. Lux Soap Flakes: This product contained 85% fatty acids. In 1936 the formulae was changed to make the flakes soluble in cold water The net filling weights per package were 115 grams and 220 grams.
g. Nurpur : Nurpur is the name for soap chips containing 78 to 80% fatty acids, which was packed in 5 kg. cartons, 25 kg. sacks, and 50 kg. sacks, which were delivered to laundries.
h. Sava: Sava was a product composed chiefly of soda and water glass which were delivered to laundries in 25 kg. sacks.
i. Vim: Vim was a scouring product in powder form. Before the war it was sold in the following sizes and weights: 230 gram box, 460 gram box, and 12 1/2 kg. drums. During the war the boxes were replaced by jars.
j. Solidox: Solidox is a non lathering toothpaste that was produced until 1943. The tubes had net filling weights of 35 grams and 75 grams.
k. Shampoos in Powder Form: Shampoos in powder form were produced from fatty acids and Igepon. The net filling weight per bag amounted to 12 grams.
l. Liquid Shampoos: Shampoos in liquid form were sold in 23 gram portions and one liter bottles.
m. Curd Soaps: Curd soaps were produced during the war for special users like hospitals. Production was limited. The net weight per bar was 200 grams.
n. Kaolin Soaps: Kaolin soaps were produced during the war in lieu of toilet or curd soaps. Initially it contained 25% fatty acids which were reduced to 14% by the end of the war. The net weight per bar was 70 grams.
o. Floating Soaps: Floating soaps were produced during the war as an alternative to Kaolin soap. The net weight per bar was 16.5 grams.
p. Product for Fine Wash: During the war a product for fine wash was produced to replace Fex. The net filling weights were 50 grams and 100 grams.
q. Washing Powder: During this war a product for normal wash was produced that contained approximately 20% fatty acids. The net filling weights of the packages were 250 grams and 500 grams.
r. Washing Powder for Heavily Soiled Work Clothes: During this war this product was used especially for cleaning clothes of mechanics etc. The net filling weight of the packages was 250 grams.
s. Bleaching Agent: The wartime bleaching agent had a net filling weight of 180 grams and 150 grams.
t. MS Soap: This soap was produced as a replacement for Nurpur. It was sold to laundries in fiber drums of 12 1/2 kg.
u. Sunovo: Sunovo is a product containing Igepon and Mersol. It was sold to commercial laundries in 25 kg. paper sacks.
v. Puck: Puck is a scouring product in solid form which was produced during the war. The net weight per bar was 150 grams.
w. Solidox Dental Soap: The manufacture of this product was started during the war, when difficulties arose in getting tubes for toothpaste. The dental powder had a net filling weight of 50 grams.

Here is a list of all known prewar and wartime products produced by Henkel and Company, Dusseldorf:

a. Persil: A prewar product. It was produced in 250 gram and 500 gram packages.
b. Henko Bleaching Soda : A prewar and wartime product. It was produced in a 300 gram package.
c. Sil: A prewar and wartime product. It came in a 180 gram package.
d. Imi: A prewar and wartime product. It came in a 300 gram package.
e. Ata Course Grade: A prewar and wartime product. It came in a 315 gram package which was reduced to 310 grams during the war.
f. Ata Fine Grade: A prewar and wartime product. During the war it came in a 340 gram package.
g. Ata Extra Fine Grade: A prewar and wartime product. It came in a 600 gram package.
h. Waschpulver with Mersolat was produced during the war. The packages had net filling weights of 250 grams and 500 grams.
i. Waschpulver with Soap was produced during the war. The packages had net filling weights of 250 grams and 500 grams.

Wartime Soap Allowance Per Person Per Month

TYPE OF SOAP	WEIGHT	FAT CONTENT	MONTHLY RATION
Einheits Soap	70 grams	9.8 grams	1 bar
or Floating Soap	16 grams	9.8 grams	1 bar
Special Floating Soap	67 grams	40 grams	1 bar
Shaving Soap			1 bar (3 months)
Soap Powder	250 grams		1 package
or Feinwasche Powder	50 grams		1 package
Bleaching Soda	250 grams		1 package
Kernseife	58 grams	36 grams	1 bar

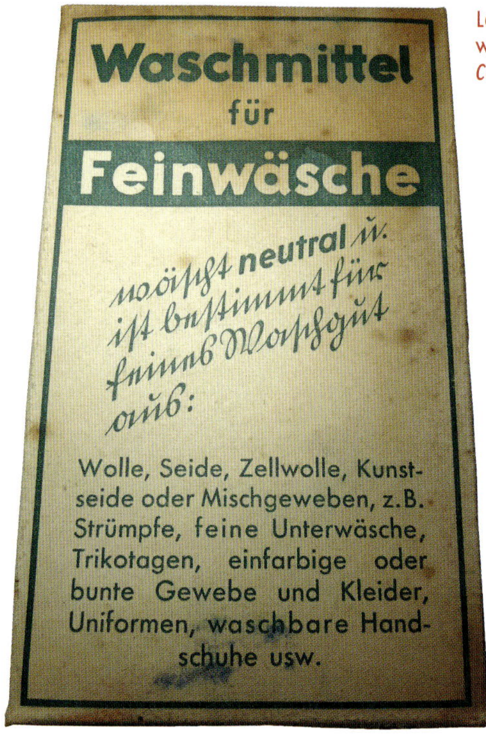

Laundry soap for fine wash. *Frédéric Ruelle Collection*

Cleaning whips. *The Collectors Guild*

Wartime instruction sheet for Waschmittel für Feinwäsche.

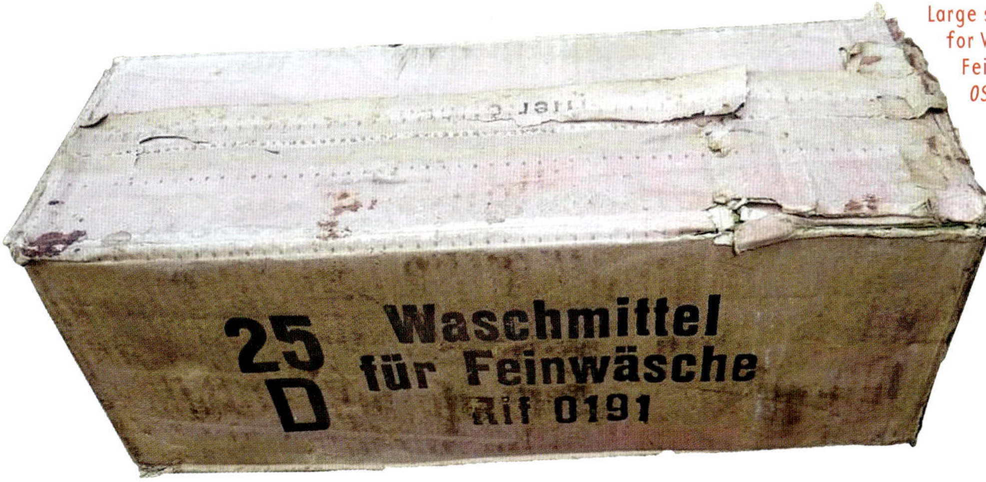

Large shipping carton for Waschmittel für Feinwäsche. *OSTFRONT Militaria*

A carton of IMI wash soap by Henkel and Company, Dusseldorf.[4] *Frédéric Ruelle Collection*

A humorous look at laundry day.

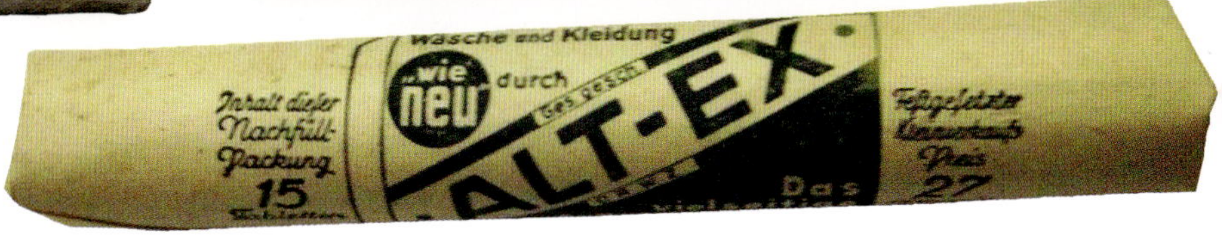

ALT-EX laundry products.[5]

Schwan soap by Henkel and Company, Dusseldorf.

Dr.Thompson's Bleach.

Sunlicht laundry soap.[6]

Special collar cleaner.

FEWA, the first fully synthetic detergent for delicate fabrics manufactured by Henkel and Company, Dusseldorf.

Pelikan brand laundry soap. *www.raskantik.com*

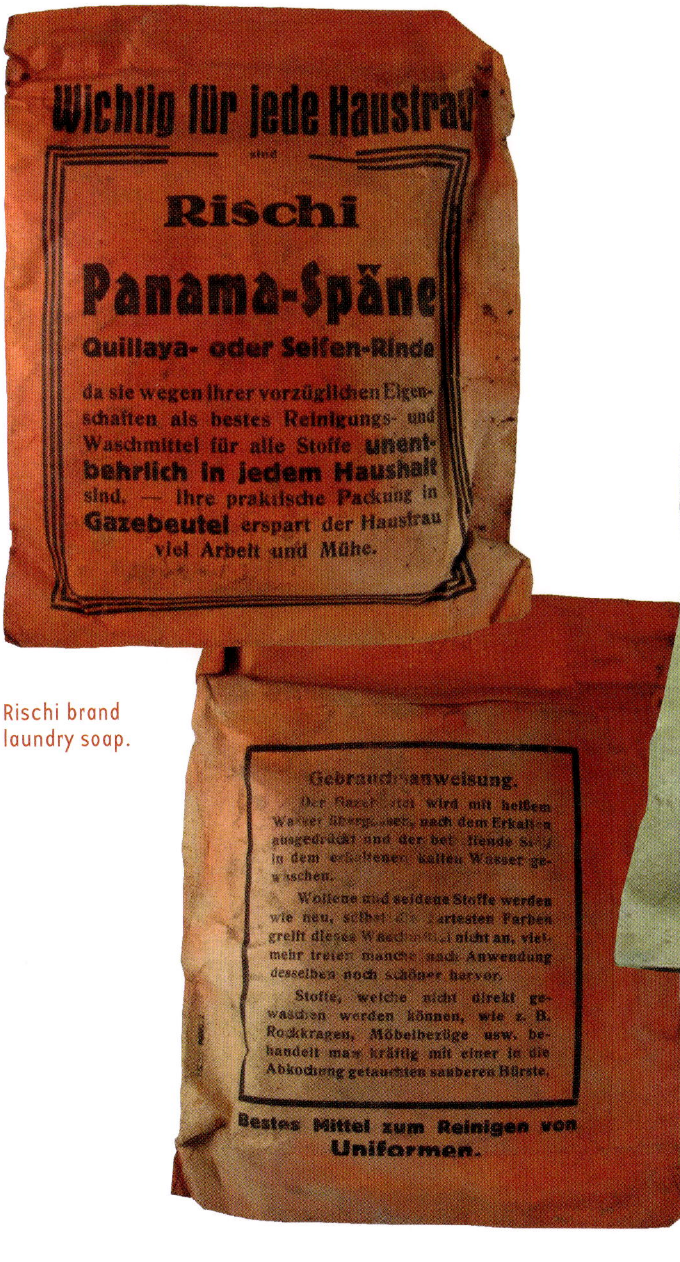

Rischi brand laundry soap.

Laundry soap for color clothing. *www.raskantik.com*

Henko bleach by Henkel and Company, Dusseldorf.

Laundry soap for whites.

Sylva brand bleach. *www.raskantik.com*

Dreiring wash soap along with a bulk shipping case. *Bunkermilitaria.com*

Lux wash soap along with a bulk shipping case. *Bunkermilitaria.com*

Sil brand wash soap.

Dali perfumed wash soap. *Frédéric Ruelle Collection*

Inka wash soap manufactured by Richard Brinkmann & Co., Wiesbaden. *Frédéric Ruelle Collection*

The campaign in North Africa presented some unique challenges. *Bunkermilitaria.com*

Presto brand wash soap. *Frédéric Ruelle Collection*

This vendor is selling a variety of cleaning products. *Bundesarchiv Bild 1011-134-0780-31, Foto: Cusian, Albert, 1941, Sommer*

Standard wash soap.
Frédéric Ruelle Collection

Wash day!

Portable clothes line reel. *The Collectors Guild*

Clothes pins.

Armored vehicles had room for the crew to dry their clothing.

Obviously an electric iron was no use in forward positions.

Cleaning brush. *Frédéric Ruelle Collection*

After washing, drying, and ironing, it is time to hang up the clothing.

Non-electric irons could be used anywhere.

CHAPTER 8 ENDNOTES

1. Milo Werke, Olmütz was situated in Moravia, in eastern Czech Republic. The town is known as Olomouc in Czech. The Heikornů family founded the factory in Olomouc in 1896, producing sugar and alcohol. By 1938, the factory was producing edible oils, vinegar, oil, margarine, soaps, and detergents. During WWII, the firm then known as Heikornovy became important for supplying the general population and the military. In January 1942, it became a limited liability company MILO-WERKE. The name is derived from MILO, an abbreviation of the German Industrie für Lebensmittel Mährisch Olmütz (Olomouc Moravian food industry). The factory was heavily damaged during the war and occupied in May 1945 by the Red Army. The company is still in operation as the Santovka SMC and Development Company.

2. The Ernst Freyberg/Chem. Fabrik Delitia, Delitzsch, Germany, was founded in 1817. The company specialized in insecticides and other pest control products. The Delicia umbrella brand name was registered in 1896. The company survived the war and in 1997, it merged with Frunol Ges. für Produktion und Vertrieb mbH to form Frunol Delicia® GmbH. Here is a wartime advertisement.

3. The Sidol-Werke in Köln-Braunsfeld, Germany, was founded in 1903. The factory produced pest control products, as well as leather good products like Seehund, Sigella, and Lodix. The factory survived the war but was heavily damaged by numerous air raids. In 1971, the company was taken over by the Henkel Corporation and closed soon after. Here is a prewar advertisement.

4. The Henkel & Cie company was founded in Aachen, Germany, on September 26, 1876. Henkel acquired a share holding in the Düsseldorf Company, Dr. Thompson's Seifenpulver GmbH, in 1929, and became the sole shareholder in 1933. In 1878, the first German brand-name detergent appeared: Henkel's Bleich-Soda. To take advantage of better transport and sales opportunities, Henkel relocated to Düsseldorf in 1878. In 1879, Dr. Thompson's Seifen-Pulver-"Marke Schwan" became one of the first German brand name products. On March 9, 1895, the lion logo was entered in the register of trademarks. Persil—the world's first self-acting detergent—was developed in 1907. In 1918, Henkel totally closed down production of Persil and replaced it with the wartime washing powder Sil. In 1920, Henkel launched Ata. In 1921, Henkel's Bleich-Soda was given the brand name Henko. Henkel's three detergents met all the requirements of the classical washing method: Henko for soaking, Persil for the main wash, and Sil for rinsing. In 1922, the Weisse Dame (white lady)—the most famous Persil advertising character—was created. In 1929, Henkel launched the household cleaner Imi. In 1933, the world's first completely synthetic, soap-free detergent (Fewa) was marketed. In 1939, just after the outbreak of the war on September 1, the German government decreed that only standard washing powders should be produced and Persil and Fewa were withdrawn from the market. Many of Henkel's factories were damaged during the war, but a few of their facilities were able to resume operations in 1945. Henkel is still in business today. Here are a few wartime advertisements.

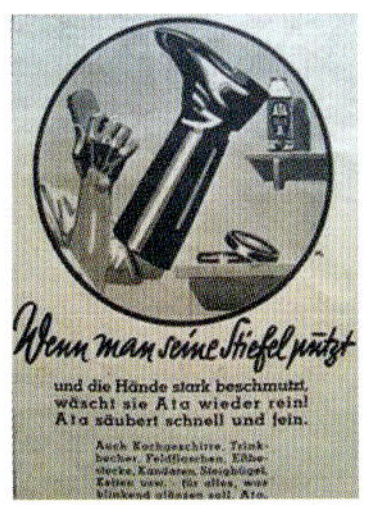

5. No history was found on the firm that produced ALT-EX. Here is a wartime advertisement.

6. The Sunlicht Gesellschaft A.G., Mannheim/Rheinau was founded in 1899. It became a Unilever brand in 2000. Here is an advertisement from the 1920s.

CHAPTER 9
MAINTAINING THE UNIFORM

In the face of ever-declining resources, Germany implemented policies to conserve raw materials and extend the life of fielded items. To compound problems, the transportation system was in disarray by the end of the war, which made resupply even more difficult. The German soldier was continually schooled on the importance of caring for issue uniforms and equipment. *Taschenbuch für den Winterkrieg* (*Handbook for Winter Warfare*) provided commanders and soldiers the following guidance about the care of clothing and equipment:

> On the march and in combat the following practices should be observed. Use breaks in the march and rest periods to exchange unserviceable articles of clothing and to make minor repairs. Garments left behind by wounded men should be collected and turned in without exception. In snowstorms wear the fur coat inside out and wrap a shelter half around it, if it does not conflict with camouflage requirements.
>
> Even during a temporary halt the troops should take time out to mend and clean their cloths. Particular attention should be devoted to drying wet cloths, and above all, footgear. Do not let boots or shoes dry near a fire or burning stove, because, in addition to the danger that they may burn, they may become hard and brittle. Wet footgear should be stuffed with straw or paper.
>
> Snow is an enemy of leather, and the best protection is to keep the leather soft. Care of the footgear is especially important in preparing for a march. The uppers should be greased daily, preferably when damp. Leather which has been greased too much, however, chills the feet and permits water to seep through. This treatment should not be applied just before marches, but well in advance.
>
> Instructions in cleaning and care of clothing while resting in permanent billets should be given by noncommissioned officers. Fix a specific hour for cleaning and mending. Clothing should be cleaned, if possible, in commercial laundries; otherwise, field laundries should be established by service units or the units themselves. If this is not possible, laundry details should be formed within the unit. Washing should be done by squads or platoons, under supervision. Prepare areas for washing and drying laundry and drying wet outer clothing. Woolens should be washed in lukewarm, not boiling water. Clean fur coats frequently by heating and brushing them. Never dry wet furs in the immediate vicinity of a stove. Clothes which are infested with lice should be deloused as quickly as possible with hot air.
>
> Clothing-repair shops must be established. If space permits, craftsmen of different sections of the same service units should be concentrated in one repair shop. Minor repairs should be made by the soldier himself. The mending of socks is very important.
>
> The troops should be taught that it is especially important to take care of footgear, in order to assure good health when the thaw occurs. If the situation permits, inspections should be held as frequently as possible to make sure that methodical care is taken of footgear. Melting snow quickly penetrates shoe leather and damages it, especially the thread in the seams. Even though the leather may not be waterproof, it may be made so to a certain degree by proper treatment.
>
> Slight damage to leather footgear should be repaired immediately. Worn out hobnails should not be pulled out, because the holes they leave will let water through. New nails should be driven in beside the old ones. Do not allow shoes to be worn until holes form in the inner soles. Wet boots should be changed (substitute with laced shoes). The inside of the shoe should be wiped dry with rags and stuffed with paper, straw, or other material which absorbs moisture. Let footgear dry slowly in moderately warm places only. The wetter the shoes, the greater the danger that the leather will crack, if they are dried too quickly near stoves or open fires.
>
> Footgear should be cleaned daily. The vamps should be slightly greased up to ankle height. Rub in the grease vigorously with a rag or, better still, with the hand. Warm grease penetrates leather more easily. Do not use too much grease, because it will penetrate the leather and soil the socks and feet. Grease should be applied freely in the groove between the upper leather and the sole in order to make the seam watertight.
>
> Once a week clean the footgear thoroughly by using luke warm water to wash off dirt and caked grease and polish. Then permit it to dry, and grease the leather. The

leg of the boot needs to be greased only once a week. Treating shoe leather with dubbing keeps it pliable. Shoe polish alone has a tendency to make leather hard and brittle and clogs the pores of the leather. This causes perspiration to condense inside the shoe and might induce frostbite.

Impregnation material for leather shoes, if available, makes them tougher and more waterproof. It is applied when the sole is dry and clean. Repeat the treatment until the sole does not absorb any more preparation. Use it once or twice a month.

Rubber boots and rubber overshoes must be treated with special care because of the shortage of raw material. Do not wear them for marching on paved roads. They should be cleaned with a soft rag and cold or lukewarm water, never with hot water, oil, or gasoline. Do not use sharp instruments for scraping dirt off them. When drying them, hang them in moderately warm places, but never near or over hot stoves. Damage must be repaired with rubber patches.

Felt boots must not be worn after the thaw begins. Wet felt boots do not keep the feet warm; on the contrary, the evaporation of moisture in the felt causes the feet to lose warmth, and frostbite will easily occur, even at moderately low temperatures. Felt boots, because they have leather parts, must be dried only in moderately warm places.

Boxes used to store cleaning supplies. *Bunkermilitaria.com* and *www.raskantik.com*

Shoe cleaning kit dated 1938.

Wartime advertisement for a shoe care kit.

Two shoe brushes. *Frédéric Ruelle Collection*

Eg-Gü brand shoe brush.[1]

Wartime advertisement for cleaning clothes.

Cleaning cloth. *Bunkermilitaria.com*

A nice color picture of a cobbler's tent.

Proper fitting and serviceable footgear was critical to the infantryman's very existence.
Photos: National Archives and Records Administration (NARA)

It was important to take care of issue equipment because replacements were not always available.

These Cossack cobblers are busy repairing equipment. *Bundesarchiv-Bild-101I-153-1989-28*

Chest for cobblers equipment.

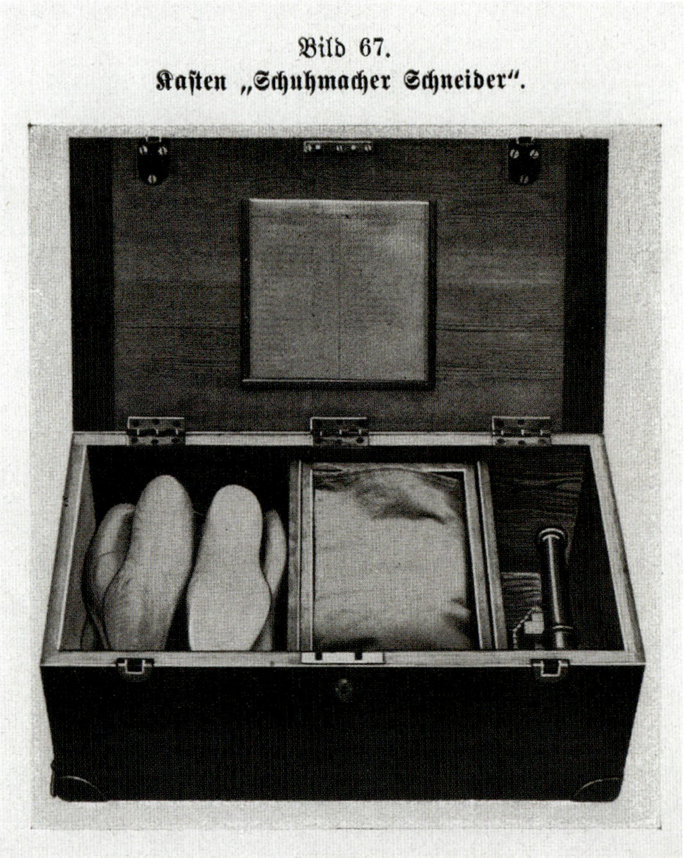

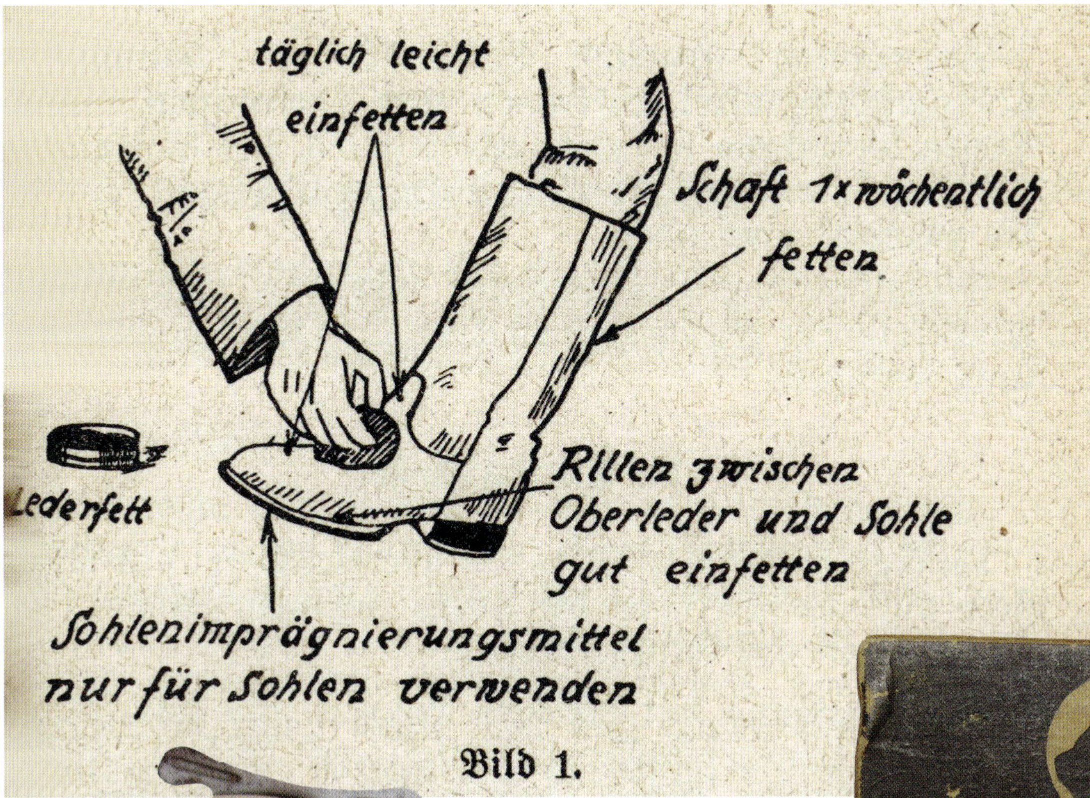

The proper method to polish shoes.

A variety of Erdal products.[2]
OSTFRONT Militaria

Möser leather care product.

Cardstock containers were used to package shoe polish and other leather treatments. *Frédéric Ruelle Collection*

Immalin brand shoe polish.[3]
Frédéric Ruelle Collection

Ternina brand shoe polish.

Paper containers were more economical to produce.

Seehund brand leather fat. *Jim Kreunen of Militaria Plaza*

Bussard brand waterproofing leather fat.

Sehr empfehlenswerte Putzmittel

r. **36560.** Bestes utz- und Poliermit-l für Metalle, äu-erst sauber und parsam. Greift die Ietalle nicht an. **18** Pf. *

Nachstehende Reinigungs- und Putzmittel für Aluminium- und Emaillegeschirre sind die besten Präparate dieser Art und in ihrer Wirkung unübertroffen!

Nr. **36561.** In keiner Küche darf dieses beliebte Aluminiumputzpulver fehlen ..... **19** Pf.

Nr. **36562.** Beliebtes Scheuerputzmittel, unentbehrlich für jede Hausfrau, sehr wirksam ... **24** Pf.

Nr. **36563.** Bestes Emailleputzmittel, reinigt spiel. leicht sämtliche Emaillegeschirre .. **19** Pf.

Nr. **36564.** Bester Messerputzschmirgel. Für Messerputzmaschine und Messerputzbank zu verwenden. **32** Pf.

Nr. **36565.** Schuhcreme, schwarz, ca. 125 g. Dose **40** Pf.

Nr. **36566.** Schuhcreme, braun, ca. 60 g. Dose **25** Pf.

Nr. **36567.** Schuhcreme, farblos, ca. 60 g. Dose **30** Pf.

Nr. **36516.** Allerbestes Bohnerwachs zum Bohnern von Parkett, Linoleum, Fußböden; gibt auch Möbeln einen spiegelblanken Glanz. ca. 250 g. Dose **52** Pf. *

Nr. **36569.** „Mixon"-Bohnerwachs, gelb. Staubbindend, trittfest und nicht glättend. ca. 250 g. Dose **42** Pf.

Nr. **36570.** Lodix-Creme, schwarz. Zur Pflege der Lackschuhe. Tube **42** Pf.

Nr. **36568.** Tranlederfett, schwarz, mit Dosenöffner. Hervorragendes Lederkonservierungsmittel, größte Ergiebigkeit. Inhalt ca. 150 g .... Dose **33** Pf.

Nr. **36571.** Schuhweiß „Lodix" in Flasche mit Schwammpinsel. Inhalt 100 g. Bestes Reinigungsmittel für **weiße Leinenschuhe.** Flasche **45** Pf.

Nr. **36572** Bester Honigfliegenfänger. 5 Stück **20** Pf.

Nr. **36573** „Diamant-Kitt." Bestes Mittel zum Kitten von Porzellan, Marmor, Glas usw. Kittet jeden Gegenstand. Flasche **47** Pf.

Nr. **36574** Ungulin-Putz-Extrakt. Unübertroffenes Putzmittel für alle Arten Metalle .... **10** Pf.

Nr. **36575** Vulkan, ausgezeichneter Ofenputz. Bestes Mittel zum Schwärzen von Eisenteilen, Öfen usw. .. **31** Pf.

Wartime advertisement for various leather care products.

Globus brand waterproof leather fat. *The Collectors Guild*

Salamander brand shoe cream. *www.raskantik.com*

Salamander advertisement.[4]

Heigöha leather wax for belts.
Frédéric Ruelle Collection

Collonil brand leather oil.[5]

Krebs leather wax. *Frédéric Ruelle Collection*

Lodix brand leather products. *OSTFRONT Militaria*

Sternolin shoe polish.[6]

Eri brand shoe polish.[7] *OSTFRONT Militaria*

Eg Gü shoe polish. *Jim Kreunen of Militaria Plaza*

Nigrin brand shoe polish.[8] *OSTFRONT Militaria*

Diamantine brand shoe polish.[9] *OSTFRONT Militaria*

Pilo brand shoe polish.[10] *OSTFRONT Militaria*

GEG brand shoe wax.
Bunkermilitaria.com

Lico shoe cream.

Unbranded can of shoe polish manufactured by G.A. Glafey, Nürnberg.[11]

Bergsteiger shoe fat.

Gloria brand
leather fat.

Gnomen wax. *OSTFRONT Militaria*

Judex brand
leather cream.

Armada brand shoe polish.
Jim Kreunen of Militaria Plaza

Morello leather balm.

Bosco leather treatment.[12] *www.raskantik.com*

Derby shoe polish manufactured in Czechoslovakia. *Jim Kreunen of Militaria Plaza*

Solo brand shoe paste.[13]

Trab-Trab leather paste.[14]

Wettruf brand shoe paste.

Columbin brand leather fat. *Michel Verberkt Collection*

Yankee brand shoe polish. *Frédéric Ruelle Collection*

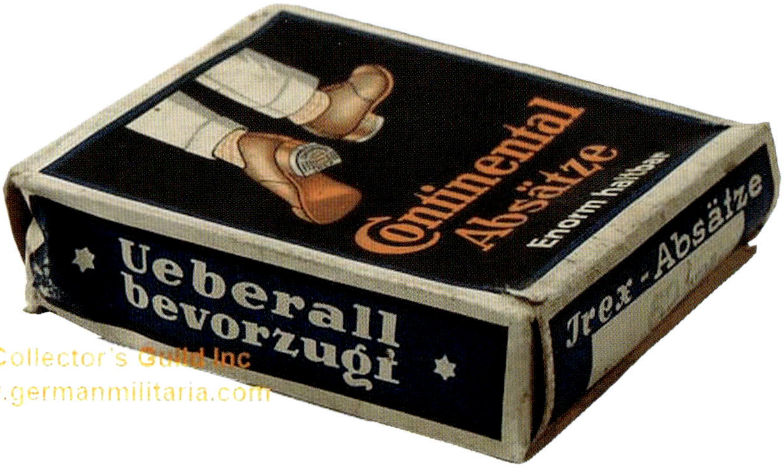

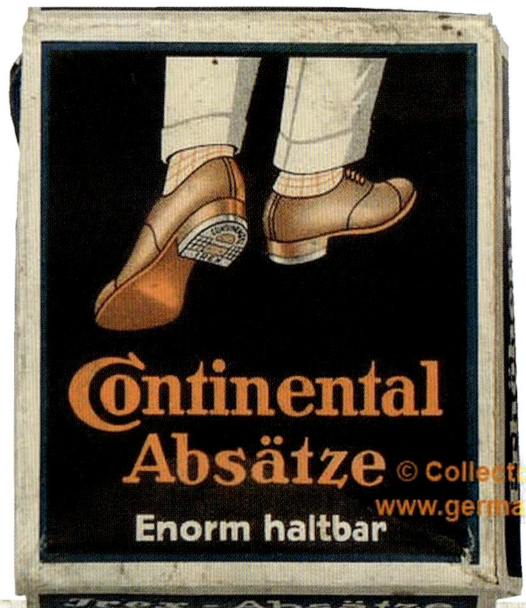

Replacement soles. *The Collectors Guild*

How to properly dry your foot wear.

Sewing kits were indispensable.

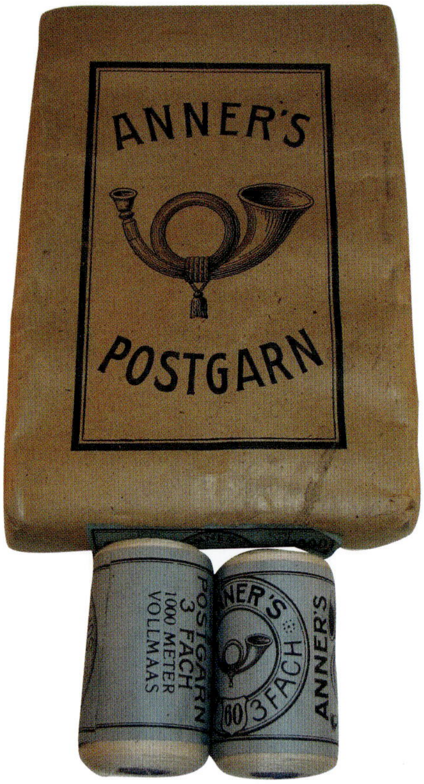

A selection of threads and yarns.

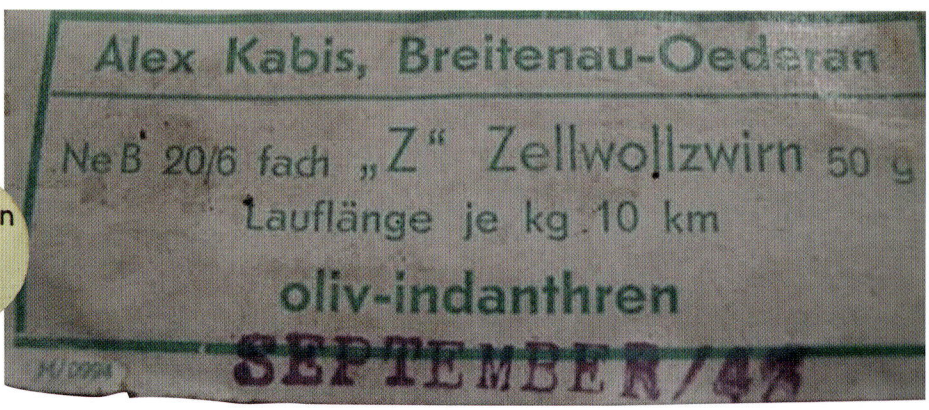

HEINRICH MITTAG AG. · MAGDEBURG u. HANNOVER

Nähgarne: Ackermann, Göggingen, Gruschwitz, Clark

Ackermann u. Göggingen

schwarz, weiß und farbig

200 m 4fach Obergarn .... Nr. 20—100
1000 m 4fach Obergarn .... Nr. 20—100
1000 m 2fach Untergarn ...... Nr. 40— 80
100 m 3fach Glanzgarn ...... Nr. 8— 12
500 m 3fach Glanzgarn ...... Nr. 24— 80
500 m 3fach Mattgarn .... Nr. 24— 80
200 m 4fach farbig .... Nr. 40
1000 m 4fach farbig .... Nr. 40

Secunda Qualitäten

in den Marken Treppe, Zange usw.

200 m 4fach schwarz und weiß Nr. 30—60
1000 m 4fach schwarz und weiß Nr. 30—60

Gruschwitz

schwarz und weiß

200 m 4fach Obergarn .... Nr. 20—100
1000 m 4fach Obergarn .... Nr. 20—100

Clark

200 m 4fach Obergarn .... Nr. 20—100
1000 m 4fach Obergarn .... Nr. 20—100
200 m 6fach Obergarn .... Nr. 30—100
200 m 6fach Inlettgarn .... Nr. 30— 50

Reihgarn (Heftgarn)

20-g-Spulen .... Nr. 24
in 10- und 50-Stück-Packung

50-g-Spulen .... Nr. 24
in 10- und 20-Stück-Packung

HEINRICH MITTAG AG. · MAGDEBURG u. HANNOVER

Gruschwitz Leinenzwirne

Gruschwitz Kristallzwirn

Der beste Haushaltszwirn

40-m-Sterne, **dreifach**, schwarz, weiß, farbig
Nr. **30 40 50 60 80 100 120 150**
sortiert **30/60** und **60/100**

Der Kasten enthält 50 Sterne

Gruschwitz Kegelzwirn

Der bekannte grüne Stern

2fach, 20 m

Nr. **20 25 30 40**, schwarz, weiß, roh, feldgrau

Gruschwitz Korallenzwirn

Der Kasten 100 Sterne

2fach, 20 m

Nr. **30 40**, schwarz, weiß, feldgrau

Gruschwitz Leinenzwirn

Gruschwitz Blauschildrollen

für Hand und Maschine
3fach, 50-g-Rollen LD.
Der Kasten = 10 Rollen

Gruschwitz Lilaschildrollen

Der bekannte Schneiderzwirn
3fach, 50-g-Rollen RD.
Der Kasten = 10 Rollen

Gruschwitz Spinnerinrollen

100 m, 2fach
Nr. **30** schwarz und weiß
Der Kasten = 20 Rollen

Gruschwitz Kopszwirn

20 m, 2fach
Nr. **16—40** schwarz, weiß, roh
Der Kasten = 48 Spulen

Gruschwitz Nadelfaden

50 m, **3fach**
Nr. **20—150** und sortiert
Der Kasten = 48 Knäuel

Gruschwitz Knäuelzwirn

100 m, 2fach
Nr. **18 20 25 30 40 50**
schwarz, weiß, rohgrau
Der Kasten = 20 Knäuel

HEINRICH MITTAG AG. · MAGDEBURG u. HANNOVER

Nähnadeln Ia Aachener Ware

25 Stück im Brief, 40 Briefe im Karton

Grün-Adler · Weißschild · Victoria-Goldöhr · Schwarzschild · Lammertz-Grünschild · Blitz

Lange · Halblange · Kurze

Grün-Adler,	Grünes Etikett (Iserlohner Ware), **nur** lang 4/8 sortiert	Ladenpreis 2½ Pf.
Weißschild,	Golddruck-Etikett, Silber-Ellipsöhr	Ladenpreis 5 Pf.
Victoria-Goldöhr,	Buntdruck-Etikett, Ellips-Goldöhr	Ladenpreis 7 Pf.
Schwarzschild,	Silberdruck-Etikett, Silber-Ellipsöhr, Qualität „Leo Lammertz"	Ladenpreis 12 Pf.
Lammertz-Grünschild,	Silber-Ellipsöhr, grüne Reichsapfelmarke „Leo Lammertz"	Ladenpreis 12 Pf.
Blitz,	Buntdruck-Etikett, Silberöhr	Ladenpreis 15 Pf.
French,	Y-Stempel, blaues Etikett, Silberöhr	Ladenpreis 5 Pf.

728 Biene-Marke, Ellips-Goldöhr, gefälliger Brief mit Zelluloidfenster, nur lang 4/8 sortiert .... Ladenpreis 10 Pf.

Taifun, Ellips-Silberöhr, nur lang 4/8 sortiert .... Ladenpreis 10 Pf.

Rotschild, Rotdruck-Etikett, Silber-Drillöhr .... Ladenpreis 12 Pf.

728 · Rotschild

Wartime advertisements for sewing supplies.

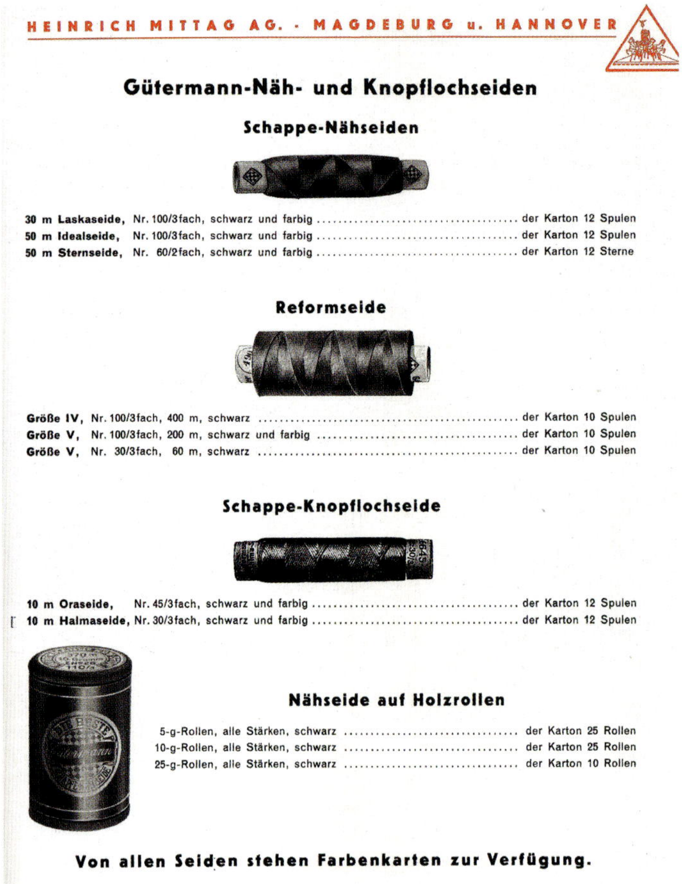

HEINRICH MITTAG AG. · MAGDEBURG u. HANNOVER

Gütermann-Näh- und Knopflochseiden

Schappe-Nähseiden

30 m Laskaseide,	Nr. 100/3fach, schwarz und farbig	der Karton 12 Spulen
50 m Idealseide,	Nr. 100/3fach, schwarz und farbig	der Karton 12 Spulen
50 m Sternseide,	Nr. 60/2fach, schwarz und farbig	der Karton 12 Sterne

Reformseide

Größe IV,	Nr. 100/3fach, 400 m, schwarz	der Karton 10 Spulen
Größe V,	Nr. 100/3fach, 200 m, schwarz und farbig	der Karton 10 Spulen
Größe V,	Nr. 30/3fach, 60 m, schwarz	der Karton 10 Spulen

Schappe-Knopflochseide

10 m Oraseide,	Nr. 45/3fach, schwarz und farbig	der Karton 12 Spulen
10 m Halmaseide,	Nr. 30/3fach, schwarz und farbig	der Karton 12 Spulen

Nähseide auf Holzrollen

5-g-Rollen, alle Stärken, schwarz	der Karton 25 Rollen
10-g-Rollen, alle Stärken, schwarz	der Karton 25 Rollen
25-g-Rollen, alle Stärken, schwarz	der Karton 10 Rollen

Von allen Seiden stehen Farbenkarten zur Verfügung.

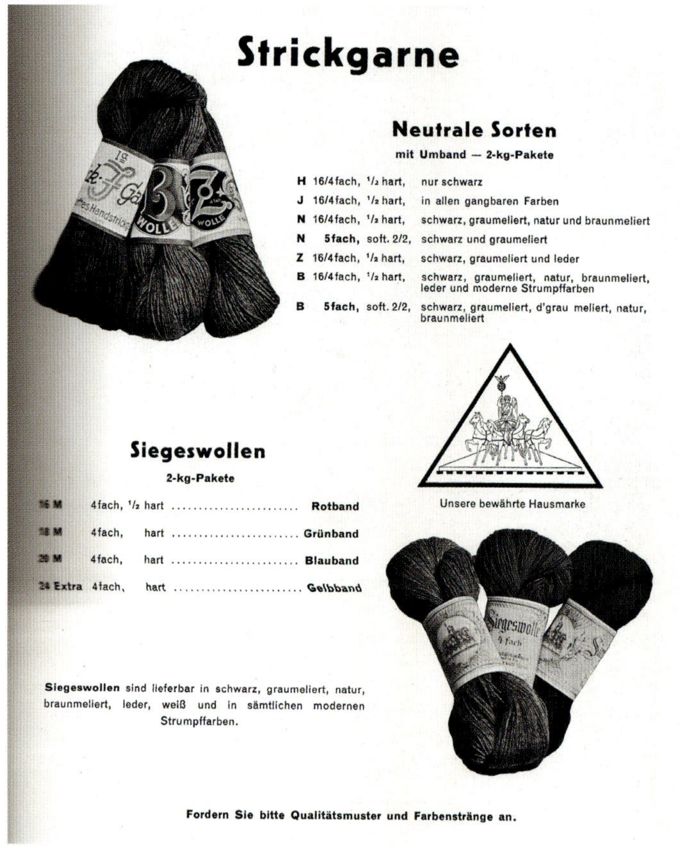

Strickgarne

Neutrale Sorten

mit Umband — 2-kg-Pakete

H	16/4fach,	1/2 hart,	nur schwarz
J	16/4fach,	1/2 hart,	in allen gangbaren Farben
N	16/4fach,	1/2 hart,	schwarz, graumeliert, natur und braunmeliert
N	**5fach,**	soft. 2/2,	schwarz und graumeliert
Z	16/4fach,	1/2 hart,	schwarz, graumeliert und leder
B	16/4fach,	1/2 hart,	schwarz, graumeliert, natur, braunmeliert, leder und moderne Strumpffarben
B	**5fach,**	soft. 2/2,	schwarz, graumeliert, d'grau meliert, natur, braunmeliert

Unsere bewährte Hausmarke

Siegeswollen

2-kg-Pakete

16 M	4fach,	1/2 hart	**Rotband**
18 M	4fach,	hart	**Grünband**
20 M	4fach,	hart	**Blauband**
24 Extra	4fach,	hart	**Gelbband**

Siegeswollen sind lieferbar in schwarz, graumeliert, natur, braunmeliert, leder, weiß und in sämtlichen modernen Strumpffarben.

Fordern Sie bitte Qualitätsmuster und Farbenstränge an.

Amann's Handarbeits-Kunstseiden

in reicher Farbenauswahl

Für Strick- und Häkelzwecke

Art. 1400 Frotté, Effektzwirn .... 50-g-Strang ein- und mehrfarbig (teilbar 2×25 g) Karton zu 5 Strang

Art. 1100 Perl-Cusir, voller Perlzwirn 50-g-Strang ein-u. mehrfarbig Karton zu 10 Strang

Art. 1001 Colomba, Crepezwirn . 50-g-Strang ein- und mehrfarbig Karton zu 10 Strang

Art. 160 Debora, Standardstärke 10-g-Knäuel Karton zu 10 Knäuel

nach Karte 20

Art. 1300 Fransen-Cordonnet, Standardstärke 50-g-Strang ... Karton zu 10 Strang

Art. 161 Debora-Dose, Standardstärke 50-g-Knäuel ... Karton zu 10 Knäuel

nach Karte 24

Art. 1350 Carola, feine Cordonnet-Seide 25-g-Knäuel ... Karton zu 10 Knäuel

Art. 1651 Cavallino, feine Cordonnet-Seide 50-g-Strang ... Karton zu 10 Strang

nach Karte 33

Für Stickzwecke indanthrengefärbt

Art. 1150 Indaperle, Perlzwirn... 10-g-Strang Karton zu 10 Strang

Art. 1050 Indakrepp, Crepezwirn 10-g-Strang Karton zu 10 Strang

nach Karte 28

Art. 157 Mouliné, 6fach teilbar . 10-m-Strang Karton zu 12 Strang

nach Karte 27

Art. 1400 Frotté

Art. 1300 Fransen-Cordonnet

Art. 151 Debora-Dose

Art. 157 Mouliné

Art. 1350 Carola

Die praktischen Verkaufskasten hierzu auf der nächsten Seite.

Stopfgarn in Haus- und Reisepackungen

Art. 217 DRGM.
„7 im Netz"
7 Knäuel je 20 m 8fach

Art. 340
Metall-Stopfbüchse
mit Nadelkissen, Spiegel, Stopftwist und Nadel

Art. 303
Praktische Nähzeugtasche
für Militär Arbeitsdienst und andere Formationen Reichhaltige Füllung

Art. 288 DRGM.
8 Knäuel zu je 20 m, 8fach, im geschmackvollen Zellophan-Beutel

Art. 217	**„7 im Netz"**	Ladenpreis ca. 25 Pf.
Art. 288	**„8 im Zellophan-Beutel"**	Ladenpreis ca. 30 Pf.
Art. 303	**„Nähzeugtasche"**	Ladenpreis ca. 50 Pf.
Art. 330	**„Nadelkissen"** klein	Ladenpreis ca. 20 Pf.
Art. 340	**„Nadelkissen"**, groß	Ladenpreis ca. 25 Pf.
Art. 777	**„Hauspackung"**	Ladenpreis ca. 30 Pf.
Art. 2080	**„Hauspackung"** in Zellophan-Packung	Ladenpreis ca. 30 Pf.

Steter Eingang neuer Strumpf-Apotheken

Seidenglanz-Stopf-Twist
Art. 2080 DRGM.
8 Knäuel je 20 m, 8fach in Zellophan-Packung

Art. 777 DRGM.
8 Knäuel zu je 20 m, 8fach

Wartime advertisements for sewing supplies.

There was a wide variety of sewing kits to choose from.

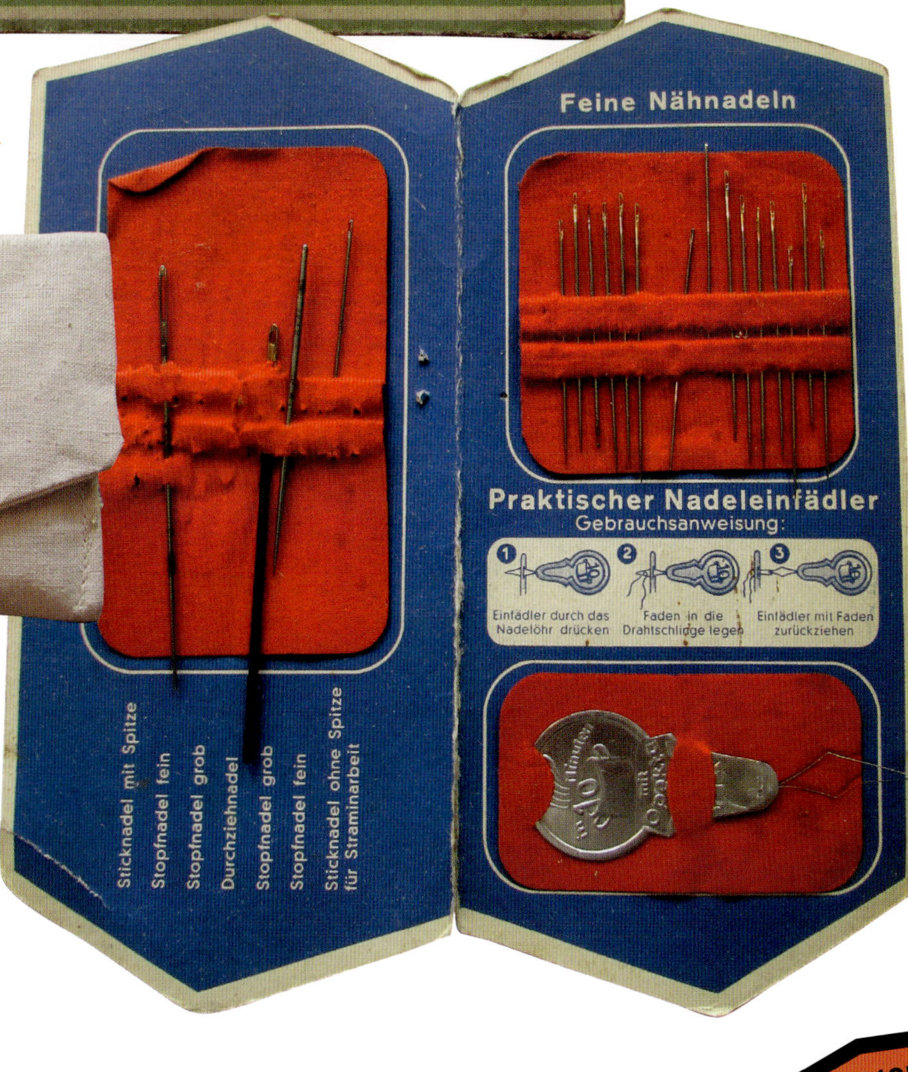

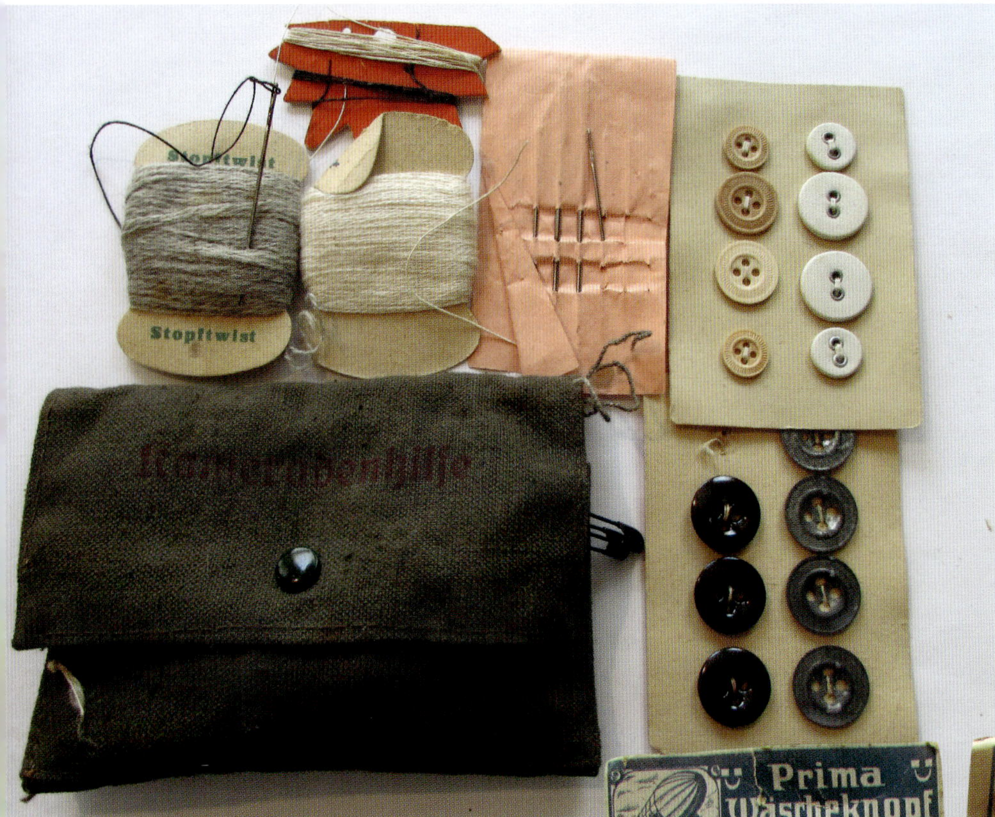

There was a wide variety of sewing kits to choose from.

Sewing needles.

This style of sewing kit is being widely reproduced.

A pair of compact scissors.

Wartime advertisement for thimbles and sewing needles.

Thimble.

Nachtrag

Rostfreie Näh-, Stick- und Stopfnadeln

in transparenten Fensterbriefen

Packung 25 Briefe im Karton

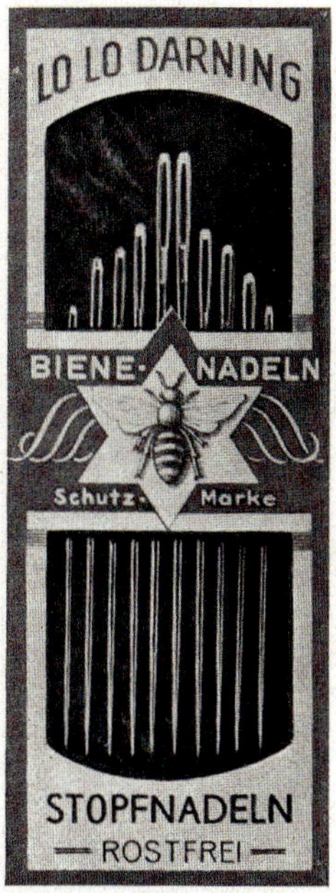

117 Woll-Stopfnadeln
10 vernickelte Nadeln
Ladenpreis . 10 Pf.

118 Florstrumpf-Stopfnadeln
10 vernickelte Nadeln
Ladenpreis .. 10 Pf.

119 Twist-Stopfnadeln
10 vernickelte Nadeln
Ladenpreis .. 10 Pf.

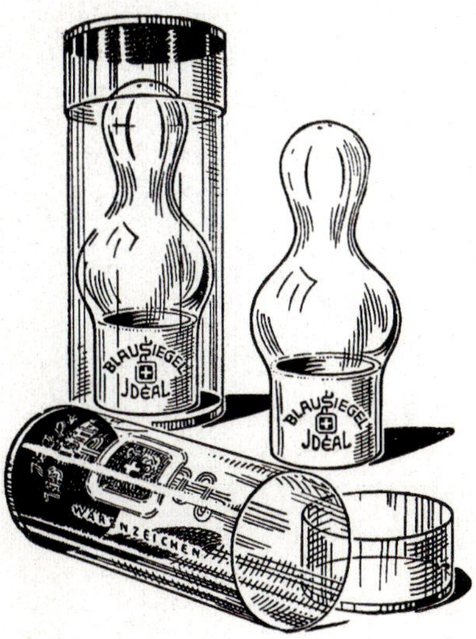

Ideal-Sauger

Art. J.

Blausiegel-Idealsauger
mit rotem Rand
Stückweis in Cellophan-Hülse
1 Dtz. im Aufstell-Karton
Ladenpreis .... 25—30 Pf.

122 Nähnadeln mit Goldöhr
20 vernickelte Nadeln
Ladenpreis .... 10 Pf.

121 Sticknadeln, mit Spitze
8 vernickelte Nadeln
Ladenpreis .... 10 Pf.

120 Straminnadeln, ohne Spitze
8 vernickelte Nadeln
Ladenpreis .... 10 Pf.

Wartime advertisement for thimbles and sewing needles.

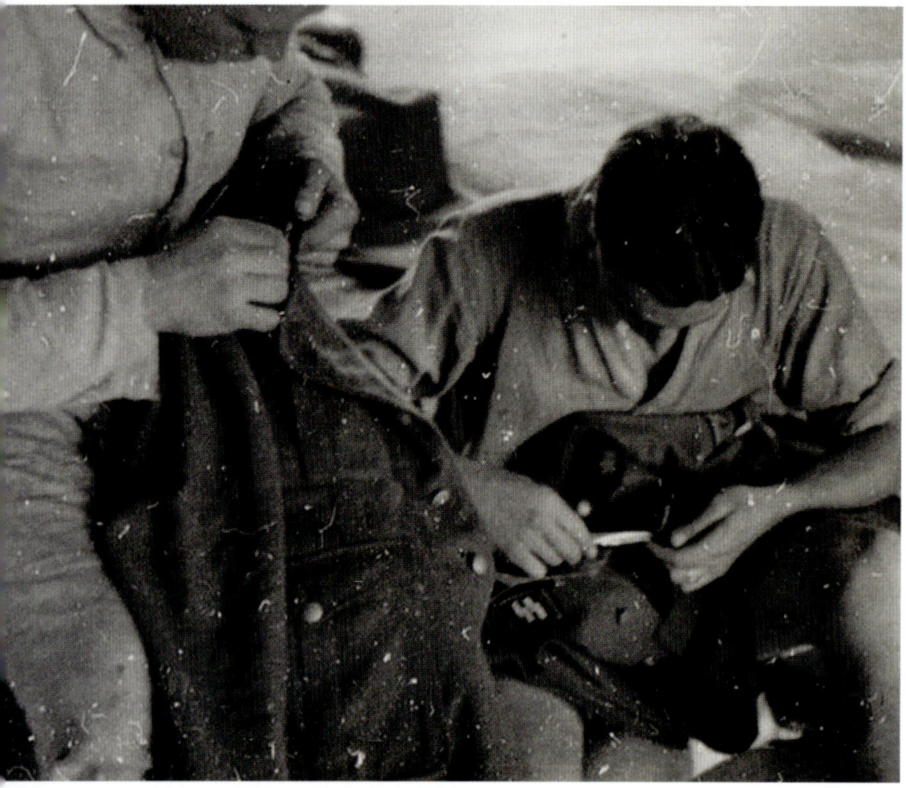

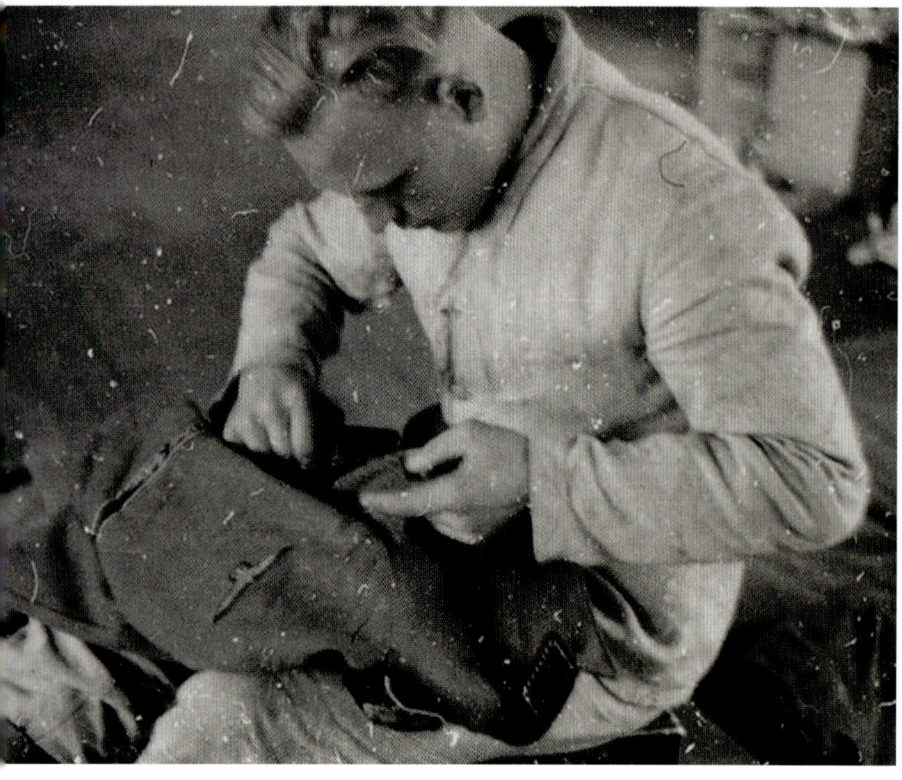

Every soldier needed to acquire sewing and darning skills out of necessity. *Photos: US National Archives and Records Administration (NARA)*

A humorous look at sewing.

Haken und Augen

gemischt

2/0 0 1

Man achte auf die Schutz-Marke

Prym's Haken & Augen No 0

extra fein gearbeitet

Größe 2/0—2, **Haken und Augen,** lackiert, 20/20 = 1/2 kg .... Ladenpreis 5 Pf.
Größe 2/0—1, **Haken und Augen,** versilbert, 20/20 = 1/2 kg .... Ladenpreis 15 Pf.
Größe 0 u. 1, **Haken und Augen,** lackiert, 50 Briefe im Karton .... Ladenpreis 5 Pf.
Größe 0, **Haken und Augen,** versilbert, 50 Briefe im Karton .... Ladenpreis 10 Pf.

Militär-Haken und -Augen

Größe 7—10 lackiert, Haken oder Augen einzeln, in 1/4-kg-Packung

Puppen-Haken und -Augen

Nr. 10 versilbert und lackiert, 1 Gros im Karton

Sewing accessories.

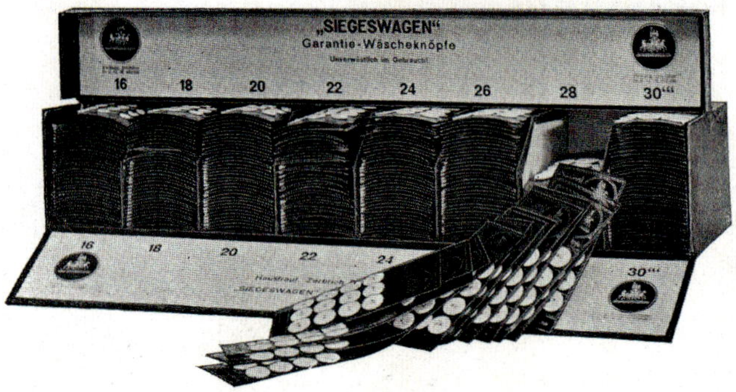

Sortimentskasten Nr. 26
pro Größe 1 Dutzend auf Karte
36 Karten pro Größe

Sortimentskasten Nr. 26½
pro Größe 1 Dutzend auf Karte
18 Karten pro Größe

Sortiment 27
eleganter Aufstellkasten, enthält 1 Gros Karten, in den Größen 16—30 lin.
Karten sind zum 10-Pf.-Verkauf geeignet.

Sortiment Nr. 25 Kasten = 24 Karten à 3 Dutzend in 6 Größen sortiert.

Porzellanknöpfe

202/16 bis 30

Art. 200 **Perlmutter-Imitation,** 4-Loch, 6 Dutzend auf Karte .... Größe 14—30
Art. 201 **Porzellan,** weiß und schwarz, 4-Loch, 6 Dutzend auf Karte .... Größe 7—50
Art. 202 **Permutter-Imitation,** 2-Loch, 1 Gros im Kasten .... Größe 14—30
Art. 203 **Bein-Imitation,** 2-Loch, 6 Dutzend auf Karte .... Größe 22—26

Beinknöpfe

1 Gros im Kasten

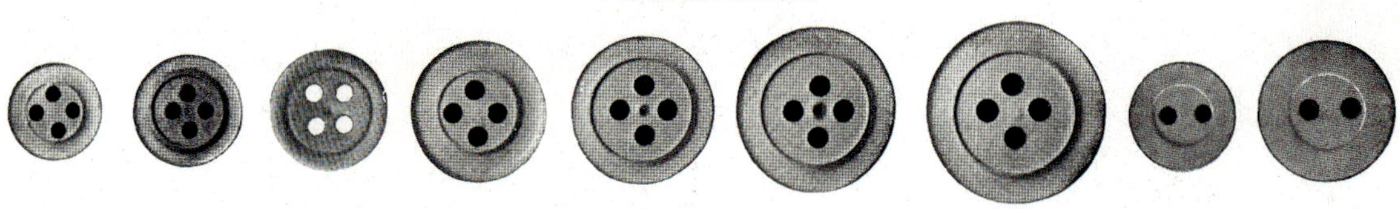

29 23½ 23 24 25 99/9 99/10 30 31

23½, 23, 24, 25 weiße 4-Loch-Beinknöpfe
26 in Größe wie 23, schwarze 4-Loch-Beinknöpfe
26½ in Größe wie 23½, schwarze 4-Loch-Beinknöpfe
27 in Größe wie 24, schwarze 4-Loch-Beinknöpfe
28 in Größe wie 25, schwarze 4-Loch-Beinknöpfe

29 weißer 4-Loch-Bein-Hemdenknopf
30 weißer 2-Loch-Leibchenknopf
31 weißer 2-Loch-Leibchenknopf
99/9 weißer 4-Loch-Jackenknopf
99/10 weißer 4-Loch-Jackenknopf

Art. 99 ist auch schwarz zu liefern

Sewing accessories.

Stahl-Sicherheitsnadeln

12 Nadeln im Karton

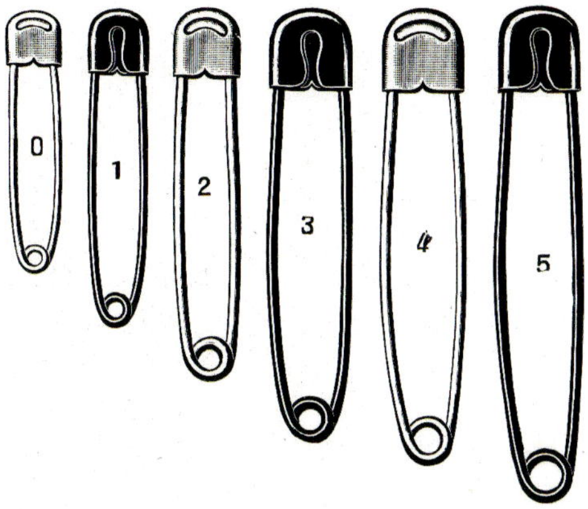

1900 und 1925

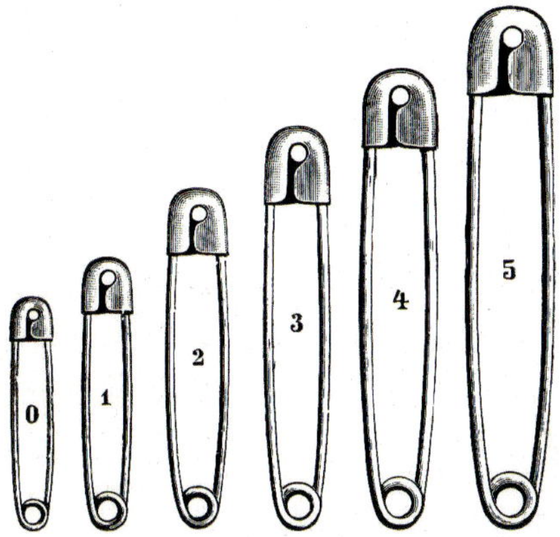

1910

1900 Stahl, vernickelt und lackiert, 2/0—5 und sortiert 0—4 .... Ladenpreis, nach Größe 5—10 Pf. das Dutzend
1925 **Stahl, Ia Qualität,** vernickelt u. lackiert, 0—5 u. sortiert 0—4 .. Ladenpreis, nach Größe 6—12 Pf. das Dutzend
1910 Stahl, doppelseitig, vernickelt u. lackiert, 0—5 u. sortiert 0—4 .. Ladenpreis, nach Größe 5—10 Pf. das Dutzend

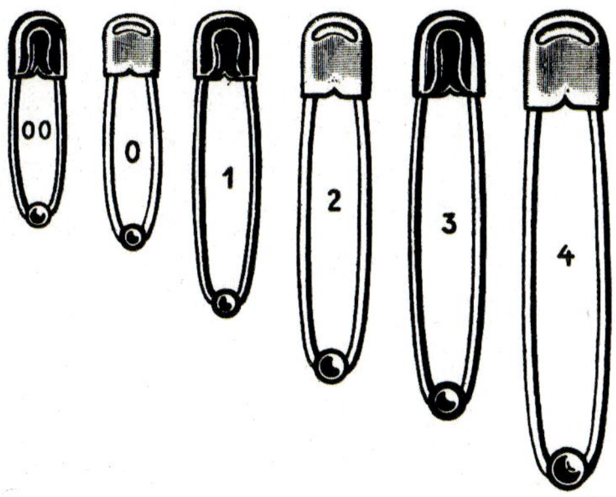

1926

Sicherheitsnadeln
auf Bügel

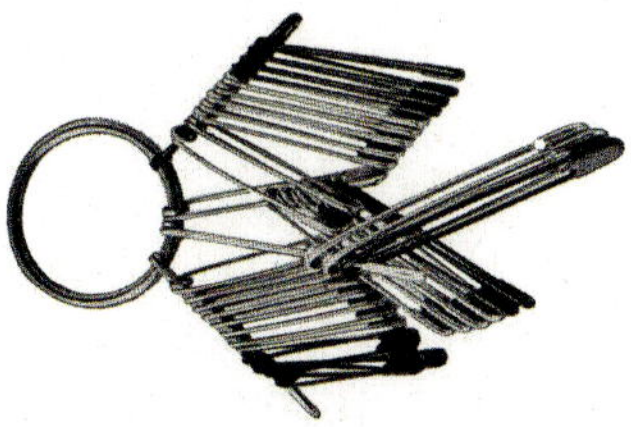

1800 1700 1901

1904

1926 **Kugel-Sicherheitsnadeln,** Stahl, vernickelt und lackiert, 2/0—5 und sortiert 0—4 Ladenpreis, nach Größe 12—20 Pf. das Dutzend
1800 **Schlüsselring** mit 36 Schildnadeln, 0—3 schwarz-weiß sortiert, 3 Dtz. im Karton .... Ladenpreis 10 Pf.
1700 **Schlüsselring** mit 24 Schildnadeln, 0—3 schwarz-weiß sortiert, 3 Dtz. im Karton .... Ladenpreis 8 Pf.
1901 **Schlüsselring** mit 36 Stahlnadeln, 0—3 schwarz-weiß sortiert, 3 Dtz. im Karton .... Ladenpreis 20 Pf.
1904 **Bügel** mit 36 vergoldeten Messingsicherheitsnadeln, 3/0—0, 3 Dtz. im Karton .... Ladenpreis 20 Pf.

102/5½

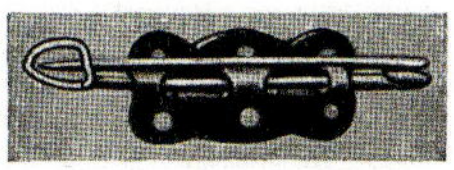

10

Schleifennadeln

Sicherheitsnadeln 102, Größe 5½ und 6, Messing versilbert
Schleifennadeln 10, mit Platte, Stahl vernickelt

Sewing accessories.

Making repairs after arriving in Africa. *Bundesarchiv-Bild-101I-782-0050-16, Foto: Borchert, Erich (Eric), 1941 Frühling*

Tailors hard at work.

CHAPTER 9 ENDNOTES

1. The Welt-Wachs-Werk, Dresden, Germany, was founded in 1890. In 1934, it was renamed Eg-Gü Werke, Günthers-Söhne, Dresden. It went bankrupt in 2005. Here are some wartime advertisements.

2. The Werner & Mertz A.G., Erdalfabrik, Mainz, Germany, was founded in 1867. The famous Erdal frog was introduced in 1903. By 1921, Erdal was the best-selling brand of shoe care products in Germany. In 1944, almost 80% of the factory was destroyed. The company is still in business. Here are a few wartime advertisements.

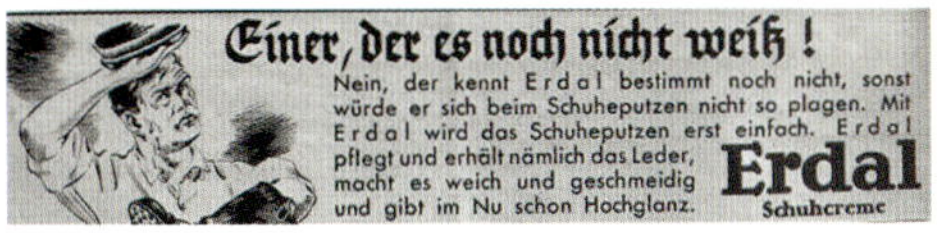

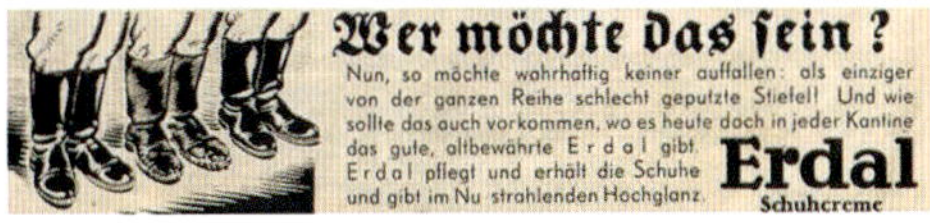

3. No history was found on the Immalin factory. Here is their listing in the 1929 Mosse Register of Firms.

IMMALIN
Putzmittel
Chem. Fabrik Eisendrath
G. m. b. H.
Fernsprecher: 851–854

4. The Salamander brand name was introduced in 1922. Salamander products are still being sold worldwide.

5. The Esslen and Company, Berlin, Germany, was founded in 1918, bringing the Collonil brand to life. In the 1930s, the first branch factory was established in Vienna. The firm started producing specialized products for skiing and mountain climbing. The company survived the war without major damage to its factories. The company is still in business. Here is the firm's listing in the 1941 Berlin phone book.

Esslen &Co.GmbH.+ chem.Fabr.
Mühlbk Kastanienallee 48 40 52
+ Mühlenbeck 2 24

6. No history was found on the Sternolin-Werke, Erkelenz, Germany. Here is their listing in the 1929 Mosse Register of Firms.

Chem.-techn. Artikel (Fabr.)
×„Sternolin" Fabrik chemisch technischer Produkte Heinrich Wilden. Ps 37559 Kn.

7. No history was found on the Eri brand name. Here is a prewar advertisement.

8. No history was found on the firm of Carl Gentner, Göppingen, Germany. It was operating in the early 1920s and most references state that the factory is closed. However, Nigrin brand car care products are still being produced. The current firm may share a history with the original firm, since it uses the "man-carrying-ladder" logo. Here are some prewar advertisements.

9. The firm of Rud. Starcke in Melle i/H, Germany, traces its history back to 1720. It is still in business as Starcke GmbH & Co. KG. Here is a prewar bill.

10. The firm of Adolf Krebs, Mannheim, Germany, was founded in 1891. In 1938, Pilo Werk was incorporated as a branch plant of the Thompson-Werke. I did not find any references for Pilo products after WWII. Here are some wartime bills.

11. G.A. Glafey, Nürnberg, Germany, was founded in 1808. They are known as producers of candles and lighting. The company is still in business today as Glafey Licht. Here is their listing in the 1929 Mosse Register of Firms.

Glafey, G. A. (Carl u. Gottlob. u. Rolf Gl., ☎ 23550, Nachtlichtefabr., Frauenholzstr. 10. Ps 140. RUC.

12. The Boston Blacking Company was founded in Oberursel, Germany, as the sister company to the Boston Blacking Company, Boston-Chelsea/Massachusetts (founded 1889). In 1930, the name "Bostik" was used for trademarked products. In 1939, the firm was classified as a war essential company. It was tasked with the repair and treatment of soldiers' boots and shoes. The firm continued to operate until 1991. Here is their listing in the 1929 Mosse Register of Firms.

Boston Blacking
Company G. m. b. H.
Oberursel b. Frankfurt a. M.

Chemische Fabrik

13. No history was found on the Solo, AG firm factory. Here is a wartime advertisement.

„Solo" Zündwaren- u. chemische Fabriken-Akt. Ges.
I/1 Hohenstaufeng 6
✶ U 2 65 95

14. Trab-Trab shoe polish was manufactured by Dr. Julius Fuchs, Stuttgart, Germany, which was founded in 1904. In 2010, the company was taken over by Detlef Weik under the name "Büdo GmbH." Here is a prewar advertisement.

CHAPTER 10
SPECIALIZED CLOTHING AND MISCELLANEOUS

This final chapter is devoted to clothing items that were worn for health, hygiene, or safety reasons. Undergarments like underwear, shirts, long underwear, etc., were generally worn under other clothing to protect the skin, prevent the outer garments from being soiled by bodily secretions and discharges, to provide support for certain parts of the body like genitalia, or as part of a layering process to keep warm. Boiler suits, coveralls, or jumpsuits are one-piece garments with full-length sleeves and legs worn to protect standard uniform items and as a safety measure while conducting certain types of work. Coveralls were manufactured in a variety of materials and colors, including camouflage. Protective clothing was also produced in leather, since it was effective against wet weather and had some fire retardant properties.

Chemical warfare was a real concern for the German military and every effort was made to prepare the military for that contingency. By the start of the war, Germany was probably the best prepared—both offensively and defensively—for chemical warfare. For the individual soldier, the gas mask and gas cape (protective sheet) were carried on his person at all times. These two items would provide the minimum protective capability during a surprise attack. The gas cape is approximately seventy-eight inches long and forty-eight inches wide. It came in several colors and was made of paper, opanol-coated fabric, or nylon (per TM-E-30-451).

If there was an escalation in chemical warfare, the Germans had a wide variety of protective gear, decontamination equipment, and offensive weapons to employ. The light protective suit, while rarely seen outside of a training environment, was available if needed. It afforded much greater protection than the gas cape. The light protective suit varied in color from grayish-green to dark blue-gray, with light tan or khaki for tropical use. The light protective suit was also manufactured in marsh pattern camouflage.

The following intelligence report discussing German chemical defense equipment was published in *Tactical and Technical Trends*, No.15, German Gas Defense Equipment:

This report on German gas defense equipment was obtained from an examination of German material captured in North Africa.

a) Gastilt (Author's note: Commonly referred to as a gas plane or cape): The German gastilt, like the gas mask, is an item of general issue. It is a rubberized sheet and is designed primarily for protection of the person in surprise attacks of liquid vesicants. Four German gastilts, complete with pouches, were found to be of the type described as "rubberized fabric," and consisted of plain rectangular sheets approximately 6 1/2 feet by 4 feet. Three were black; the fourth was khaki in color. The khaki one bore the marking "Tp," a special German marking for supplies intended for use in the tropics. Three were contained in gray-green or gray canvas pouches; the fourth (not the one marked "Tp"), in a pouch of black American cloth-like material. Each gastilt has two corners marked with white-this indicates the corners which are held when the gastilt is opened for use-which bore the following markings: (bps 1140-80 op), (evw 12342 40/X, 80 op), (80 op 4/40/9 bft) and (bft-7-41/6-80 op-Tp) respectively. In every case the bottom corners were marked with a small square of green paint-presumably detector paint. The weight of the complete outfit (i.e., a single gastilt in pouch) was about 2 pounds. Regarding the material of which the tilts were made, it seems from the marking: 80 op and 80 op (Tp), taken in conjunction with the appearance of an item "gasplanen, oppanol" in a captured German ledger of antigas supplies, that these specimens are made of fabric treated with oppanol, a synthetic material consisting mainly or wholly of polymerized isobutylene, which is highly resistant to both mustard gas and lewisite and is made by the I.G. Farben Industrie at Oppau-hence the name oppanol.

b) German Light Antigas Clothing: The information at present available indicates that this outfit consists of a one-piece suit with short legs and an open back, thigh boots, gloves, and hood. The material of the suit is described as having an external fabric layer, the inner layer consisting of hardened gelatine. Penetration of vesicants through seams and creases is immediate, but unworn portions resist mustard gas up to 3 hours. The gloves and hood are described as being made of rubberized fabric. The seams appear to offer little or no resistance to penetration by vesicants. The legs of the boots appear to be of similar material to that of the gloves. This material resists vesicants well, but seams or creases, caused by folding, offer little resistance. The soles of the boots are of thick rubber and give long resistance to penetration by mustard gas (14 hours).

c) German Wax-Paper Gas Capes: This cape of green waxed paper measures about 70 by 46 inches and folds into about 6 by 7 1/2 inches. The paper consists of about 90 to 95 percent Swedish sulphite pulp, the balance of fibers being rag or jute waste. In its waxed state, 31 percent of the paper's total weight consists of white wax and 7 1/2 percent of a water extract which is almost certainly an alginate, and quite possibly sodium alginate. The purpose of the wax is to act as an external waterproofing agent and to counteract the brittle feel of the alginate. The alginate is employed as a binder instead of colophony (rosin), and as an inherent waterproofing agent to protect the paper at those points where creasing or cracking has impaired the efficiency of the wax. The green vegetable dye of a chlorozol type does not react as a gas detector. It is reported that when subjected to field trials, the paper cape was found to provide a high initial resistance to mustard gas, but resistance was considerably lowered by creasing.

The majority of the items pictured are manufactured for the army. Other members of the armed forces wore similar items.

The shapeless toque was a simple but effective means of protection from the cold. *Ed Stroh Collection*

The toque could be worn with almost any headgear. *Bundesarchiv-Bild-101I-287-0872-11, Foto: Koll, 1941/1942 Dezember-Januar*

Many different styles of ear protection were worn. *Ed Stroh Collection*

Panzer crew wearing ear protection. *Bundesarchiv-Bild-101I-215-0354-12A, Foto: Gebauer, 1941*

Wollsachen
FÜR UNSERE SOLDATEN

Abb. 1

Abb. 1. Der warme **Kopfschützer,** aus dicker weicher Wolle im Streifenmuster gestrickt, wird unter dem Helm getragen. Erforderlich: etwa 80 Gramm Dreidrahtwolle. Arbeitsbeschreibung auf dem Schnittbogen.

Wool balaclava. *Helmut Weitze, Hamburg*

6

ZUM SCHUTZ
gegen die Winterkälte

Abb. 14

Abb. 15

Abb. 16

Loved ones at home were encouraged to knit items for soldiers at the front.

Commercial ear protectors are frequently seen in wartime pictures. *OSTFRONT Militaria*

This photograph shows a pair of ear muffs in wear. *OSTFRONT Militaria*

A wide variety of gloves and mittens were issued to the German soldier.

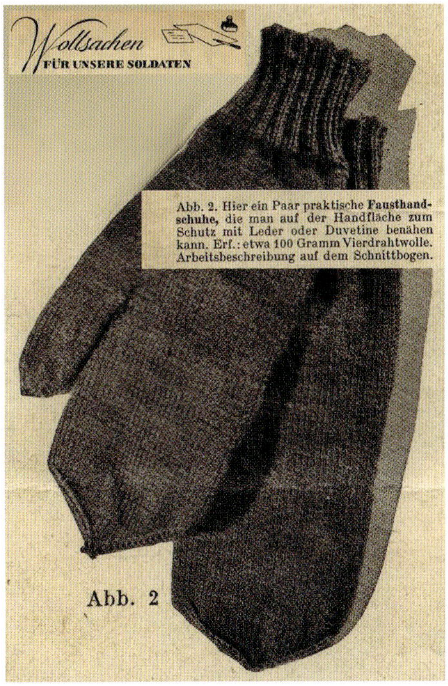

Wollsachen
FÜR UNSERE SOLDATEN

Abb. 2. Hier ein Paar praktische **Fausthandschuhe,** die man auf der Handfläche zum Schutz mit Leder oder Duvetine benähen kann. Erf.: etwa 100 Gramm Vierdrahtwolle. Arbeitsbeschreibung auf dem Schnittbogen.

Abb. 2

A style of mitten knitted by loved ones and mailed to the front.

Wristlets. *Ed Stroh Collection*

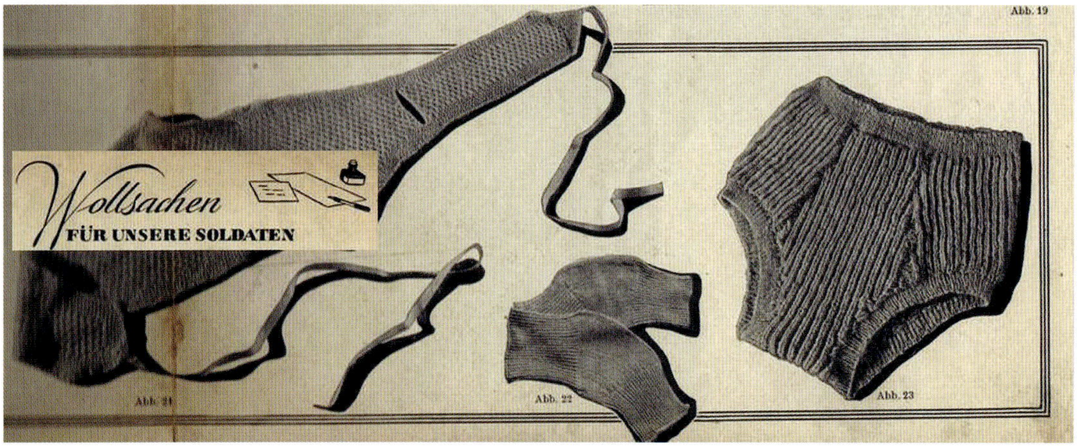

Knitted underwear, kidney warmers and anklets were popular knit items.

A complete set of quilted cold weather underwear. *The Collectors Guild*

Quilted underclothing as pictured in a US Army intelligence report.

A wide selection of cold weather underwear, both commercial and issue, were worn by the military.

Several knitted sweaters with green size rings.
Michael Davis of VirtualGrenadier

Two sweaters without size rings. *Helmut Weitze, Hamburg*

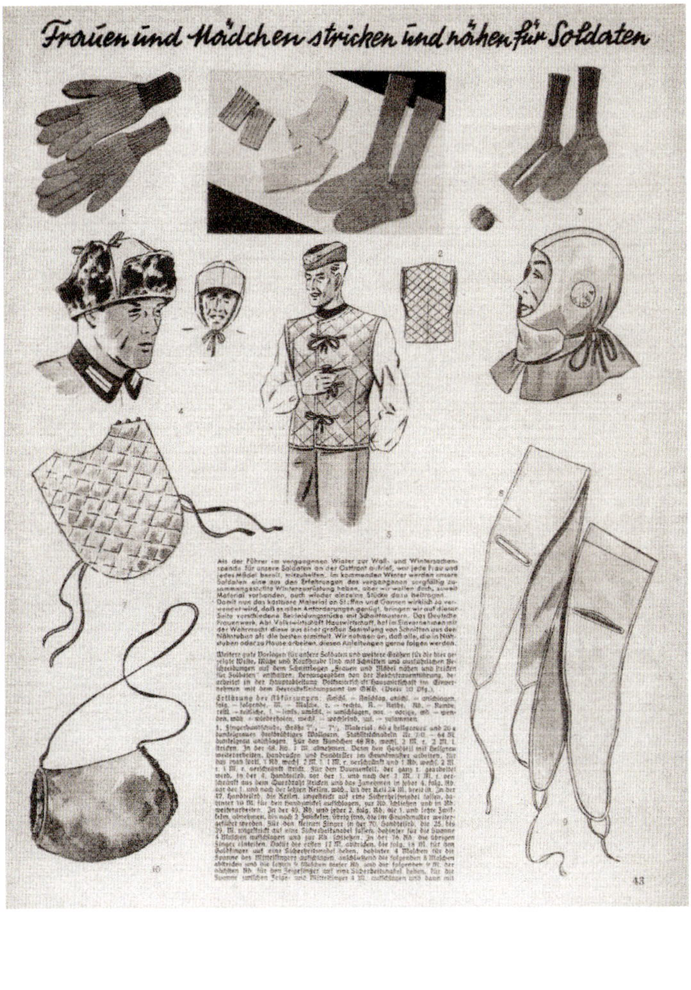

Frauen und Mädchen stricken und nähen für Soldaten

Sweaters and vests were popular items to knit for the troops.

Sweaters in wear.

Lightweight underwear for use in warm climates. *Ed Stroh Collection*

White shirts—both long and short sleeves—were manufactured for wear with dress and field uniforms.

Grey tricot shirts were manufactured with and without pockets.

White shirts were a common item of wear in the field.

Various styles of shirts in wear.

Various styles of shirts in wear.

A small selection of shirts manufactured for the German soldier.

It was fairly common to wear insignia on shirts.

The gas mask was carried at all times. *The Collectors Guild*

In the event of chemical warfare, the German soldier would have been issued the lightweight chemical protective suit.

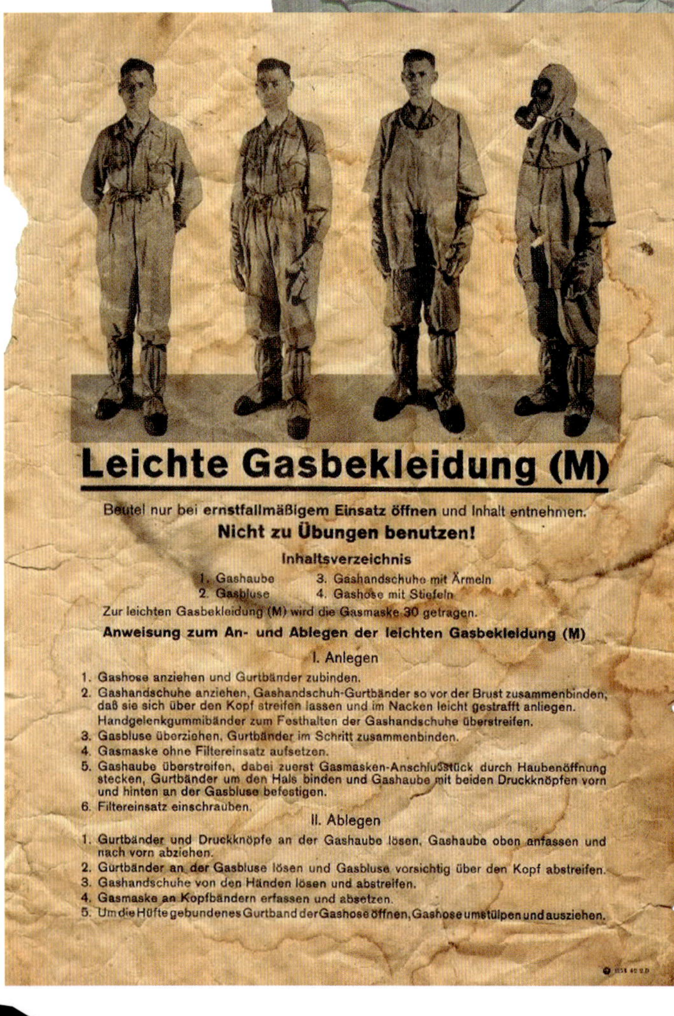

Leichte Gasbekleidung (M)

Beutel nur bei **ernstfallmäßigem Einsatz öffnen** und Inhalt entnehmen.

Nicht zu Übungen benutzen!

Inhaltsverzeichnis

1. Gashaube
2. Gasbluse
3. Gashandschuhe mit Ärmeln
4. Gashose mit Stiefeln

Zur leichten Gasbekleidung (M) wird die Gasmaske 30 getragen.

Anweisung zum An- und Ablegen der leichten Gasbekleidung (M)

I. Anlegen

1. Gashose anziehen und Gurtbänder zubinden.
2. Gashandschuhe anziehen, Gashandschuh-Gurtbänder so vor der Brust zusammenbinden, daß sie sich über den Kopf streifen lassen und im Nacken leicht gestrafft anliegen. Handgelenkgummibänder zum Festhalten der Gashandschuhe überstreifen.
3. Gasbluse überziehen, Gurtbänder im Schritt zusammenbinden.
4. Gasmaske ohne Filtereinsatz aufsetzen.
5. Gashaube überstreifen, dabei zuerst Gasmasken-Anschlußstück durch Haubenöffnung stecken, Gurtbänder um den Hals binden und Gashaube mit beiden Druckknöpfen vorn und hinten an der Gasbluse befestigen.
6. Filtereinsatz einschrauben.

II. Ablegen

1. Gurtbänder und Druckknöpfe an der Gashaube lösen, Gashaube oben anfassen und nach vorn abziehen.
2. Gurtbänder an der Gasbluse lösen und Gasbluse vorsichtig über den Kopf abstreifen.
3. Gashandschuhe von den Händen lösen und abstreifen.
4. Gasmaske an Kopfbändern erfassen und absetzen.
5. Um die Hüfte gebundenes Gurtband der Gashose öffnen, Gashose umstülpen und ausziehen.

Instruction sheet for the light chemical protective suit.

The chemical protective suit was also manufactured in camouflage. *The Collectors Guild*

The Gas Plane was carried by the German soldier as an emergency measure against chemical attacks.

Flamethrower in action.

The chemical protective suit in wear. *Jim Kreunen of Militaria Plaza*

This leather suit was manufactured for flamethrower operators. *Espenlaub Militaria*

Scarves were effective in keeping out dust.

Numerous styles of coveralls were produced for the German military.

This blue denim work jacket was worn by Panzer crews. *Gerard Stezelberger of Relic Hunter Militaria*

The soldier second from the right is wearing the blue denim work jacket. *Bundesarchiv-Bild-146-2005-0185, Foto: Broenner, 1943*

ANNEX 1
MICA AND LICO KITS

The Mica kit was a compact, compartmentalized, personal hygiene and grooming case that was very popular with military members. It was manufactured so that it could be transported in a mess kit. It contained everything a soldier would need to take care of his body, as well as his uniform. The firm of Willi Bilke, Hannover, applied for the patent for what became known as the Mica kit on July 28, 1933. The patent application read:

> [Class 18] A box or case for toilet and like articles has two hinged lids 2, 3 and an insert 6 which forms a false bottom and partitions dividing the two parts of the box into further compartments. One of the compartments, for material, such as soap, which becomes smaller in use, has a cover which fits within the compartment so as to clamp the soap in position. The partitions may be slidable to vary the capacity of the compartments. Clips 37 may be provided within one lid for holding post cards, a pencil, etc.

The firm of Gunther Wagner Blechwerk, Hannover, also manufactured the Lico kit, which was almost identical to the Mica kit.

Cover page for the Mica kit manual.

Mica kit in its original box.

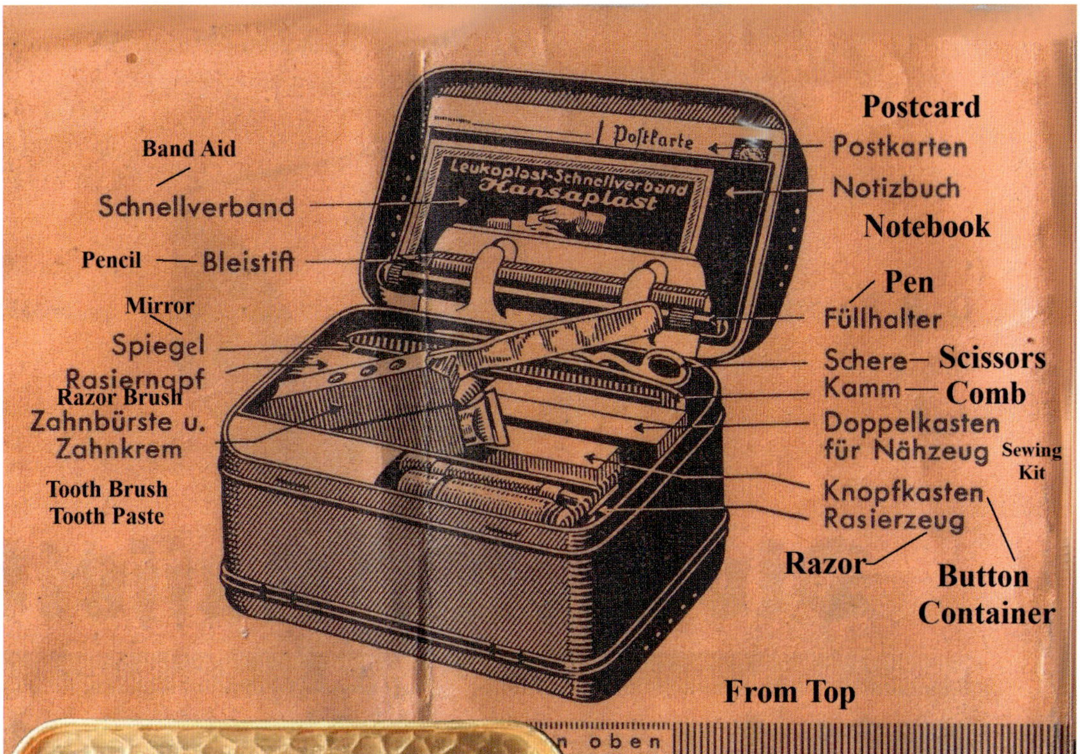

Contents of the upper portion of the Mica kit.

The upper portion of the kit with items properly stowed. *Thomas Bock Collection*

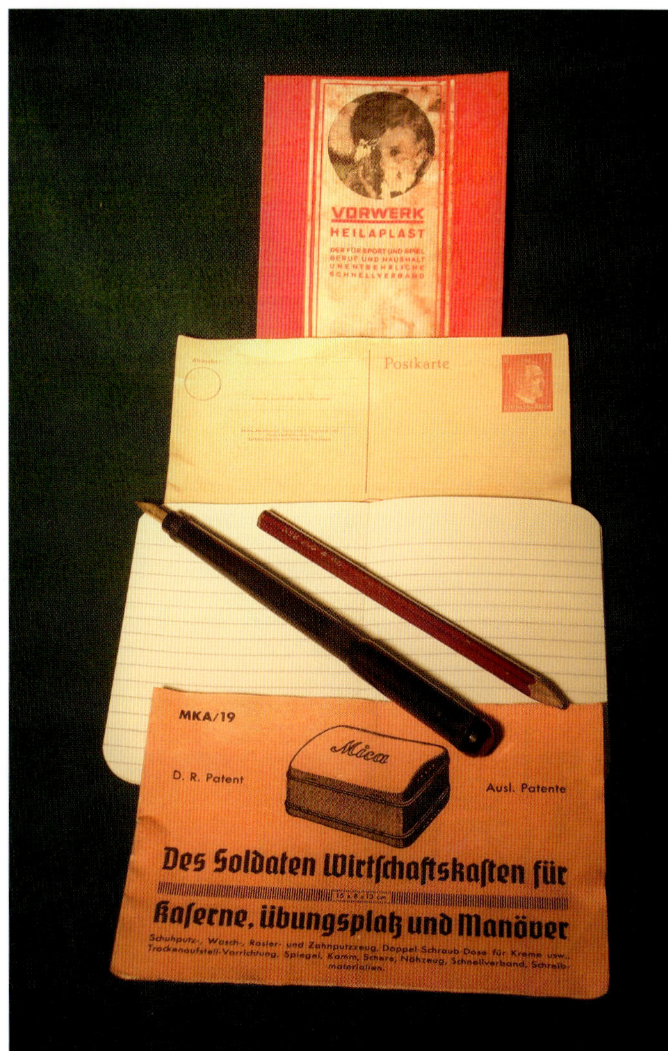

Writing materials and band aid. *Thomas Bock Collection*

Shaving gear. *Thomas Bock Collection*

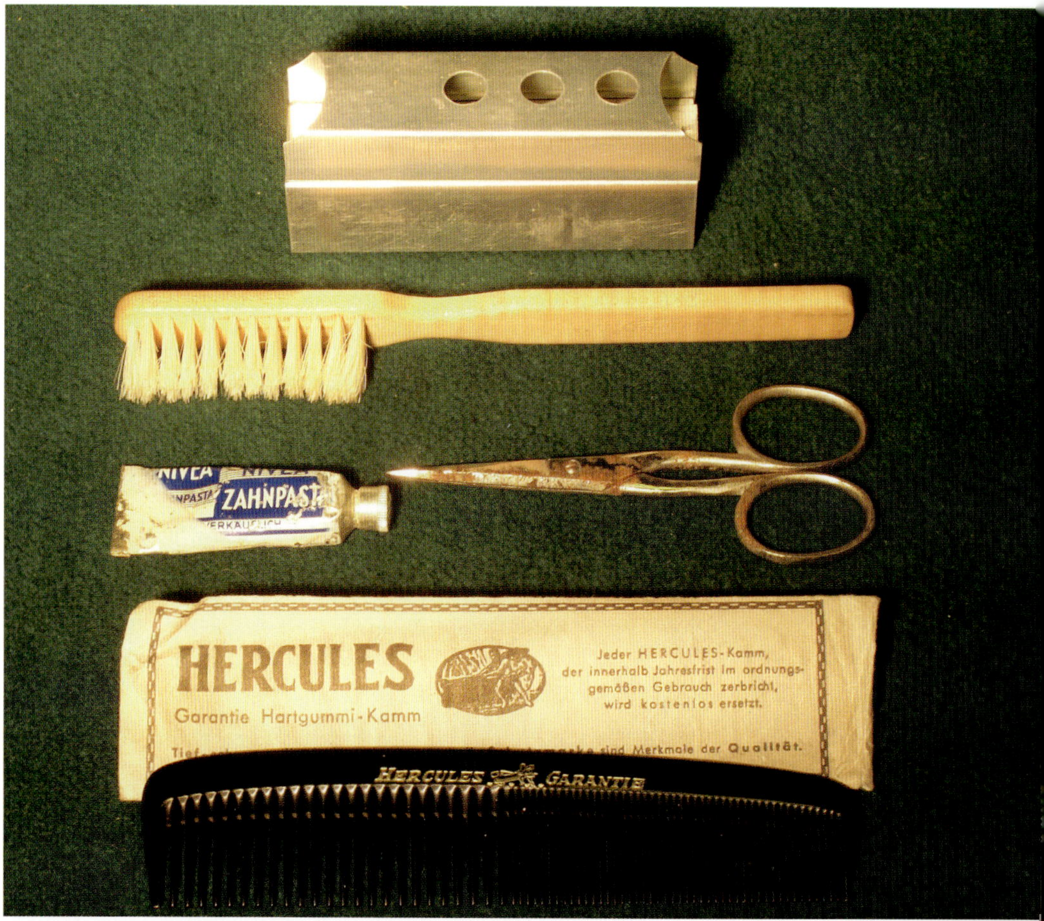

Shaving and grooming items. *Thomas Bock Collection*

Sewing items. *Thomas Bock Collection*

Miscellaneous items. *Thomas Bock Collection*

Contents of the lower half of the Mica kit.

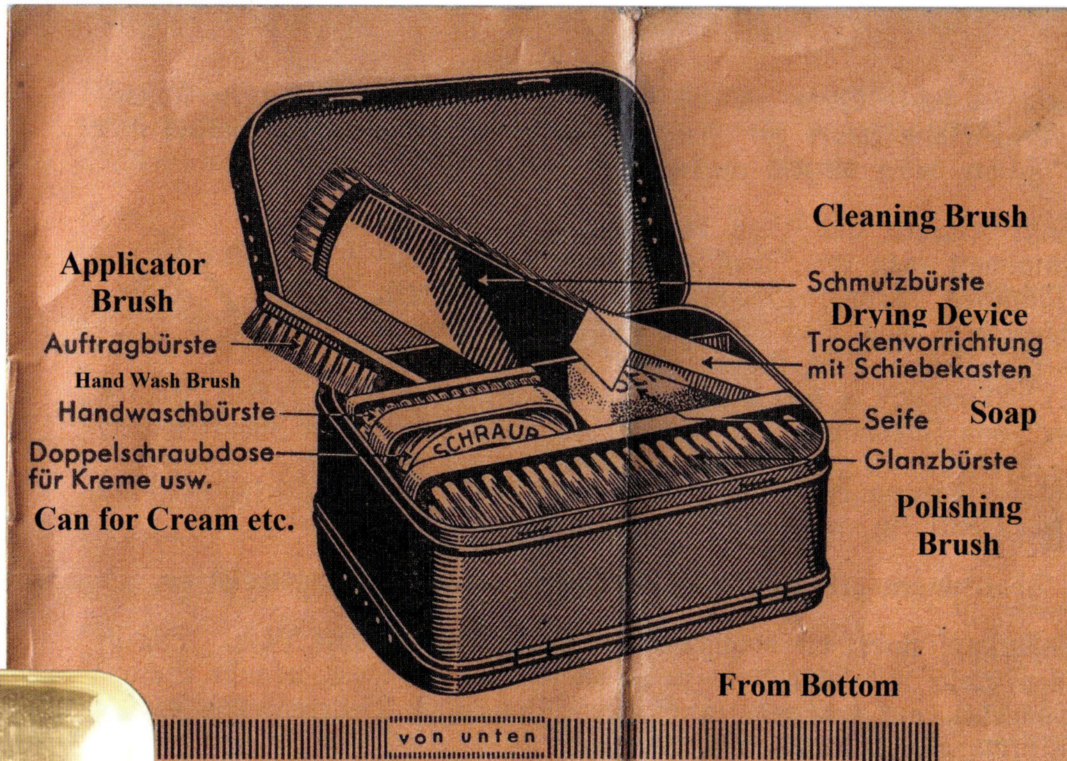

The bottom half of the kit with contents. *Thomas Bock Collection*

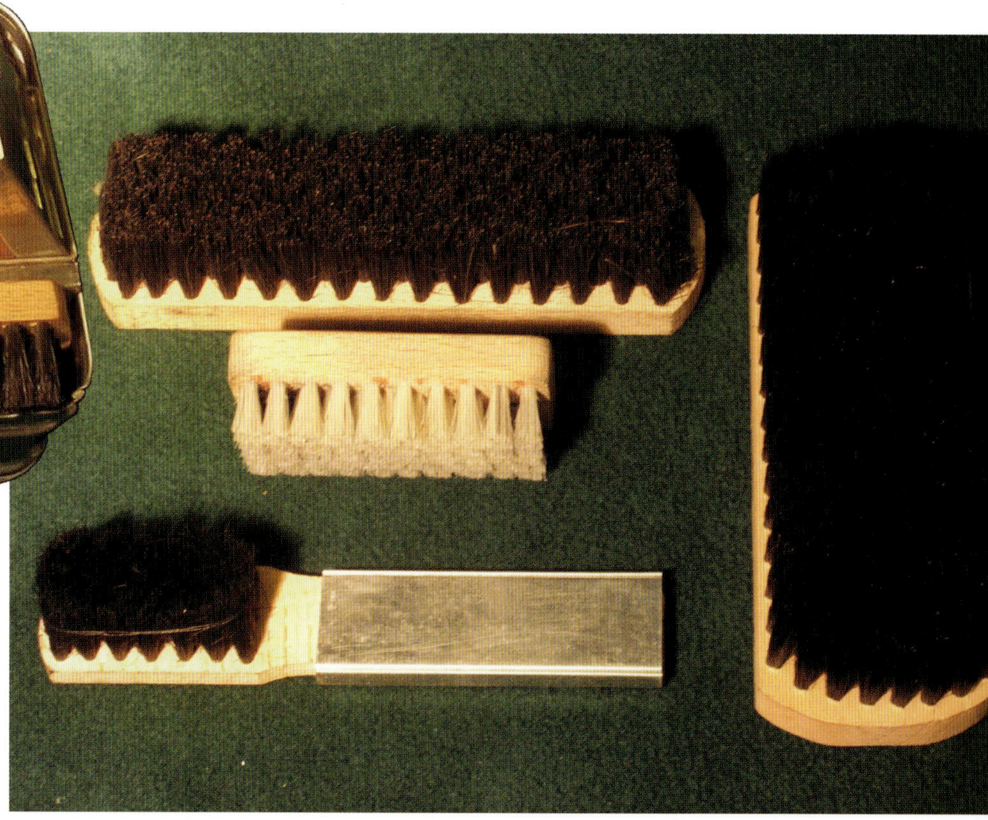

Brushes. *Thomas Bock Collection*

Soap. *Thomas Bock Collection*

Instructions on how to transport the kit.

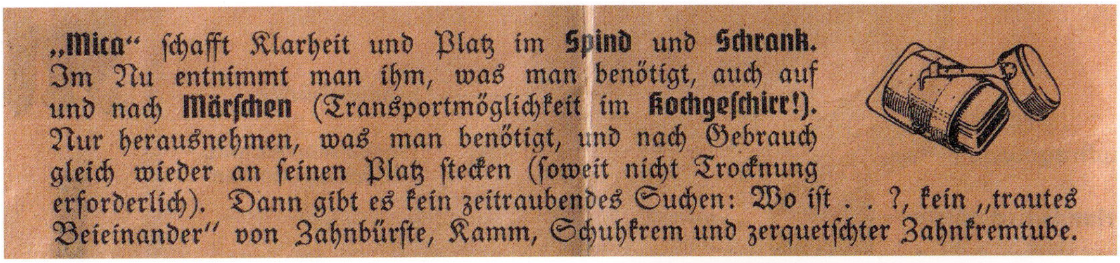
„**Mica**“ schafft Klarheit und Platz im **Spind** und **Schrank.** Im Nu entnimmt man ihm, was man benötigt, auch auf und nach **Märschen** (Transportmöglichkeit im **Kochgeschirr!**). Nur herausnehmen, was man benötigt, und nach Gebrauch gleich wieder an seinen Platz stecken (soweit nicht Trocknung erforderlich). Dann gibt es kein zeitraubendes Suchen: Wo ist . . ?, kein „trautes Beieinander“ von Zahnbürste, Kamm, Schuhkrem und zerquetschter Zahnkremtube.

A variation of the Mica kit with smooth cover. *OSTFRONT Militaria*

Mica kit stored inside a mess kit. *Thomas Bock Collection*

The Lico kit.

Lico kit. *OSTFRONT Militaria*

Diagram for the upper half of the kit.

The upper half of the Lico kit. *OSTFRONT Militaria*

Diagram of the lower portion of the kit.

The lower half of the Lico kit. *OSTFRONT Militaria*

ANNEX 2
MILITARY ARCHEOLOGY - ONE MAN'S STORY

Archaeology is the study of human activity in the past, primarily by recovering and analyzing cultural and environmental data left behind, including artifacts, architecture, human remains, etc. Archaeology is considered both a science and humanity and is a subfield of anthropology.

Military archaeology is a subfield of archaeology and deals with the excavation and study of artifacts relating to the military history of various cultures, wars, and regions. This includes weaponry, military buildings, rations, personal items, and warrior customs. From a collector's perspective, battlefield finds are another tool in determining the originality of specific artifacts. Another very important aspect of military archaeology—especially in respect to modern wars—is to recover and identify human remains and to ensure their proper burial.

Battlefield archaeology is the study of an area where a military action occurred. This may include battlefields with distinct boundaries where troop dispositions, numbers, and the order of battle are known from documented sources and also from undocumented evidence of a conflict. It is distinct from military history, in that it seeks to answer different questions, including the experiences and lives of ordinary soldiers. Battlefield archaeology generally avoids the reasoning behind a conflict or the strategy and tactics involved in a conflict, even though findings could reinforce, dispute, or offer different theories on how a battle was fought. The most famous example of battlefield archaeology was Dr. Douglas D. Scott's metal detecting and evaluation of the Little Bighorn Battlefield National Monument in 1983.

Jean-Loup Gassend (author of *Operation Dragoon: Autopsy of a Battle*) is a modern-day amateur military archaeologist who specializes in excavating the battlefields of WWII. In cases where bodies or ID tags are found, he works under the control of the Volksbund Deutsches Kriegsgräberfürsorge (the Volksbund, or German War Graves Commission). He has been involved in exhuming fifteen bodies in South France and finding an ID tag forgotten at a former exhumation site that enabled the soldier to be identified; ten identifications in all. The rest of this story, as well as the accompanying photographs, were provided by Jean-Loup Gassend:

> WWII was the most deadly conflict in the history of mankind, causing the deaths of over sixty million people. Germany alone suffered approximately eight million dead, of which approximately 5.5 million were members of the German Army. Most of these soldiers were buried in the general area where they were killed; in other words, close to the battle fronts—sometimes in organized military cemeteries, but often in field graves or trenches at the very place where they died. In cases when the dead were buried by civilians or enemy troops, standard administrative and identification procedures were not always followed and the fates of these men remained unknown to their next of kin. When soldiers died in remote areas (mountains, swamps, deserts), they sometimes simply remained undiscovered where they fell, without even being buried. In the Soviet Union, German cemeteries were deliberately destroyed by the Soviet government. The result is that after the war, large numbers of missing in action cases remained to be solved and millions of unmarked or clandestine German military graves were present all over Europe and North Africa.
>
> The German Volksbund is a private organization tasked with tending to German military graves. Their mission includes:
>
> a. Maintaining existing German military cemeteries.
> b. Finding as many unmarked and clandestine graves as possible, exhuming and identifying the bodies they contain, and reburying them in German military cemeteries.
> c. Informing the next of kin of the locations of the graves.
>
> Today, the Volksbund maintains 827 cemeteries in forty-five countries and performs roughly 30,000 exhumations per year—mostly in Russia. Insufficient funding, coupled with a large workload, has forced the Volksbund to utilize what some might call rather primitive methods to exhume and identify remains. Identification is almost invariably conducted using two methods: the first is the search for the identification tag (ID tag) or other artifacts that may have personal information about the soldier on them. If no such objects are discovered, the body is declared unknown. This is where the second identification method comes in: information about any identified bodies and units in close proximity of the unknown remains are cross-checked with data in the Deutsche Dienststelle (German Military Archive, also

known as WASt). If unknown soldiers are found in the same area as identified bodies they are checked to see if they belonged to the same unit. If a match is found, the search is expanded to see if there were any soldiers listed as missing in action. These missing soldiers are then considered to be amongst the unidentified bodies. Because of the lack of funds and the lack of any proper databases for comparison, no other identification methods—such as dental records or DNA—are normally used. No attempt is made to discover the cause of death or to do any type of anthropological analysis of the remains.

The great majority of identifications are made thanks to the ID tag that every German soldier was required to carry around his neck. WWII-era German ID tags were composed of a disk that was precut down the middle so that it could easily be broken in half. The soldier's personal information was stamped onto each half of the tag. In the event of death, one half of the tag was to be kept for administrative purposes, while the other half was to be buried with the body to allow for future identification. The personal information stamped onto the tag was a unit number and a serial number. The soldier's actual name, date of birth, or hometown was never written on the tag. The decoding of the information on the tag can only be done by the WASt in Berlin, a process which usually takes a few months.

A standard identity disc for a member of the army.

Jean-Loup Gassend in his element.

A member of the Volksbund talking to journalists about the progress of an excavation.

The following is the account of one of Jean-Loup's digs in Southern France.

1. Background: The Maritime Alps region is located in the southeastern corner of France, adjacent to the Mediterranean coast and Italy. In 1944, the region was occupied by 15,000 German soldiers of the 148th Reserve Division. On August 15, 1944, the Allied 7th Army performed a massive landing just west of the Maritime Alps. While most of this army headed west and north, a small detachment—the 1st Airborne Task Force (FABTF)—was given the mission of liberating the Maritime Alps. Between August 15 and September 6, 1944, the FABTF liberated 90% of the region, pushing back the 148th Reserve Division. The remaining 10% of the region—mostly composed of mountains—was only liberated in April 1945.

During the fighting against the FABTF, approximately 300 German soldiers were killed in the Maritime Alps. Most were buried by French civilians, usually in local cemeteries or in graves on the battlefields. These graves were normally marked and the local administration was aware of their existence. In the postwar years, the Volksbund and local town halls cooperated with each other concerning information on the existence of graves. In 1958, the Volksbund sent several teams of workers to the Maritime Alps who, in a few months, located and exhumed all the known graves of German soldiers and reburied them at the Dagneux German Military Cemetery near Lyon, France.

However, a few graves remained undiscovered. For unknown reasons, a large mass grave near the village of Villeneuve-Loubet was not found by the Volksbund, although the inhabitants of Villeneuve-Loubet were well aware of its existence. Villeneuve-Loubet is located near the Mediterranean coast, 10km [6.2 miles] west of the city of Nice. Fighting between the 1st Special Service Force and units of the 148th Reserve Division occurred there between August 24 and 26, 1944. After the battle, local civilians dug a large mass grave in a field near the town in which they buried the bodies of all the Germans who had been killed. When interviewed in 2006, the elders of Villeneuve-Loubet willingly told us about the existence of the grave, so it was decided to attempt to locate it.

2. Purpose: To describe all the steps that were required for the full investigation of a mass grave dating from August 1944 that contained the bodies of fourteen German Army soldiers of the 148th Reserve Division. This description will include the often overlooked aspect of the actual search for the exact grave site and will also present the results of the exhumation and identification process. I will then discuss several particular points of interest that arose in the process of our work. The main goal of the exhumation was to identify and rebury the bodies and inform the next of kin of their recovery.

3. Methods:
3.1. Techniques used to locate clandestine graves: Searching for a clandestine grave after sixty-two years can be an extremely difficult task that the average forensic worker has no experience with. For this reason, I will describe the search process in detail. Several methods can be used to attempt to locate a clandestine or unmarked grave, including:

a. Analysis of witness accounts and archival information.
b. Observation of the area to spot a depression, abnormal vegetation, or anything remarkable.
c. Use of a metal detector to try to locate relevant objects in or near the grave.
d. Use of a metallic probe inserted into the earth to feel differences in earth density at the grave site or to actually "feel" bones or other buried artifacts.
e. Observation of old or modern aerial photos to attempt to see the grave.
f. Use of cadaver dogs to attempt to smell the presence of the grave.
g. Use of "ground penetrating radar" to locate objects in the ground or disturbances in the earth.

3.2. Initial interviews: We started by interviewing all available elder inhabitants of Villeneuve-Loubet. These witnesses agreed the grave had been dug by locals and was located beside a small creek named the Mardaric, but the accounts varied greatly concerning exactly where along the Mardaric the grave was and how many bodies it contained. The probable location after the interviews was a square approximately 20m [65.6ft] large and 500m [1,541ft] long parallel to the Mardaric, in a wooded area that was formerly a field. Estimates of the number of bodies varied between fourteen and more than thirty.

3.3. Methods used in Villeneuve-Loubet: The area where the grave was supposed to be located was overgrown with trees, weeds, and bushes. Observation of the area did not yield any clues to the presence of the grave. Metal detecting proved fruitless, since the area was heavily polluted with modern metallic debris. Probing such a large area with a metallic probe was extremely difficult due to the large area to be covered, the presence of stones and roots, and the possibility the grave may be very deep. Ground penetrating radar and archival information was not available. Cadaver dogs would be of no use considering the age of the grave. When it comes to bodies that have been buried for several decades, ethical questions are frequently brought up by members of the public. The purpose of conducting an exhumation is not always so obvious. However, we were able to explain that the exhumation was necessary in order to identify the bodies, inform the next of kin, answer historical questions, and to provide the soldiers a dignified burial worthy of their sacrifice. Family members were located for four out of the seven identified men, although contacting them was more difficult than for the average German soldier's family because of the Silesian origins of most of them. Siblings or children were still alive in three cases. Most of these next of kin expressed gratitude about our work.

I believe every country has a responsibility to search for their missing soldiers to bring closure to any next of kin and provide them a proper burial worthy of their sacrifice. Today, hundreds of thousands of missing German soldiers are still buried in field graves throughout Europe. Often the local authorities are aware of the presence of these graves but remain inactive. Even the grave of the father of former German Chancellor Gerhard Schröder was only recently found in Romania.

A variety of items were recovered from German grave sites near the southern France invasion beaches. The German soldiers were killed in encounters with American airborne units and the First Special Service Force.

ANNEX 3
THE GERMAN TEXTILE INDUSTRY, FIBERS, AND DYES

As the prices of German militaria continue to rise, so do the activities of counterfeiters trying to fool unsuspecting collectors. The more information the average collector has about period manufacturing techniques and raw materials the less susceptible they will be to being conned.

While writing Volume II of *Rations of the German Wehrmacht in World War II*, I stumbled upon a treasure trove of wartime intelligence reports. These reports were written by the British Intelligence Objectives Sub Committee (BIOS) and covered a wide spectrum of subjects, from food to rockets. The reports were a joint venture between British and American intelligence communities. While the reports are pretty detailed, they should not be considered all inclusive. Many documents were destroyed during the war and the analysts had to rely on personal accounts that cannot be considered 100% reliable. The analysts also did not have access to factories, personnel, or information in the Soviet occupation zone. The following BIOS reports were used in writing this Annex: *The Development of New Dyes and Colour Application Processes in Germany and Italy during World War II and Der Zellwolle-Lehrspinnerei G.m.b.H.-Its Potential Value to Dyestuff and Textile Chemical Auxiliary Development, Infra Red Reflectance of Coloured Textiles and Other Materials, Dyes-Intermediates and Pharmaceutical Processes, Report on the Progress of the German Textile Industry during the War, German Progress in Products and Processes for Cellulosic Textiles, Textile Printing in Germany*, and *German Textile Industry*.

The intelligence reports did not provide a good overview of the German textile industry as far as production totals, number of mills, etc. I was able to piece together some of that information from the various reports. In 1938, the German production of artificial silk was 72,000 tons and spun rayon was 189,000 tons. During 1943–44, the following production figures were provided: 96,000 tons of continuous filament rayon of all types and 320,000 tons of Zellwolle (rayon staple) of 178 different types, origin, denier, staple lengths, and characteristics; 200,000 tons of all sorts of reclaimed fibers; 13,000 tons of wool and angora (no artificial casein fiber due to the necessity of conserving the protein food supply); practically no cotton, versus a prewar consumption of 350,000 tons accounting for 40% of the total fiber used; six tons of silk produced at home, along with an effort to increase the production of Perlon (Nylon) and PeCe (Polyvinyl chloride)—no production figures were available on the production of Perlon and PeCe—; and 75,000 tons of flax and hemp, of which 10,000 was domestic.

While a good overview of the wartime German textile industry proved elusive, excellent studies of countries occupied by Germany were provided in the eleven-volume series *Elimination of German Resources for War, Volumes 1-11*. I decided to concentrate my discussion on France to demonstrate how the economies of the occupied countries operated under German control. What follows is an analysis of the French textile industry as part of the overall German war effort. This information was mostly derived from hearings conducted by the United States congress after the war. I also integrated information from other intelligence reports into the congressional report where needed.

The German invasion of France in 1940 was so swift that large stocks of raw materials and mills fell into German hands before they could be destroyed. German economic officers quickly took control of mill warehouses, conducted inventories of all warehouses and manufacturers, and in some locations began moving supplies to Germany. However, the practice of moving stocks and semi-finished goods to Germany was quickly stopped to save labor costs. It was decided to have the materials manufactured in France. In August 1940, it was estimated there were 550,000 bales of cotton in France. There was no information on the amount of wool and other fibers captured by the Germans in 1940.

The Kehrl plan (named for Hans Kehrl, secretary in the Ministry of Armament) was negotiated to cover the delivery of textiles to Germany for the period June 1940 to October 1941. Under this plan, the French delivered one-third of the 1940 wool clip, two-thirds of the 1941 clip, and large quantities of semi-finished textiles as follows: 30,000 metric tons of greasy wool, 5,593 metric tons of carded wool, 6,000 metric tons of wool combings and waste, 2,217 metric tons of wool cloth and yarn, 24,000 metric tons of cotton, 2,500 metric tons of jute, and 50,000 metric tons of rags (one-half wool). In return, the Germans made available 80,000 metric tons of wood pulp for rayon manufacture. This would allow France to triple its output of artificial fiber, but part of the output was to be returned to Germany in the form of fiber or cloth.

A second Kehrl plan was negotiated for the period October 1941 to October 1942. Under this plan, it was assumed that 150,000 metric tons of materials would be available in France, with one-third to be delivered to Germany in the form of raw, semi-finished, or finished materials. Although the German deliveries of wood pulp under the first Kehrl plan were not completed until midsummer 1942, the French were not excused from shipping the negotiated quantities of rayon to

Germany by October 1941. The second Kehrl plan, on the presumption that future deliveries of wood pulp would be on time, called for the rayon shipments by the French equivalent to those made under the first plan. The Germans were also allowed to purchase "manufactured textile products which are not indispensable for French needs, such as decorative fabrics for theaters and cinemas, tapestries, carpets, upholstery fabrics" up to a total of 10 million Reichsmarks. In a related agreement, the Germans—facing their first winter in Russia—demanded 100,000 woolskins a month, but after six months of negotiation, the quantity was reduced to 50,000 a month.

A third Kehrl plan was negotiated for the period October 1942 to October 1943. Under this plan, the Germans were able to get 78% of the estimated wool, 50% of the estimated cotton, and 67% of the estimated flax supplies—both raw and manufactured goods—along with quantities of other textile materials and goods as follows: 7,800 metric tons of wool (washed or manufactured), 3,100 metric tons of cotton (raw or manufactured—half had to be American cotton), 8,400 metric tons of flax tow (in yarn or fabrics), 20,000 metric tons of rags (one-third wool), 2,200 metric tons of animal hair, and 20,000 metric tons of rayon (fiber or in fabrics).

The wool requisition was based on 10,000 metric tons of washed wool being available (80% from sheep in France and the remainder from North Africa). The French were able to cheat the occupiers by under-reporting the sheep population and using a lower wool yield per sheep figure (1,000 grams of wool per washed sheep versus the prewar figure of 1,200 grams).

The cotton requisition was based on 6,200 metric tons of cotton being available.

The flax tow requisition was based on a production level of 13,200 metric tons. If actual production exceeded the estimate then 50% of the excess would go to Germany.

As in previous plans, the Germans would deliver "subject to deliverability" 60,000 metric tons of wood pulp for rayon manufacture (one-third of which was to be returned to Germany in the form of fiber or cloth). The French were also allowed to purchase 20,000 metric tons of bisulphate wood pulp; 18,000 metric tons of "soda pulp paper" (used to make binder twine); 10,000 metric tons of binder twine manufactured in Germany, Belgium, or Holland; 20,000 metric tons of bisulphate paper for twisting into cord; and 200 metric tons of bemberg rayon. None of the twine or cord had to be sent back to Germany. Above and beyond the requisitioned items, the Germans were also allowed to purchase "manufactured textile products which are not indispensable for French needs" up to a total of ten million Reichsmarks. In all, the third Kehrl plan contemplated that over 60,000 metric tons of true textile fabrics were to go to Germany and over 70,000 would be available for the French.

The third Kehrl plan had barely gone into effect when the Allies invaded North Africa. This reduced the amount of wool requirement by 20% and lessened the supplies of other fibers, such as animal hairs. When other French possessions like Madagascar, West Africa, etc., were captured, supplies of cotton, sisal, and other fibers were no longer available.

After the loss of these French colonies, the supplies of textile materials available for metropolitan France (excluding hidden stocks and the German allocation) for the period ending October 1943 were: 3,000 metric tons of cotton; 2,000 metric tons (mostly black market) of washed wool; 9,000 metric tons of flax tow; 4,000 metric tons of hemp and neglected hard fibers; 6,000 metric tons of alpha grass; 2,000 metric tons of sisal; unknown quantities of hair (the collection of human hair from barber shops and beauty shops was compulsory in towns of 10,000 people or more); 10,000 metric tons of rags, mostly non-wool; 28,000 metric tons of rayon and 100 metric tons of lanital/nylon (mostly lanital). (Author's note: It is interesting to see that nylon/perlon, even in such small quantities, was available to the French civilian population.) It should be mentioned that the Germans purchased a lot of the available supplies under the guise "indispensable for French needs," as well as through the black market.

A fourth Kehrl plan was introduced to cover the period October 1943 to April 1944. Under this plan, the Germans were to get 4,000 metric tons of wool uniform cloth equivalent to 7,250 metric tons of raw wool, 15,000 metric tons of flax tow, and 7,000 metric tons of wool rags. The Germans would deliver "subject to possibilities of delivery" 60,000 metric tons of wood pulp for the manufacture of artificial fiber. By the second half of 1943, the Germans were relying less on the Kehrl plan for supplies and buying what they needed at high prices through semi-official German organizations, as well as the black market. The overall effect of these practices was the reduction of stocks of textiles for the French population to negligible levels.

Shortly after the armistice of 1940, the French textile industry, along with other industries, was reorganized along German lines. All national labor, employer, and other organizations harmful to economic activity were dissolved and all industrial activities were placed under the Minister Secretary of Industrial Production and Labor. A number of implementing decrees were issued that dissolved existing labor organizations and created Comites d'Organisation (organizing committees) for various industries and commercial enterprises. By late 1940, all national confederations for textile workers or employers were dissolved. A decree of October 26, 1940, created the organizing committee for the textile industry based in Paris. The goal of this reorganization was to centralize control of the textile industry and to make the most efficient use of plants, materials, and labor to meet the needs of the German occupation. Textile production and distribution were prioritized as follows:

a. German Military Requisitions (Rustung)
b. Other German requisitions and private orders (Verteidigt)
c. Colonial requirements (i.e., trade goods, etc., needed to obtain colonial products used largely by the Germans). This priority was eliminated after the Allies invaded North Africa.
d. French official requirements.
e. French technical and industrial requirements.
f. French civilian goods.

Members of the industry were organized into regional and local groups and paid dues. Only members in good standing could obtain the raw materials, fuel, power, etc., to market their goods. Jews and other groups or persons deemed undesirable were excluded from membership.

The "Social organization of occupation" law was passed on October 4, 1941 (it established an elaborate network of organizations for employers and workers), strictly regulating labor and industrial relations. The active population was divided into professional (occupational) "families," one for each section of French industry or commerce. Each "family" was divided into five classes: Employers, Managerial agents, Technical Administrative and Commercial personnel, salaried employees, and Workers. In each locality, the "family" members in each class would belong to a single "syndicate." Each syndicate was governed by an administrative council that selected a union to represent it at the regional level. Each union selected members to represent it in the national organization or "federation."

In addition to this organizational hierarchy, there was another interlocking system of social committees at the plant, as well as at the local, regional, and national levels. The social committees had authority over occupational and social issues, but not political or religious activities. They handled questions over salaries, education, hiring and firing practices, etc., but not plant management. Strikes and lockouts were banned.

After the Germans occupied France, the French textile industry could either comply with the German occupation forces or close their plants. For the most part plant owners accepted the German occupation. The Germans paid well for items they needed and there were ample opportunities to acquire properties put on the market by owners fleeing the country or forced out of business. Firms with overseas assets usually sent someone to manage their assets from abroad. Provisions were put in place preventing or limiting the ability of Germans acquiring French properties or moving equipment to Germany. French textile officials and mill owners also took steps to help their fellow citizens avoid the German labor draft.

When Germany occupied France in 1940, there were approximately 12,000 textile companies or firms in operation. The number of plants or shops involved in the textile industry was estimated at around 25,000. By the end of 1942, approximately 8,500 textile companies or firms were still in operation. There was no estimate given for the number of plants or shops in operation during the same time frame, however, it appears that smaller plants and home work shops were more impacted by the occupation than larger firms. The principal cause for the decline in the number of operating plants was a lack of raw materials and supplies, some of which was due to the allocation system dictated by the Germans. Other factors, such as fuel, power shortages, lack of specialized machinery, Allied bombings, German confiscation of equipment, sabotage, etc., led to the temporary or permanent closure of plants. Despite the number of firms that went out of business, most large plants were operational to some degree through war's end.

During the occupation, the Germans were the French textile industries' largest customer. It should be no surprise that the types of goods produced were driven by German orders. Military cloth for uniforms was the largest requirement. Mills in Sedan and elsewhere worked full time to turn out such fabric. To extend the quantities of natural fibers, the Germans instructed the French mills to mix an increasing percentage of reworked fibers and rayon staples with the natural fibers. Under the third Kehrl plan, wool cloth consisted of 50% wool, 30% rayon staple, and 20% rag ravelings (wool). Cotton goods for the Wehrmacht consisted of 16.6% cotton, 16.6% rayon, and 66.8% rayon staple. Civilian goods used a similar mix.

Mills in the Roubaix-Tourcoing region produced blankets for the Wehrmacht. In 1943, the flax and linen mills were engaged in producing linen fire hose linings. The net-making facilities, especially those at Calais and Caudry, manufactured mosquito netting and other camouflage nets.

The silk and rayon mills in the Lyon area produced parachute cloth for the Wehrmacht. Initially, they produced the cloth and manufactured the parachutes. However, since the finished products proved to be so defective, final assembly was transferred to Germany.

Strange as it may sound, *haute couture* (high fashion) thrived under the German occupation. The Germans showed an extraordinary interest in the industry, even trying to have the whole French *haute couture* industry moved to Berlin. Obviously this failed, but it might explain how the industry managed to acquire a generous share of the textiles set aside for the general French population. In 1941, the *haute couture* industry received 800 metric tons of supplies. In 1942, when German fashion houses were closed, the French industry still received 160 metric tons of supplies. Even in 1943, the industry received eighty metric tons of supplies, equivalent to the annual ration for 80,000 civilians.

The French civilian was granted 100 ration points a year for clothing. Even the poorest quality suit cost thirty ration points and a suit in exchange. But customers of the French fashion houses—many of them the wives or girlfriends of prominent German officials—only had to surrender fifteen ration points a season and contribute an additional 5% of the purchase price to the National Relief in exchange for a complete wardrobe.

The Germans never really attempted to gain full control over the French textile industry, except when it came to rayon production. The French Gillet-Carnot organization representing French rayon interests worked closely with the German Kunstseide und Zellwolle Ring before the war, laying the foundation for further collaboration under the occupation. In December 1940, most of the rayon production facilities in France were united under the France-Rayonne

The Germans showed a lot of interest in the French *haute couture* industry.

consortium. It was reported that the German Kunstseide und Zellwolle Ring contributed 33% of the capital in the form of patent rights and technical advice. A ten-year agreement was reached between the German Kunstseide und Zellwolle Ring and the France-Rayonne consortium, covering raw materials, processes, prices, and domestic and international markets.

After forming the France-Rayonne consortium, the French Textile Committee standardized the nomenclature for artificial fibers to correspond with the system used by the German Kunstseide und Zellwolle Ring. All types of artificial filaments (not just those having a cellulose base) were called Rayonne and all types of staple made from such filaments were called Fibranne. The compositions of the various filaments and staples were indicated by an accompanying word, for example, rayonne-nylon, rayonne-viscose, fibranne-acetate, fibranne-lanital, and so on.

From studies conducted in the immediate aftermath of the war, it appears that German yarn and cloth manufacturing industry was not as sophisticated as Britain or the United States. However, in the field of synthetic fibers, Germany was still a leader in research and development. Most of the machinery used in German factories was of British origin dating from 1932–34. These machines were manufactured specifically for cotton and wool products. As Germany's supplies of raw cotton and wool continued to dry up, German scientists and chemists produced synthetic fibers to replace them. However, very little in the way of resources was devoted to develop the machinery to properly use these new fibers. The old machinery and methods were simply modified to accommodate the new fibers. The Germans built an experimental plant at Denkendorf, near Stuttgart, to develop and test new machinery and fibers. This plant was financed jointly by the state and private industry. The following information was taken from the BIOS report *German Textile Industry*:

> There is one phase of this pilot plant's service which is very important, and that is that they actually test samples from every batch of synthetic fibers made by the fiber producers from a point of view of spinability. If these samples do not measure up in every way to the various tests, including spinning qualities, it is then up to the chemist who produces these fibers to make changes in this quality so that the fibers going to the textile mills will give them a minimum of trouble.
>
> Due to the almost lack of cotton and the scarcity of wool in Germany during war years, it was necessary to devise ways and means of bolstering the available natural fibers, such as wool and hemp and flax with synthetic fibers.

German Textile Industry's analysis of the German knitting industry was confined to the mills in the British, American, and French zones of occupation. The story of the German knitting mills during the Third Reich was one of substitution. In 1934, German yarn mixtures containing at least 30% Rayon Staple Fiber (Zellwolle) were made compulsory. The percentage of other fibers in cotton was raised to 50%, then 70%, and by September 1945, yarns containing any cotton are unknown. Wool yarns contained less than 50% staple fibers by the end of the war. This proved to be a hardship for makers of quality underwear and outerwear like Jantzen and Jaeger, whose brands were nonexistent by war's end.

Rayon could be blended with wool without seriously affecting the quality of the resulting fabric. A 20% mixture of rayon and wool had little effect on quality and even a 30% wool/rayon blend provided excellent results.

Another yarn that saw use during the war was *Flockenbast*, manufactured from seed flax, flax waste, and hemp. Garments made from this yarn were of very low quality due to unevenness and the quantity of shives. (A shive is a small piece of plant after it is crushed and broken into pieces before the fibers are extracted and combed.) This yarn was hard on the knitting machines and rough on the wearer's skin.

Streichgarn (shoddy, or inferior materials) were used in large quantities to produce coarse, low-grade garments. The bulk of this type of yarn was manufactured entirely from rags. Filament rayon was used in large quantities, both alone and mixed with Streichgarn and Flockenbast.

The training of German workers was excellent, as reflected in the quality of workmanship on finished garments. The apprenticeship period was eighteen months and included the study of fibers and training on various machines and techniques. Hand embroidery was very common in the garment business. Most mills employed a large number of home workers.

Prior to 1884, all textile staple fibers were made from natural fibers: wool, silk, cotton, and linen. By WWII, many fabrics were manufactured entirely of synthetic fibers or mixed with the natural fibers. Prior to the war, Germany was part of a robust global economy and freely traded on the open market. The I.G. Farben Company was one of, if not the largest chemical company in the world, with assets throughout Europe, North America, and South America. This partially explains why research and development in the field of chemistry was similar throughout the world. During the course of the war, Germany still had some access to the global market via occupied countries, neutral countries, and Axis allies.

Unless noted, the majority of the following information on fibers was taken from Bulletin 300, *Synthetic Fibers and Textiles, Agriculture Experiment Station, Kansas State College of Agriculture and Applied Science, April 1942.* The synthetic fibers described in the report are American, but German chemists produced similar products:

> A. Classification and Identification of Natural Fibers: Natural fibers are fibers derived from plants or animals. There are other natural fibers Hemp, Kenaf, Jute, Ramie, Alpaca, Sisal, Mohair as well as other fibers derived from animal hair which are not discussed.

NAME: Wool
DATE INTRODUCED: The oldest wool cloth ever found was discovered in a bog in Denmark and was dated to 1500 BC
DESCRIPTION: Wool is the hair, or fleece, of sheep.

NAME: Silk
DATE INTRODUCED: The process of raising silkworms and collecting the silk has been practiced in China for over 10,000 years.
DESCRIPTION: Silk is the fiber secreted by certain caterpillars and spiders to make their cocoons and webs.

NAME: Cotton
DATE INTRODUCED: Cotton has been grown in India/Pakistan for more than 6,000 years.
DESCRIPTION: Cotton is a soft fiber that grows around the seeds of the cotton plant.

NAME: Linen
DATE INTRODUCED: Common flax was one of the first crops humans cultivated for use. It is thought to have originated in the Mediterranean region of Europe.
DESCRIPTION: Linen is made from the flax plant.
OTHER NAMES: Flax

The following discussion was taken from *Classification and Identification of Synthetic Fibers*:

> Practically all synthetic textiles manufactured on a commercial basis from 1891 to 1938 were rayon, which are all kinds of synthetic fibers made from cellulose. Experimenters turned to sources other than cellulose from which to produce fibers. Casein from milk and soybeans are used to make protein fibers in much the same way as cellulose is utilized for rayon. The synthetic fibers which have attracted the most interest prior to WWII are those produced from plastics or resins. These are produced by completely synthetic methods, for they are made from raw materials such as coal, oil, natural gas, or other sources of organic compounds.
>
> The following classification of synthetic textiles has been proposed:

A. Rayons-Fibers made from a natural cellulose base: viscose, acetate.
B. Prolons-Fibers made from a natural protein base: casein, soybean, chitin.
C. Synthons-Fibers made from organic substances which have been synthesized from simple raw materials: nylon, vinyon.
D. Glass-Fibers of fine glass filaments.
E. Miscellaneous-Fibers made from other natural bases: alginate, cuprammonium.

> The period of 1884 to 1939 saw the development of rayon's from cellulose. A patent was granted in 1884 by the French government to Count Hilaire de Chardonnet (1840-1924) of Besacon, France, for making of artificial silk from nitrocellulose. In 1891 this became the first synthetic textile to be produced on a successful commercial basis. Developments of synthetic fibers were spectacular and rapid both in the United States and the European countries. The late Dr. Arthur D. Little (1863-1935) of Boston, Mass., one of the pioneer textile chemists, in 1921 spun silk-like fibers in his laboratory made from pig's ears which were in turn woven into fabric for a purse, thus refuting the ancient proverb that "You can't make a silk purse out of a sow's ear."
>
> After the factories were set up in France to produce synthetic textiles, chemists and physicists in Germany, England and the United States worked to perfect a fiber. The product at first was undesirable and went under the name of 'artificial silk' because it resembled silk and was regarded as a cheap substitute for this superior fiber. The synthetic textile fibers by 1920 had made a place for themselves and now are not regarded as substitutes for the natural fibers. They have inherent values of their own; some are superior and even preferred to the natural fibers. The term "rayon" was adopted in the United States in 1924 for the various kinds of synthetic textile yarns which were known as artificial silk. By WWII the rayon's constituted the bulk of the synthetic fiber production in the world. Rayon is a textile fiber made from cellulose. It is manufactured from spruce wood and cotton linters, the short fine fibers that cling to the cotton seed after the long fibers have been removed. It's manufactured by dissolving spruce wood and cotton linters to produce spinning solution about as thick as molasses. This solution is forced through small holes of a spinneret. The streams of liquid from the spinneret are drawn out and solidified into filaments in a chemical bath or on exposure to air. The filaments from a single spinneret are twisted slightly into a yarn which contains as many filaments as holes in the spinneret. Rayon filaments can be made finer than those of silk or coarser than wool. This yarn can then be woven into cloth. There are four kinds of rayon: nitrocellulose, viscose, cuprammonium and cellulose acetate. All are made from a cellulose base, but each is manufactured by a different process. The first three are regenerated cellulose rayon's because the cellulose solution is regenerated or solidified back into pure cellulose in the form of filaments. The cellulose acetate rayon is a nonregenerative cellulose rayon, for the cellulose solution has not been changed back to pure cellulose, but is a derivative of cellulose.

FIG. 1.—Cotton linters, spruce wood chips and wood pulp are the raw materials used in the production of rayon.

Materials used in manufacturing rayon.

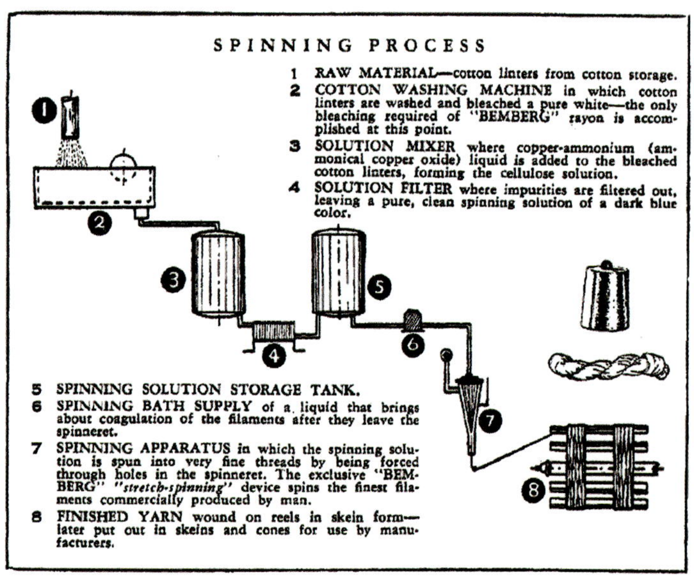

Courtesy American Bemberg Corporation.

FIG. 18.—Diagram showing the manufacture of cuprammonium rayon yarn.

Diagram showing how rayon yarn is manufactured.

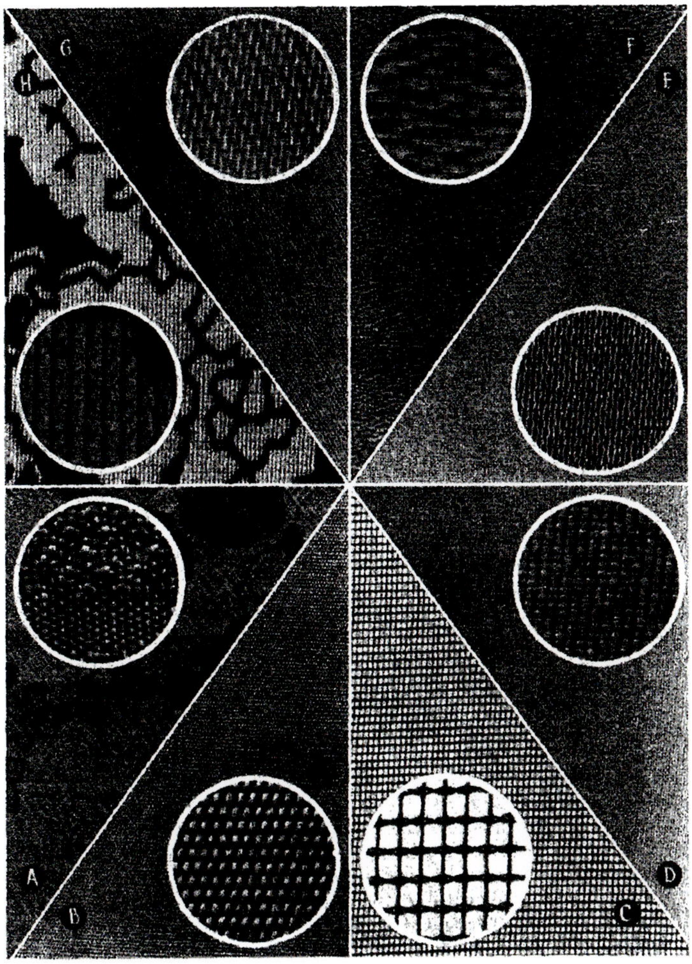

FIG. 5.—Fabrics made of continuous filament rayon: A, viscose crepe; B, viscose taffeta; C, viscose marquisette; D, cuprammonium twill; E, cuprammonium sheer; F, acetate granite cloth; G, acetate satin; H, acetate jersey. (Inserts magnified 4 ×.)

Magnified view of various types of rayon.

The following is a list of wartime natural cellulose-based fibers and their properties:

NAME: Viscose
DATE INTRODUCED: Viscose rayon was discovered by the English chemists Charles F. Cross and E. J. Bevan, who secured a patent for the process in 1892.
DESCRIPTION: Cellulose based. Most abundant form of rayon produced in the United States during the war. It is not as strong when wet as when dry. It does not scorch easily and can be ironed in much the same way as cotton.
IDENTIFICATION: Burns like cotton or paper.

NAME: Cellulose Acetate
DATE INTRODUCED: Cellulose acetate was discovered in 1869 by the German chemists Naudin and Schutzenberger. It was patented in Europe in 1894. In 1902 the first acetate rayon was made in the United States.
DESCRIPTION: Second most abundant rayon produced in the United States during WWII. Cellulose acetate rayon is second in importance to viscose rayon as far as the amount manufactured. TECA is another form of cellulose acetate. In its staple form it has a permanent kink or wavy appearance.
OTHER NAMES: Celanese, acetate, and cellon in Germany.
IDENTIFICATION: When held in a flame it melts and forms a hard crisp ash ball. Will dissolve in acetone and melt when ironed with a hot iron.

NAME: Cuprammonium
DATE INTRODUCED: Was discovered by Schweitzer, a German chemist, in 1857. A French chemist, Louis Henri Despaissis, was granted the first patent for making cuprammonium rayon yarns in 1890. The first factory to produce it commercially was built in Germany in 1897, and in 1924 it was manufactured in the United States.
DESCRIPTION: Cellulose based. Least abundant of the three rayons produced in the United States during the war.
OTHER NAMES: Bemberg
IDENTIFICATION: It burns like paper or cotton.

NAME: Nitrocellulose fiber
DATE INTRODUCED: Initially developed in France during 1891, this became the first synthetic textile to be produced on a successful commercial basis.
DESCRIPTION: Nitrocellulose is formed by treating cellulose with nitric acid. This was the chief method of rayon manufacture in Europe for a period of twenty years after it was first started in 1891, and one company in the United States manufactured this rayon from 1920 to 1934. Nitrocellulose is highly flammable. By WWII it was no longer manufactured or available commercially in the United States.
OTHER NAMES: Artificial silk

There were several synthetic fibers made during the war that used raw materials other than cellulose. These consisted of protein fibers made from the casein of milk and soybeans, nylon and vinyon made from synthetic resins of organic origin, and glass fibers. The following is a list of wartime protein fibers and their properties:

NAME: Lanital
DATE INTRODUCED: Lanital was the first successful fiber made of milk casein. Italian Antonio Ferretti perfected the process and was issued a patent by the Italian government in 1935. In 1938 a patent was granted to the United States Department of Agriculture for making of casein fiber using a different production method. In 1940 a casein fiber known as aralac was announced. The physical and chemical properties are similar to the Italian product, lanital.

DESCRIPTION: First successful commercial fiber made of milk casein. Chemically, lanital is quite similar to wool and can be dyed with the same kinds of dyes. Moths will not attack it, and it does not shrink as much as wool but mildews easily when damp.
OTHER NAMES: Arlac in the United States.
IDENTIFICATION: It burns with the same characteristic odor as wool, but does not have the surface scales that wool fibers have. The casein fibers cannot be distinguished from wool fibers by chemical or burn tests. They have practically the same chemical composition as wool and both have the odor of feathers when burned, leaving a black crisp ash. Both wool and casein fibers are easily dissolved in alkalis and are resistant to acids.

NAME: Soybean fiber.
DATE INTRODUCED: The first attempts to manufacture textile fibers from soybean protein were carried out in Japan during the 1940s.
DESCRIPTION: Is white to light tan in color and has an appearance and texture similar to silk or wool. It does not absorb moisture as easily as wool or casein fiber. Thus it will not mold as easily as the casein fiber. The chemical and dyeing properties of soybean fiber are similar to wool.

There were other protein fibers produced during WWII that have not been discussed. Many were just experimental in the United States. One of these is produced from zein, a material derived from cornmeal. Animal bones, hides, and muscles are other sources of protein that were used. Silk waste and fish were also utilized as raw materials. Seaweed was used in countries outside the United States to make textile fibers. Alginate fibers are fireproof and are nearly as strong as those of rayon. Chitin was another material from which textile fibers were made. This substance is found in the shells of lobsters, crabs, and certain insects.

Nylon, perlon, and other synthetic fibers from petroleum products hold a special interest for collectors of German militaria. It has always been assumed, and rightly so, that the Germans did not use fibers that burned like modern polyesters. This has always been a key method to determine if a uniform was of wartime manufacture. The Germans did manufacture petroleum-based fibers that can be easily mistaken for modern polyester by the untrained eye.

Remember that modern polyesters are manufactured from petroleum, just like nylon and perlon. Wallace Carothers, the inventor of nylon, also worked with the polymer that became polyester as early as 1929. Further research on polyesters was delayed until the end of the war and it was not until 1950 that the first modern polyester (dacron, a nylon derivative) was introduced. Modern polyesters will catch fire, melt, and give off a black smoke when held under a flame. The residue is initially a hard cream-colored bead that becomes darker.

Bulletin 300, *Synthetic Fibers and Textiles*, states:

> Nylon differs radically in its physical and chemical properties from other synthetic fibers. It resembles silk more closely than it does any of the other natural fibers. The great strength, elasticity, and wearing qualities claimed for it have aroused considerable interest. The advantages of nylon are its high strength and elasticity, its lack of sensitivity toward moisture and various chemical agents, and its ability to be spun into fine filaments. It is stronger and more elastic than silk. It is nearly as strong when dry as when wet. Because it does not absorb moisture readily, garments made of it dry quickly. Mineral acids deteriorate it and phenol and formic acids are active solvents. No common dry cleaning solvents affect it, and it is quite resistant to alkalis' even in concentrated form and also to mildew, molds and moths. Nylon does not burn. When held in an open flame it reacts similarly to silk, wool or acetate rayon. The fibers melt and fuse into a glassy round-shaped mass. Varied commercial uses have been made of nylon and it probably will replace silk to a great extent in the textile field. This fiber can be made into fine hosiery and other knit goods such as underwear. Some other uses are sewing thread, brush bristles, racquet and violin strings, surgical sutures, fishing lines, woven dress goods and velvets.

In 1938 perlon—a synthetic fiber similar to American nylon—was invented by German chemist Dr. Paul Schlack at I.G. Farben. In the summer of 1938, the LBO firm (Louis Bahner Oberlungwitz), under Imperial Patent 748.253, produced the Perlon "test stocking." Soon after, the first well-engineered fine lady stockings were produced. LBO became better known as the ELBEO firm. Perlon was declared a military defense material under the code name "Perluran" during Hitler's preparation for war. Perlon was used as fabric for high pressure hoses in airplane tires, as stiff bristles for brushes, for cords and ropes for parachutes, and as reinforcement in socks used by the German armed forces. In 1943, lady's stockings were presented as Christmas presents for the wives of I.G.-Farben managers. Perlon burns in a similar manner to nylon.

The extent to which perlon was used in the German textile industry may never be known. The Italians also had some experience with dyeing nylon because the BIOS report titled *The Development of New Dyes and Colour Application Processes in Germany and Italy During World War II*, dated October 1945, references an Italian publication entitled *La Tintura del Nailon* (The Dyeing of Nylon), which showed selected dispersed and developed acetate and acid colors on nylon. The fact that nylon or perlon was manufactured

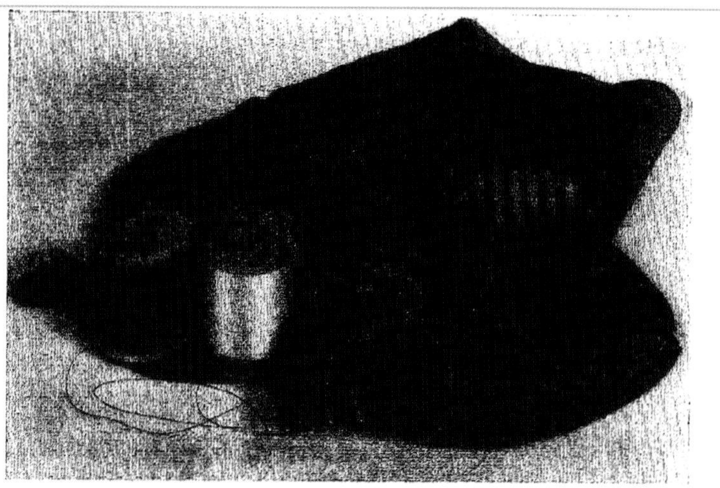

Fig. 6.—Nylon used for toothbrush bristles, hose and sewing thread.

This is a wartime picture of a spool of Nylon thread.

for the civilian population in France as late as October 1943 and that rayonne-nylon was manufactured by the France-Rayonne consortium may indicate a wider use than the collecting community is aware of. While I would approach any uniform or insignia item utilizing nylon or perlon thread with caution, I would not condemn it solely on that factor alone.

There were three types of perlon produced in Germany during the war: Perlon-L, a polyamide fiber manufactured from e-caprolactum; Perlon-T, a polyamide fiber produced from adipic acid hexamethylenenediamine (corresponds closely to nylon); and Perlon-U, a polyurethane fiber produced from hexamethylenenediisocyanate and 1.4 butanediol. Wartime perlon burns in a particular way that unfortunately most people mistake for modern polyester. Modern polyesters tend to melt erratically into a ball. Some polyester will sizzle or pop as it burns, while some will also catch fire and melt like plastic. Other polyesters may have an ash residue with a hard ball underneath. Perlon, on the other hand, melts slowly into a hard black bead, consistently exhibiting a grey center. Nylon fibers melt and fuse into a glassy, round-shaped mass.

None of the references I had access to specifically address what items were manufactured from perlon, but they did provide additional clues about this miracle fiber:

a) From the BIOS report *Textile Printing in Germany*: The Germans conducted pattern and fastness tests on a number of printed fabrics. Pigment and resin fixation to Perlon was found to be extremely effective.

b) From the BIOS report *The Development of New Dyes and Colour Application Processes in Germany and Italy During World War II*: This particular report stated that most of the documents related to perlon were destroyed during the war. Interviews revealed there were no tests conducted comparing nylon to perlon by either country. For the purposes of this report, it was assumed that the dyeing properties of Perlon and Nylon were similar, even though there were some differences in the chemical makeup. The I.G. Farben personnel who were interviewed stated that the fastness properties of acid, chrome, and metalized colors on perlon do not necessarily correspond with the fastness properties of the same dyes on wool. The following types of dyes were suitable for perlon: Acetate dyes known as Celliton or Cellitonecht penetrated the Perlon fiber and worked well; some acid and chrome dyes were acceptable as a surface dye, since they did not penetrate the fiber; and Perlon Fast Dyes known as Perlonecht (this consisted of a complete range of shades). The Perlonecht line of dyes consisted of: Perlonechtdunkelblau RS (Perlon Fast Dark Blue RS), Perlonechtgelb G (Perlon Fast Yellow G), Perlonechtgelb R (Perlon Fast Yellow R), Perlonechtgelb RS (Perlon Fast Yellow RS), Perlonechtgrau B (Perlon Fast Grey B), Perlonechtgrün BT (Perlon Fast Green BT), Perlonechtgrün 3B (Perlon Fast Green 3B), Perlonechtmarineblau RS (Perlon Fast Navy Blue RS), Perlonechtorange R (Perlon Fast Orange R), Perlonechtorange RRS (Perlon Fast Orange RRS), Perlonechtrot B (Perlon Fast Red B), Perlonechtrot BS (Perlon Fast Red BS), Perlonechtrot 3BS (Perlon Fast Red 3BS), Perlonechtrot G (Perlon Fast Red G), Perlonechtrotviolett R (Perlon Fast Red Violet R), Perlonechtviolett BT (Perlon Fast Violet BT), Perlonechtviolett RTS (Perlon Fast Violet RTS), Perlonechtblau FFB (Perlon Fast Blue FFB), and Perlonechtblau FFR (Perlon Fast Blue FFR). The light and wash fastness of these colors on Perlon was satisfactory. The Perlonecht dyes also penetrated the fibers like the Cellitonecht dyes did. Other dyes were also tested and found to be either inferior or never produced commercially. According to this report, I.G. Farben did not conduct any tests on mixed fiber fabrics containing perlon. Even though US personnel did not find any evidence of mixed fiber fabrics containing perlon being produced, they still found it strange the Germans did not attempt to dye perlon yarns simultaneously with yarns of other fabrics. This was a fairly standard practice and I.G. Farben must have anticipated that perlon would eventually find its way into mixed fiber fabrics. The only explanations that US personnel could provide were that the war interfered with dye application research and that the quantities of perlon were relatively small. It has to be reiterated that many of the records on perlon were destroyed during the war. It is fairly certain that perlon was mixed with wool to reinforce high-wear areas in socks. *Das Bekleidungswesen der Luftwaffe*, dated 1943, also infers that perlon was mixed with rayon staple.

c) From *Camouflage Fabrics both Plain and Printed for Military Use* by the German SS and German Army: The report states: "Fairly large quantities of nylon were printed as parachutes for the German Air Force. The cloth used was very much the same as that used by the U.S. Army Air Forces."

d) The reference *Das Bekleidungswesen der Luftwaffe* (1943) specifically addressed German Air Force clothing and offered the following information about perlon: "Perlon(Perluran) is lighter/more delicate and around 50% stronger than natural silk. The scrubbing firmness is particularly large. The fiber can be washed in hot water and ironed; it can be mixed with Zellwolle (Perlon blended with rayon staple). Perlon is extremely suitable for the manufacture of clothing. Since 1941 the fiber has been bulk manufactured for use by the armed forces." (Author's note: This confirms that perlon was likely used as a blended yarn for the manufacture of uniform items, in contradiction to statements made by I.G. Farben personnel in paragraph b) above.)

Bulletin 300, *Synthetic Fibers and Textiles*, states:

> Vinyon is a synthetic fiber having remarkable properties. It is thermoplastic and when heated above 117° F. will shrink. If held in a flame it melts and chars but does not burn. Concentrated acids or alkalis will not injure vinyon fabrics. The fabric does not absorb moisture; consequently it will not mildew and will be quite useful in damp climates. This fiber has high elasticity and breaking strength; and because it is not affected by water, its strength is the same wet as when dry. Vinyon has been put to many uses. Short fibers of vinyon have been mixed with cotton, wool, glass or other fibers to form felts. The most extensive use is for industrial filter cloth because of its high dry and wet breaking strength and its resistance to acids and alkalis. Some other uses are fish lines, nets, seines, acid and alkali-resistant clothing, electric insulation, shower curtains, bathing suits, waterproof clothing, fireproof awnings and curtains. Vinyon has also been used for shoe fabrics and gloves. Stains are readily removed from vinyon fabrics in a soap solution, and the material dries quickly.

In Germany, Vinyon is referred to as "PeCe," an I.G. Farben synthetic fiber produced from chlorinated vinyl chloride. I.G. Farben developed a series of dispersed, water insoluble dyes specifically for PeCe. The dyes came in a range of yellows, oranges, scarlets, reds, and browns. There was reference to PeCe in *Das Bekleidungswesen der Luftwaffe*, which basically stated the fiber was suitable for use in the chemical industry for fishnets, fishing line, and sails, but not for standard clothing. It is unknown what specific line of products were manufactured from PeCe, except for suits used in chemical plants and for chemical warfare clothing (as referenced in *The Development of New Dyes and Colour Application Processes in Germany and Italy During World War II*).

The following is a list of wartime synthons, glass fibers, and miscellaneous fibers.

NAME: Nylon
DATE INTRODUCED: Dr. Wallace H. Carothers (1896-1937) directed the research program which resulted in the discovery of nylon. Nylon first appeared in the United States market in the form of brush bristles and sewing thread. In 1940 nylon hose was available.
DESCRIPTION: Nylon was the name applied to all materials that are synthetic fiber-forming polymeric amides having a protein like chemical structure, derivable from coal, air, and water or other substances. It's characterized by high strength and elasticity, lack of sensitivity toward moisture and various chemical agents and it can be spun into fine filaments. It is stronger and more elastic than silk. It is nearly as strong when dry as when wet. It is resistant to alkalis, even in concentrated form, and also to mildew, molds, and moths.
OTHER NAMES: Nylon 6, Nylon 6.6
IDENTIFICATION: The fibers melt and fuse into a glassy round-shaped mass.

NAME: Perlon
DATE INTRODUCED: In Germany a fiber similar to nylon was developed in 1938. It was named perlon.
DESCRIPTION: It is characterized by high strength and elasticity, lack of sensitivity toward moisture and various chemical agents and it can be spun into fine filaments. It is stronger and more elastic than silk. It is nearly as strong when dry as when wet. It is resistant to alkalis even in concentrated form, and also to mildew, molds, and moths.
OTHER NAMES: Perlon-L, Perlon-T, Perlon-U, Perulan
IDENTIFICATION: The fiber melts slowly into a hard black bead, consistently exhibiting a grey center.

NAME: Vinyon
DATE INTRODUCED: The patent for vinyon was granted by the United States government in 1937.
DESCRIPTION: It is thermoplastic and will shrink at temperatures above 117° F. Concentrated acids or alkalis will not affect it. The fabric does not absorb moisture, so it will not mildew. This fiber has a high elasticity and breaking strength. Moisture does not degrade its strength.

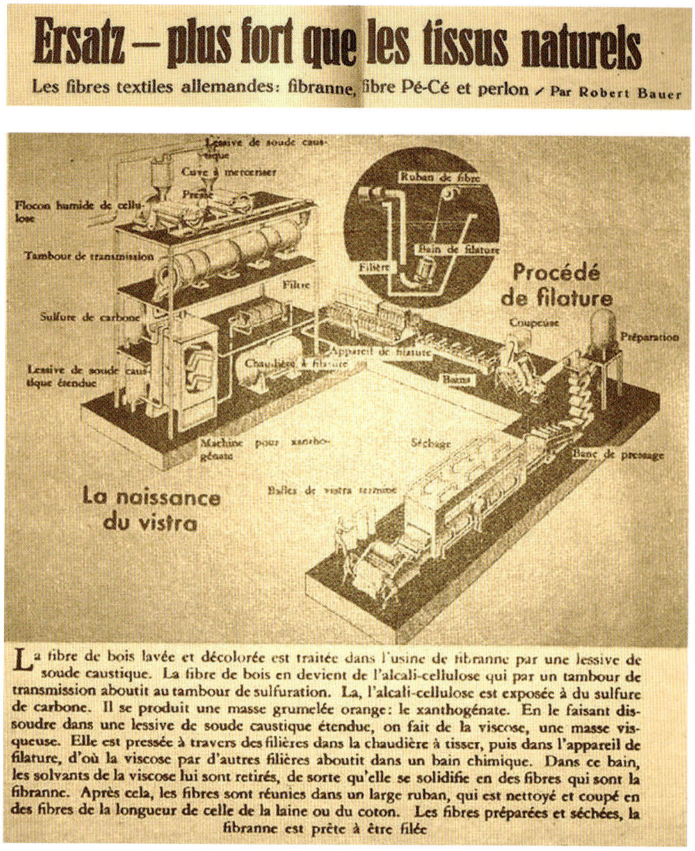
Ersatz – plus fort que les tissus naturels

Les fibres textiles allemandes: fibranne, fibre Pé-Cé et perlon / Par Robert Bauer

La fibre de bois lavée et décolorée est traitée dans l'usine de fibranne par une lessive de soude caustique. La fibre de bois en devient de l'alcali-cellulose qui par un tambour de transmission aboutit au tambour de sulfuration. La, l'alcali-cellulose est exposée à du sulfure de carbone. Il se produit une masse grumelée orange: le xanthogénate. En le faisant dissoudre dans une lessive de soude caustique étendue, on fait de la viscose, une masse visqueuse. Elle est pressée à travers des filières dans la chaudière à tisser, puis dans l'appareil de filature, d'où la viscose par d'autres filières aboutit dans un bain chimique. Dans ce bain, les solvants de la viscose lui sont retirés, de sorte qu'elle se solidifie en des fibres qui sont la fibranne. Après cela, les fibres sont réunies dans un large ruban, qui est nettoyé et coupé en des fibres de la longueur de celle de la laine ou du coton. Les fibres préparées et séchées, la fibranne est prête à être filée

Articles about Perlon and PeCe were published in *Signal* and *Der Adler* magazines.

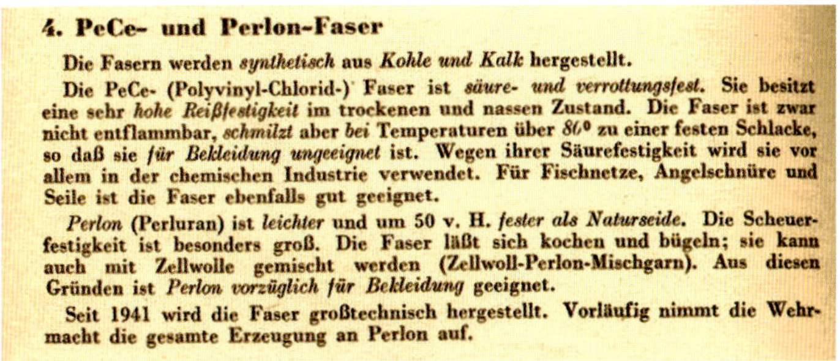

4. PeCe- und Perlon-Faser

Die Fasern werden *synthetisch* aus *Kohle und Kalk* hergestellt.

Die PeCe- (Polyvinyl-Chlorid-) Faser ist *säure- und verrottungsfest.* Sie besitzt eine sehr *hohe Reißfestigkeit* im trockenen und nassen Zustand. Die Faser ist zwar nicht entflammbar, *schmilzt* aber *bei* Temperaturen über 80° zu einer festen Schlacke, so daß sie *für Bekleidung ungeeignet* ist. Wegen ihrer Säurefestigkeit wird sie vor allem in der chemischen Industrie verwendet. Für Fischnetze, Angelschnüre und Seile ist die Faser ebenfalls gut geeignet.

Perlon (Perluran) ist *leichter* und um 50 v. H. *fester als Naturseide.* Die Scheuerfestigkeit ist besonders groß. Die Faser läßt sich kochen und bügeln; sie kann auch mit Zellwolle gemischt werden (Zellwoll-Perlon-Mischgarn). Aus diesen Gründen ist *Perlon vorzüglich für Bekleidung* geeignet.

Seit 1941 wird die Faser großtechnisch hergestellt. Vorläufig nimmt die Wehrmacht die gesamte Erzeugung an Perlon auf.

Passage from *Das Bekleidungswesen der Luftwaffe* discussing Perlon and PeCe.

OTHER NAMES: PeCe.
IDENTIFICATION: The fiber melts and forms a hard irregular bead.

NAME: Glass Fibers
DATE INTRODUCED: In 1893, Edward Drummond Libbey exhibited a dress at the World's Columbian Exposition incorporating glass fibers with the diameter and texture of silk fibers.
DESCRIPTION: Glass in its solid state has hardness, strength, cleanliness, durability, and has characteristics of plastic when molten. It is a poor conductor of heat and electricity and can be subjected to temperatures of 1,000° F without melting. It does not absorb moisture; resists decay, does not mildew and vermin will not eat it. They are very resistant to alkalis, acids, and other chemicals. By the middle of the war glass filaments as small as 0.00025 of an inch were produced. Yarns of glass fiber can be used to make cloth of any weave.
IDENTIFICATION: They will not burn or melt, except at temperatures over 1,000°F.

I have restricted my identification methods to those that the average collector could conduct. Conclusive results can only be obtained by viewing the fibers under high magnification or through chemical analysis. It is important to remember that fibers were often mixed to meet specific needs. Burn test results will be skewed if you are testing a mixed fiber. Fabrics are often chemically treated to make them resistant to luster, fire, mildew, shrinking, etc. These chemicals may also affect test results. The following information was taken from Bulletin 300, *Synthetic Fibers and Textiles*, Agriculture Experiment Station, Kansas State College of Agriculture and Applied Science, April 1942:

> It has become difficult to ascertain the fiber content of fabrics by their appearance and handle or by chemical and burning tests. Formerly, it was a simple matter to determine whether a fabric was silk, cotton, linen, or rayon. Many of the new finishes give the synthetic fabrics the appearance of wool, linen, or silk. Furthermore, there has been an increasingly large production of fabrics composed of two or more kinds of fibers. Experienced textiles workers have frequently been unable to determine fiber content without using exacting methods of identification. Because the kinds of fibers used cannot be determined without reliable laboratory techniques, fabrics on the market should have labels stating accurately the fiber content. The textile technologist employs many tests to identify fibers. The burning tests are the easiest to use, but are not exacting, especially for mixed fabrics. Chemical tests are often helpful, but these are usually not applicable except in a chemical laboratory. The microscopically identification of fibers is the most reliable and satisfactory. For this a microscope of high magnification must be available. Also, one must be equipped with the necessary apparatus to make mounts of the fibers both in longitudinal and cross-sectional views.
>
> Viscose and cuprammonium rayons can be distinguished from cellulose acetate by the burning test. The acetate rayon melts to a crisp black bead, and the other rayons burn quickly like paper or cotton with no odor and no ash. Viscose and cuprammonium rayons are difficult to distinguish by chemical means, for they are both regenerated cellulose. They are best identified by the shape of their cross sections. All three fibers appear like smooth glass rods, but the cross sections have characteristic shapes. The cuprammonium fiber is round; the acetate has a clover-leaf appearance with three or four lobes; and the viscose has saw tooth edges. Acetate rayon is easily distinguished from the natural and synthetic fibers because it is readily dissolved in acetone and the others, except vinyon, are not. Acetone is the base of nail polish remover and a drop of remover on acetate rayon or vinyon fiber will dissolve it, but has no effect on the other fibers. Strong acids will attack acetate rayon, but will not attack vinyon.
>
> The casein fibers cannot be distinguished from wool fibers by chemical or burning tests. They have practically the same chemical composition as wool and both have the odor of feathers when burned, leaving a black crisp ash. Both wool and casein fibers are easily dissolved in alkalis and are resistant to acids. The wool fiber is readily distinguished from other fibers under a microscope because it has scales on the surface which is not characteristic of any other fiber. The surface of lanital is smooth and the cross section is round.
>
> Soybean fibers react similarly to casein fibers and wool by chemical and burning tests. The fiber is smooth in appearance and has no scales. The cross section is round.
>
> Both nylon and vinyon melt at high temperature and are practically nonflammable. They are easily distinguished by the shape of their cross sections. Nylon is round, and vinyon is shaped like a dumbbell. Vinyon is not attacked by either strong acids or alkalis'; nylon is resistant to alkalies, but is injured by strong acids.
>
> Glass fibers are readily identified because when held in a flame, they will not burn or melt, except at extremely high temperatures of over 1,000°F. All other fibers when held in a flame will either burn or melt. Glass fiber has a round cross section and is the smallest of all the textile fibers.

"Celleon" is a term widely used within the collecting community to describe thread introduced during the war to replace the more expensive metal-based threads and bullions in various insignia. The term has been further complicated by the use of the German terms Cellophan and Cello that are sometimes used when describing German uniforms, etc. The description for Celleon provided in *Uniforms and Traditions of the Luftwaffe, Volume I*, by John Angolia and Adolf Schlicht provides the answer:

> The insignia, etc., of general officers and officials of general's rank was made of gold, and were frequently pure hot gilding. To "eliminate the need of gold, to reduce purchase costs, and to increase the wearing periods," gold was substituted by a newly-developed material "Celleon" by an order (HV 38B, No. 258) dated 15 July, 1938. Celleon web, celleon lace and cord, etc., was made of a silver-plated web on a golden-yellow or white artificial silk base with a golden-colored textile-cellophane spinning. Bright Celleon had a base of silver-plated web, and matte Celleon had a white silk base.

The base fibers were covered with cellophane to give it a bright finish. Unissued celleon insignia with paper tags, etc., are sometimes annotated with the term cellophan (cellophane). Remember, cellophane is simply a thin, transparent sheet made of regenerated cellulose. From a burn test perspective, the cellophane coating burns like any other cellulose based product, such as rayon. Sometimes uniform advertisements used the term *cellon*, which is the German term for cellulose acetate.

Breast eagle manufactured using celleon thread.

Wartime advertisement for cellon.

For the average collector, the most common means of determining the type of textiles an item is manufactured from are the black light and burn test. There is plenty of information available on the shortcomings of the black light test and its use is very limited. Certain wartime dyes will glow under a black light and certain modern cleaning products will cause textiles to react under a black light. In fact, the Germans identified and described certain finishes used on fabrics by the color it fluoresced under UV light. Burn testing is better than black lighting, but certainly has its limitations. Forensics laboratories can determine the exact contents of any textile, but are beyond the financial means of most collectors, and the quantity of materials required to make an accurate test has to be considered.

I have attempted to point out some of the factors that complicate fiber identification. The physical composition of the actual fiber is the most important factor. Other factors, such as dyes and the method of finishing, may influence the outcome of a black light or burn test. Germany took serious steps to improve their finishing techniques, largely due to the fact that artificial cellulose fibers had a number of undesirable characteristics. Softening agents like Soromin brands were used to reduce the papery feel of rayon. Paraffin emulsions like ramasit, impragnol, hydrophobol, persistol, etc., were used as waterproofing agents. Several resins were developed to increase the wet strength and crease resistance of rayon. Inorganic salts were used to improve the flameproofing capability of synthetic fibers. Polyvinyl acetate was used to obtain a stiff finish. The world of German wartime finishes is obviously much more complex than I can convey in a single paragraph. However, it is largely a study of chemistry that is beyond my capability to present. The point I am trying to make is that finishing chemicals might influence the outcome of a burn test or black light test.

Repairing large rips or tears in a uniform would require a patch of cloth. Wartime pictures show that repairs were often made with any available cloth. The following discussion on standard uniform cloth was obtained from an intelligence report titled *German Army "Einheitstuch" - Standard Cloth Field Gray*, 19 June 1945.

In 1926, the Reichswehr adopted two field grays: a greenish gray for tunics and a bluish gray for trousers. In 1940, the bluish gray color was discontinued. Here are the vat dye specifications for the Reichswehr adopted field grays:

NAME: COAT FIELD GRAY BLEND
COLOR 1:
2% Indigo MLB vat 60% pieces
2.88% Helindon Brown CV vat Pdr.
1.37% Helindon Yellow CG vat Pdr.
BLEND
75 parts of Color 1
25 parts White

NAME: TROUSERS NEW GRAY CLOTH BLEND
COLOR 2:
5% Helindon Black 3 B vat Pdr.
4.5% Helindon Black T vat Pdr.
COLOR 3:
0.27% Helindon Black T vat Pdr.
BLEND
50 parts of Color 2
25 parts of Color 3
25 parts White

In 1944, a new brownish gray color was adopted. The justification was based on better camouflage properties. The Hoechst factory worked out the official mixture, which was initially based on four ground shades (tan, green, brown-green, and gold) and 8% white wool. This combination did not work properly and only three shades were selected as shown below:

NAME: FIELD GRAY 1944

30 parts Yellow
20 parts Olive Gray
40 parts Field Green
8 parts White

The original specifications limited the cloth manufacturer to the use of vat dyes for the dyeing of wools (virgin or new). This restriction did hold true for wool waste and reworked wools, which could be dyed with vat or chrome colors. (Author's note: Vat dyes are essentially insoluble in water and incapable of dyeing fibers directly. The original vat dye is indigo. Mordant/Chrome dyes require a mordant, or a substance used to set dyes on fabrics. Most natural dyes are mordant dyes; however, the most important mordant dyes are the synthetic mordant dyes, or chrome dyes, used for wool. These dyes are especially useful for black and navy shades.) For the rayon staple portion of the fabric, the dyeing could be done with either vat or sulphur dyes, or dyed directly in the spinning solution. It appears that vat-dyed wool was preferred over chrome-dyed wool.

The infrared sensitivity of all dyes in question were studied, and indigo was found to be the main offender. With the reduction of the blue component in the 1944 shade, a considerable reduction in the infrared sensitivity took place.

When the war began, the Germans looked closely at the economic aspect of cloth production. The vat-dying process for wool had the advantage of higher production in dyeing, better running in spinning, and shorter fulling time (which meant a savings in time and labor, as well as a savings in steam because of the low temperatures necessary in vat dying) versus the chrome-dyeing process.

The major economic challenge was how to stretch the available stocks of wool, since Germany only produced 10% of its requirements. The only other sources for wool were wool wastes, tailor clippings, and rags. Chrome dyes worked best on reworked wool. However, it was left up to the manufacturer whether to use chrome or vat dyes. Towards the end of the war, the largest percentage of waste and reworked wool was field gray in color, which eliminated the need for dyeing.

Indanthren dyes were widely used in the manufacture of uniforms.

TABLE 1.—*Key to identification of synthetic fibers*

KIND OF FIBER.	Burning test.	Microscopical appearance.	Chemical properties.	Physical properties.
Viscose rayon.	Burns like cotton with flame, no odor, little ash.	Cross section has sawtooth edges.	Dissolves in strong acids.	Breaking strength decreases when wet, not very elastic.
Cellulose acetate rayon.	Melts when burned and forms crisp black bead.	Cross section has lobes similar to clover leaf.	Dissolves in acetone and strong acids.	Wet breaking strength does not decrease as much as viscose, more elastic.
Cuprammonium rayon.	Burns like cotton.	Resembles glass rod, cross section is round.	Dissolves in strong acids.	Similar to viscose.
Casein.	Burns like wool with odor of burning hair.	No surface scales, cross section is round.	Damaged readily by alkalies.	Not as strong or as elastic as wool, mildews easily.
Soybean.	Burns like wool.	Cross section is round.	Damaged readily by alkalies.	Similar to casein fiber, mildews less easily.
Nylon.	Melts and forms round hard bead.	Resembles glass rod, cross section is round.	Damaged by acids, quite resistant to alkalies.	High dry and wet breaking strength, great elasticity.
Vinyon.	Melts and forms hard irregular bead.	Resembles glass rod, cross section shaped like a dumbbell.	Resistant to acids and alkalies, dissolves in acetone.	High dry and wet breaking strength, very elastic.
Glass	Does not burn.	Smallest of all fibers, cross section is round.	Resistant to chemicals.	Strong, brittle, does not absorb moisture.

This wartime burn chart shows that different types of rayon reacted differently to flames and chemicals. The same would hold true of different nylon and perlon threads.

BIBLIOGRAPHY

Absolon, Rudolf. *Die Wehrmacht im Dritten Reich, Band VI. 19 Dezember 1941 bis 9 Mai 1945.* Boppard Am Rhein: Harald Boldt Verlag, 1995.

Der Adler. (Magazine Various Issues).

Amtliches Fernsprechbuch fur den Bezirk der Reichspostdirektion Berlin 1941.

Amtliches Fernsprechbuch fur den Bezirk der Reichspostdirektion Berlin 1943. (CD Version).

Amtliches Fernsprechbuch fur den Bezirk der Reichspostdirektion Hamburg 1941. (CD Version).

Amtliches Fernsprechbuch fur den Bezirk der Reichspostdirektion Nurnberg 1938. (CD Version).

Amtliches Fernsprechbuch fur den Bezirk der Reichspostdirektion Potsdam 1941. (CD Version).

Amtliches Fernsprechbuch fur den Bezirk der Reichspostdirektion Wien 1943. (CD Version).

Angolia, John R., and Adolf Schlicht. *Die Kriegsmarine- Uniforms and Traditions.* 3 vols. San Jose, CA: Roger James Bender, 1991-1993.

Angolia, John R., and Adolf Schlicht. *Uniforms and Traditions of the German Army, 1933-1945.* 3 vols. San Jose, CA: Roger James Bender, 1984-1987.

Angolia, John R., and Adolf Schlicht. *Uniforms and Traditions of the Luftwaffe.* 3 vols. San Jose, CA: Roger James Bender, 1996-1998.

Böddrich, E., and W. Zimmermann. *Einführung in die Dinormen.* Leipzig und Berlin: Verlag und Druck von B.G. Teubner, 1941.

Borsarello J., and D. Lassus. *Camouflaged Uniforms of the Wehrmacht.* ISO-GALAGO Publications, 1988.

Buckner, Alex. *The German Infantry Handbook 1939-1945.* Atglen, PA: Schiffer, 1991.

Classified List of OTS Printed Reports PB 81500. Department of Commerce, October 1947.

Camouflage Fabrics both Plain and Printed for Military Use by the German SS and German Army. Reported by Francis S. Richardson, QMC Consultant, 20 July 1945.

Davis, Brian L., *Uniforms and Insignia of the Luftwaffe, Volume 2, 1940-1945.* London: Arms and Armour Press, 1995.

Cuthbertson, D.P., and J.A.C. Knox. "The Effects of Analeptics on the Fatigued Subject." *J. Physiol.* 106, 42-58, (1947) received 1 August 1946.

Defalque, Ray J. MD., and Amos J. Wright, MLS. "Methamphetamine for Hitler's Germany: 1937 to 1945." *Bulletin of Anesthesia History,* 29, No 2, (April 2011).

De Lagarde, Jean. *German Soldiers of World War Two.* Poole, Dorset, UK: Histoire Et Collections, 2005.

Das Deutsche Mädel. (Magazine Various Issues).

Design Investigation in Selected German Consumer Goods Industries. BIOS Final Report No.952, item no.22, nd.

The Development of New Dyes and Colour Application Processes in Germany and Italy During World War II. British Intelligence Objectives Sub-Committee Misc.Report No.20, October 1945.

DIN Normblatt-Verzeichnis 1942. Berlin SW 68: Beuth-Vertrieb GmbH.

DIN Normblatt-Verzeichnis 1956. Berlin W 15, Köln: Beuth-Vertrieb GmbH.

DIN Taschenbuch 4, Werkstoffnormen, Berlin SW 68: Beuth-Vertrieb GmbH, July 1941.

The Dying of Glass Fibre Textiles. British Intelligence Sub Committee Final report No.981, 1 November 1946.

Elimination of German Resources for War, Hearings before a subcommittee of the Committee on Military Affairs. 2 vols. Washington: United States Government Printing Office, 1945-1946.

Filmwoche. (Magazine Various Issues).

FM-E 101-10 Staff Officers' Field Manual Enemy Forces Organization, Technical, and Logistical Data. Washington: United States Government Printing Office, *1942.*

Frauen-Warte. (Magazine Various Issues).

Gassend, Jean-Loup, *Operation Dragoon: Autopsy of a Battle: The Allied Liberation of the French Riviera August-September 1944.* Atglen, PA: Schiffer, 2014.

German Clothing, Equipment and Rations. Office of the Quartermaster General Military Planning Division Research and Development Branch, 5 September 1945.

German Comb Industry. BIOS Final Report No.857, item no. 22, nd.

German Cutlery Case, Canteen and Cabinet Industry. BIOS Final Report No.1135, item nos. 22 and 31, nd.

German Divisional Emblems. London :Military Intelligence Research Section, 1 January, 1945.

German Fountain Pen Industry. BIOS Final Report No.911, item no.35, nd.
German Glass or Enamelled Lined Equipment on Mild Steel and Cast Iron for Chemical-Food-Drink and Allied Industries. BIOS Final Report No.569, item nos.21, 22 and 31, nd.
German Glass Industry. BIOS Final Report No.403. item no.22, nd.
German Lead,Copying &Coloured Pencil Manufacture, and Allied Industries. BIOS Final Report No.472, item no.35, Undated)
German Light Metal Industry-Fancy Goods. British Intelligence Objectives Sub-Committee-BIOS., Final Report No.836. Item No.36, nd.
German Military Timepieces of World War II. Ulric of England, 1996.
German Mountain Warfare. Special Series, No. 21, 29 February, 1944. Prepared by Military Intelligence Division War Department.
German Papermaking Industry. Final Report No.312, item no.22, nd.
German Papermaking Industry. BIOS Final Report No.1041, item No.22, 27 April, 1946.
German Progress in Products and Processes for Cellulosic Textiles. BIOS. Final Report No.1773, item no.22, nd.
The German Rubber Footwear Industry and The German Sole and Heel Industry. BIOS Miscellaneous Report No. 3, September 1945.
The German Soap Industry. BIOS Miscellaneous Report No.25, September 1945.
German Spectacle Frame Industry. BIOS Final Report No.480, item no. 24, nd.
German Textile Industry. BIOS Final Report No.514, item nos. 22 and 31, nd.
German Tinplate Industry. BIOS Final Report No.610, item no.21, February 1946.
Gesetze und Verordnungen Deutsches Reich. (Various issues).
Handbook on German Military Forces TM-E-30-451. Washington: United States Government Printing Office, 1945.
Hauptvogel, Curt. *Das Bekleidungswesen der Luftwaffe.* Braunschweig/München/Berlin: Franz Heß Verlag, 1943.
H.Dv. 86/1. Regulations for the Rations of the Armed Forces with Specific Deployment. (Revised version from June 20, 1940)
Infra Red Reflectance of Coloured Textiles and Other Materials (Part 1) and Dyes, Intermediates and Pharmaceutical Processes (Part II), BIOS Miscellaneous Report No.55, October 1945.
Internationales Militaria-Magazine. 66482 Zweibrucken: Verlag Heinz Nickel, (Various issues).
Investigation of Certain German Paper and Board Mills with Particular Reference to the Production of Leatherboard, Carton and Shoe Board and Coated Papers. BIOS Final Report No.838. item no.22, nd.
Light Alloys. British Intelligence Objectives Sub-Committee-BIOS Final Report No.981, item no.21, nd.
Madeja, Victor W. *Hitler's Dying Ground: Disintegration of the German Armed Forces in World War 2.* Allentown, PA: Valor Publishing Co. 4th edition, 1992.
Maier, Curtis E. *A Survey of the Practices of the German Can Industry During the Second World War.* Combined Intelligence Objectives Sub-Committee, Item No. 21 and 22, File No. XXX-85, London: HM Stationary Office, nd.
The Manufacture of Cigarettes, Cigars and Pipe Tobacco in Germany. BIOS Final Report No.780, item no. 22, nd.
Manufacture of Harmonicas (Mouth Organs) and Accordions. Final Report No.227, item no. 34, nd.
Manufacture of Pulp Paper and Related Products from Wood in Western Germany. FIAT Final Report No.487, 9 November, 1945.
Mason, Chris. *Personal Effects of the German Soldier in World War II.* Atglen, PA: Schiffer, 2006.
Merkblatt 18a/17 Taschenbuch für den Winterkrieg. 1943.
Military Improvisations During the Russian Campaign. Department of the Army Pamphlet No. 20-201, August 1951.
Mosse, R. *Deutsches Reichs-Adressbuch für Industrie, Gewerbe, Handel und Landwirtschaft.* Berlin: Druck und Verlag Rudolf Mosse, 1929. (Five Volume CD Version).
Palinckx, Werner with Dr. J.F. Borsarello, *Camouflage Uniforms of the German Wehrmacht*, Atglen, PA: Schiffer, 2002.
Paper Pulp Moulding Industry in Germany. BIOS Final Report No.1589, nd.
Pool, Jim and Tom Bock. *Rations of the German Wehrmacht in WWII.* Atglen, PA: Schiffer, 2010.
Pool, Jim. *Rations of the German Wehrmacht in WWII, Volume 2.* Atglen, PA: Schiffer, 2012.
Report on the Progress of the German Textile Industry During the War. British Intelligence Objectives Sub-Committee Misc. Report No.6, nd.
Reibert. *Der-Dienstunterricht-im-Heere-Ausgabe-fur-den-Panzerjager.* Berlin: Verlag von Mittler und Sohn, 1941.
Sáiz, Agustín. *Deutsche Soldaten.* Philadelphia and Newbury: Casemate, 2008.
Signal. (Magazine Various Issues).
Some Aspects of the German Glass Industry in 1946. BIOS Final Report No.1780, item no.22, nd.
Special Series NO. 3, German Military Training. Prepared by Military Intelligence Division War Department, 17 September, 1942.
Special Series NO. 8, German Tactical Doctrine, Prepared by Military Intelligence Division War Department, 20 December, 1942.
Special Series NO. 17, German Doctrine of the Stabilized Front, Prepared by Military Intelligence Division War Department, 15 August, 1943.
Special Series NO. 21, German Mountain Warfare, Prepared by Military Intelligence Division War Department, 29 February 1944.
Synthetic Detergents and Related Surface Active Agents in Germany. F.I.A.T. Final Report No.1141, nd.
Synthetic Detergents and Washing Agents. BIOS Miscellaneous Report No.11, October 1945.
TACTICAL AND TECHNICAL TRENDS. Issues 1-40, Prepared for Army Ground and Air Forces and Services of Supply by Military Intelligence Service, War Department, 1942-1945.
Textile Printing in Germany. BIOS Final Report No.1088. item no.31, nd.
Uniformen-Markt. (Magazine Various Issues 1935-1945).
Weaver, W. Darrin. *Kunststoffe: A Collectors's Guide to German World War II Plastics and their Markings.* Atglen, PA: Schiffer, 2008.
Wehrmacht-Verwaltungsvorschrift IV. Berlin: Druck und Verlag der Reichsdruckerei, 1939.

Williamson, Gordon, *World War II German Women's Auxiliary Services*, Osprey, 2003.
Die Woche. (Magazine Various Issues).
Young, Jeffrey F. and Daniel W.Meinz. *German Third Reich Era Documents, Volume Two: Military Documents*, Published by Authors, 1998.

WEBSITES

1. 4711, http://en.wikipedia.org/wiki/4711 (1 February 2012)
2. LUHNS, http://de.wikipedia.org/wiki/Luhns (1 February 2012)
3. Kappus, http://www.kappus-seife.de/e_index.html (1 February 2012)
4. Saubere Geschäfte, weiße Westen und Persilscheine, http://www.cocon-verlag.de/books/regional/sauberegeschaefteinfo.htm (1 February 2012)
5. Pfeilring, http://www.markenmuseum.de/index.php?id=854 (1 February 2012)
6. Dalli Group, http://www.dalli-group.com/dalligroup/index.php (1 February 2012)
7. Nivea, http://www.niveausa.com/about-us/beiersdorf/history (1 February 2012)
8. 2500 Companies-Slave Holders in the Nazi Camp System, December 4 1999, http://www.labournet.de/diskussion/geschichte/zwa-firmenliste.htm, (13 March 2008)
9. Glossary of the Third Reich, 10 March 2008, http://en.wikipedia.org/ wiki/Glossary_of_the_Third_Reich (17 March 2008)
10. Trade mark register, https://dpinfo.dpma.de/protect/mar_e.html (3 September 2008)
11. Images from the German Federal Archive by Year, http://commons. wikimedia.org/wiki/Category:Images from the German Federal Archive by year (23 December 2008)
12. Propaganda Leaflets of WWII, http://ww2propaganda.eu/ (25 January 2009)
13. Vasenol, http://de.wikipedia.org/wiki/Vasenol (1 February 2012)
14. "You've Come to a Family of Perfumers" The Cosmetic Companies Scherk and Dr. Albersheim, http://www.jmberlin.de/main/EN/06-Press/01-Press-Releases/Press-Releases-2010/2010_08_18.php (1 February 2012)
15. Blendax, http://de.wikipedia.org/wiki/Blendax (1 February 2012)
16. ARYA LAYA, http://www.diaderma.de/ (1 February 2012)
17. Pigmentan, http://www.pigmentan.de/ (1 February 2012)
18. Chlorodont, http://de.wikipedia.org/wiki/Chlorodont (1 February 2012)
19. Mack verschwindet vom Firmenschild, http://www.augsburger-allgemeine.de/neu-ulm/Mack-verschwindet-vom-Firmenschild-id3228606.html (1 February 2012)
20. EDUARD GERLACH GmbH, http://www.gehwol.de/, (7 February 2012)
21. Florena , http://de.wikipedia.org/wiki/Florena (7 February 2012)
22. Wolff & Sohn, http://ka.stadtwiki.net/Wolff_%26_Sohn (7 February 2012)
23. Queisser Pharma, http://de.wikipedia.org/wiki/Queisser_Pharma (7 February 2012)
24.A/S Lilleborg Fabrikker, http://en.wikipedia.org/wiki/Lilleborg (7 February 2012)
25. August Friedrich Mouson, http://de.wikipedia.org/wiki/August_Friedrich_Mouson (7 February 2012)
26. Auergesellschaft, http://en.wikipedia.org/wiki/Auergesellschaft (7 February 2012)
27. Perfumes, http://parfuemseite.wb4.de/ (7 February 2012)
28. Odol, http://de.wikipedia.org/wiki/Odol (7 February 2012)
29. Barnangens Vademecum GmbH, http://www.barnangen.se/fotoutstallning/index.html (7 February 2012)
30. New York Hamburger Gummi-Waaren Compagnie, http://de.wikipedia.org/wiki/New-York_Hamburger_Gummi-Waaren_Compagnie (8 February 2012)
31. Schwarzkopf, http://www.schwarzkopf.com/sk/en/home/schwarzkopf.html, (8 February 2012)
32. Colgate-Palmolive, http://en.wikipedia.org/wiki/Palmolive_(soap) (8 February 2012)
33. Vasenol, http://de.wikipedia.org/wiki/Vasenol (8 February 2012)
34. Engelhard Arzneimittel, http://www.engelhard-am.de/deutsch/index.asp (11 February 2012)
35.Togal, http://www.togal.de/ (11 February 2012)
36. Razor Makers, http://www.archivingindustry.com/cutlers&toolmakers/razormakers.htm (13 February 2012)
37. A. Riebeck'sche Montanwerke AG Halle, http://de.wikipedia.org/wiki/A._Riebeck%E2%80%99sche_Montanwerke (17 February 2012)
38. Die Seifenwerke Flammer, http://www.stadtarchiv-heilbronn.de/stadtgeschichte/stichworte/f/flammer/ (17 February 2012)
39. Schering AG, http://en.wikipedia.org/wiki/Schering_AG (17 February 2012)
40. Bayer, http://www.bayer.com/ (17 February 2012)
41. Historie ŠANTOVKA, http://www.santovka.cz/historie/ (18 February 2012)
42. Delitia , Delitizsch, http://frunol-delicia.de/site/html/de/common/index.php??page=historie&folder=unternehmen (18 February 2012)
43. Objektführer - Rheinische Industriekultur, http://www.rheinische-industriekultur.de/objekte/koeln/Sidol/koeln_sidol.htm (18 February 2012)
44. c. lück, ostseebad kolberg, http://www.pharmaziegeschichte.at/ichp2009/vortraege/vortraege_volltext_pdf/L43.pdf (18 February 2012)
45. Globus-Werk, http://de.wikipedia.org/wiki/Fritz_Schulz_jun._AG (18 February 2012)
46. Werner & Mertz, http://de.wikipedia.org/wiki/Werner_%26_Mertz (18 February 2012)
47. Salamander Schupflege, http://www.melvo.de/unternehmen/geschichte/ (18 February 2012)
48. Collonil, http://www.collonil.com/en/ (18 February 2012)
49. Rud. Starcke in Melle i/H, http://www.albert-gieseler.de/dampf_de/firmen0/firmadet9594.shtml (18 February 2012)
50. Pilowerke Adolf Krebs, http://www.albert-gieseler.de/dampf_de/firmen0/firmadet9575.shtml (19 February 2012)
51. Henkel, http://www.henkel.com/about-henkel/company-history-11789.htm (19 February 2012)
52. G.A. Glafey, GmbH & Co.KG, http://www.glafey.de/ (19 February 2012)
53. Boston Blacking Company, Oberursel, http://www.ursella.info/obu_in_han/Bostik/Bostik_Oberursel.htm (19 February 2012)

54. Büdo GMBH, http://www.firmen.tv/buedo-gmbh_cgnrpn (19 February 2012)
55. Prym, http://www.prym-consumer.com/prym/proc/docs/0H0H003XX.html?nav=0H0H003YA (19 February 2012)
56. Hartmann Group, http://de.wikipedia.org/wiki/Hartmann_Gruppe (20 February 2012)
57. Condoms, http://en.wikipedia.org/wiki/Condom#Rubber_and_manufacturing_advances (21 February 2012)
58. Ritex Gummiwarenfabrik GmbH, http://www.ritex.de/ (21 February 2012)
59. Blausiegel kondom, http://www.blausiegel.de/blausiegel.php (21 February 2012)
60. Leipzig State Archive, http://www.archiv.sachsen.de/archive/leipzig/4243_3230373035.htm (21 February 2012)
61. Temmler Werke, http://en.wikipedia.org/wiki/Temmler (21 February 2012)
62. Toothbrush, http://en.wikipedia.org/wiki/Toothbrush (18 May 2013)
63. Toothpaste, http://en.wikipedia.org/wiki/Toothpaste (18 May 2013)
64. What is Military Archaeology, http://www.wisegeek.com/what-is-military-archaeology.htm (19 May 2013)
65. Battlefield archaeology, http://en.wikipedia.org/wiki/Battlefield_archaeology (19 May 2013)
66. Archaeology, http://en.wikipedia.org/wiki/Archaeology (19 May 2013)
67. The Nazi Death Machine: Hitler's Drugged Soldiers by Andreas Ulrich, http://www.spiegel.de/international/the-nazi-death-machine-hitler-s-drugged-soldiers-a-354606.html. (1 May 2013)

TRADEMARK INFORMATION

Most of the items and products in this book may be covered by various copyrights, trademarks, and logotypes. Their use herein is for identification purposes only. All rights are reserved by their respective owners. I used a trademark symbol (® or ™) if my research determined the symbol is integral to the name of a particular product or firm.

The text and the products pictured in this book are from the collection of the authors of this book, its publisher, or various private collections. The book is not sponsored, endorsed, or otherwise affiliated with any of the companies whose products are represented herein.